T0046082

The Modern Witchcraft Grimoire

The

MODERN WITCHCRAFT Grimoire

YOUR COMPLETE GUIDE TO CREATING YOUR OWN *Book of Shadows*

Skye Alexander

Adams Media
New York London Toronto Sydney New Delhi

Adams Media
An Imprint of Simon & Schuster, Inc.
100 Technology Center Drive
Stoughton, MA 02072

For information about special discounts for bulk purchases, please contact Simon & Schuster Special Sales at 1-866-506-1949 or business@simonandschuster.com.

The Simon & Schuster Speakers Bureau can bring authors to your live event. For more information or to book an event contact the Simon & Schuster Speakers Bureau at 1-866-248-3049 or visit our website at www.simonspeakers.com.

Interior images © F+W Media, Inc.; iStockphoto.com/Nocturnus; iStockphoto.com/ilbusca; iStockphoto.com/ARTappler; iStockphoto.com/VeraPetruk.

Manufactured in the United States of America

8 2022

Library of Congress Cataloging-in-Publication Data
Alexander, Skye, author.
The modern witchcraft grimoire: your complete guide to creating your own book of shadows / Skye Alexander.
Avon, Massachusetts: Adams Media, 2016.
Includes bibliographical references and index.
LCCN 2016007697 (print) | LCCN 2016017136 (ebook) | ISBN 9781440596810 (pob) | ISBN 1440596816 (pob) | ISBN 9781440596827 (ebook) | ISBN 1440596824 (ebook)
LCSH: Witchcraft.
LCC BF1566.A54732016 (print) | LCC BF1566 (ebook) | DDC 133.4/3--dc23

LC record available at https://lccn.loc.gov/2016007697ISBN 978-1-4405-9681-0
ISBN 978-1-4405-9682-7 (ebook)

To the witches of the next generation—
you are the torchbearers who illuminate our future

Acknowledgments

Many thanks are due to my astute and supportive editors Rebecca Tarr Thomas and Peter Archer, to Stephanie Hannus for her beautiful book design, and to the rest of the Adams Media staff—no author could work with a better team.

CONTENTS

Introduction

RECORDING YOUR MAGICKAL JOURNEY

Perhaps you're accustomed to keeping a journal in which the story of your life unfolds. There you confide your hopes and dreams as well as the events that make up the fabric of your existence. In *The Modern Witchcraft Grimoire*, you'll learn how to keep another book. Although it's similar in some ways to a journal, it is much more. It is your *grimoire* (pronounced grim WAR).

If you are Wiccan or follow another magickal path, your grimoire is an essential tool—an intimate account of your spiritual journey, the steps you take on the road to self-discovery, and what you learn along the way about the Craft of the Wise. As well, it's a resource for you, containing spells and other magickal lore that are aids in finding serenity and happiness.

Between its covers you reveal your soul's secrets, as well as your expressions in the outer world—particularly those of a magickal and spiritual nature. Here you pen information about your practice as a witch, the spells and rituals you perform, and your ongoing exploration of the mysteries that lie beyond the ordinary mundane world. Insights, visions, dreams, meditations, and musings all may grace the pages of your grimoire. Your experience is both personal and universal, for as a witch you know that everything in the cosmos is connected, wisdom is timeless, and truth is enduring.

Perhaps you feel inspired to discuss how you interpret the presence of the Divine Feminine in your life. How does she reveal herself to you and guide you on your spiritual path? Your grimoire is also the place to relate the magickal knowledge you've gained and the revelations you've discovered. As a practitioner of the Craft, you are continually unfolding and growing and transforming. You are continually deepening your relationship with yourself, the Goddess, nature, the universe, and everything around you. Each day opens new doors; each moment the spirit world slips extraordinary messages into your psychic mailbox. And you don't want to forget a single thing, so write it down!

The Modern Witchcraft Grimoire is a guide to designing and using this amazing resource. Part I explains the tradition of keeping a grimoire and why you'll want to create your own. I discuss various ways to fashion your book, how you might like to organize it, and what things you may consider including in it. Are you an artist? Perhaps you'll enjoy adding illustrations, photographs, and other inspiring imagery to enrich your book. Are you a poet? Compose original incantations to call up the magickal forces in the cosmos and write your poems in your grimoire. Do you have a dramatic bent? Choreograph personal rituals and record what you did, with whom, and what resulted. You can even fabricate your own grimoire from scratch. This is your chance to be creative and to express yourself, without fear of criticism or censorship.

In Part II I suggest ways to work with your grimoire. Celebrate and chart the sacred holidays. Catalog your spells. Discuss your interactions with deities, spirits, and other nonphysical entities. Let the spark within you shine, let the music in you sing. All the details of your quest here on earth and beyond could end up on the pages of your book.

I also share things here that I've found worth including in my own book: favorite spells and rituals, chants and affirmations, signs and symbols, insights and inspirations. I offer them as suggestions only, to help you get started in this wonderfully creative and richly rewarding endeavor. Take what you like and leave the rest. Your grimoire can contain anything you feel is significant to you as a witch and as a person. It is a record of your awakening and your evolution, what you've received and what you're giving back. It is uniquely yours—no two witches will create a grimoire in the same way.

Above all, I urge you to embrace your own truth. Delve deeply into your heart of hearts. Engage your imagination. Enjoy knowing that you are part of a long-standing, time-honored, and incredibly exciting tradition that connects you with witches past, present, and future. Invite the Goddess to join you in the process. Whatever you do will be amazing! Blessed be.

> *"You have more than enough to do, be, create and have everything you desire! In order to have EVERYTHING you desire, you must shift your beliefs and begin to see yourself in a new and strong way. It's about creating a powerful mindset shift . . . the first step is connecting with your Inner Goddess."*
>
> —*Lisa Marie Rosati*

PART I

Designing Your Grimoire

Chapter 1

WHY CREATE A GRIMOIRE?

A grimoire is a witch's personal journal of her or his magickal experiences. Here, you keep track of your spells, rituals, and other things related to your development as a magick worker. It's like a cook's collection of recipes. Some people refer to it as a "book of shadows." Old grimoires served as collections of spells and rituals. A book of shadows today might also include its author's musings and insights related to a spell, as well as her dreams, feelings, poems, lore, and other asides.

Your grimoire is a record of your growth and of the changes you and others bring about in your life. Above all, it is a tool you can use in your search for and discovery of the path of the Goddess.

THE WAY OF THE GODDESS

The Egyptians called her Isis. The Sumerians knew her as Inanna, the Babylonians as Ishtar. Long before the advent of Christianity, Islam, and other patriarchal religions, our ancestors stood in awe of the Goddess's power and revered her in all her splendor. For as much as 30,000 years they drew nurture from her spirituality and strength. Now you have chosen to tread a special path in this world, a path rooted in antiquity that respects the Goddess as well as the God. You seek to know her, to learn of her great mysteries and feel her hand guiding you as you journey through life in the manifest world. Call to her and she will welcome you.

The Reawakening of the Goddess

In recent years we have seen a great re-emergence of interest in the Divine Feminine. Our modern world, where science and logic and materialistic thinking dominate, has become increasingly unbalanced. Many of us experience a thirst for deeper wisdom, a hunger in our souls, and realize that something essential has been missing from our lives. We seek a stronger connection with nature and the spiritual realm, and long to rediscover our true place in the universe. In our quest for a more fulfilling way of life, many of us have turned within and found the Goddess waiting there for us.

Wicca and Neopaganism, belief systems that honor the Goddess, resonate with us because they speak to issues about which we feel most deeply: respect for the environment, gender equality, and overcoming religious biases and narrow-minded thinking. They also encourage us to respect and develop our own, unique powers so we can take charge of our lives and be everything we choose to be.

Growing Wiccans

A growing number of both women and men now follow the Wiccan path. According to an American Religious Identification Survey in 2008 (the 2008 ARIS), 682,000 people in the United States identified themselves as Wiccan or Neopagans, although the real figure is probably much larger. Even the U.S. military now recognizes Wicca as a bona fide religion.

As you progress along your chosen path, you'll want to chronicle your spiritual journey—just as you might keep a travel log while on a trip. For Wiccans, your grimoire is the tool you use to do this. In writing your story, you preserve the intimate details of what you do and experience along the Wiccan Way, as well as your unique relationship with the Divine. You also make it possible for other seekers to share in your search for wisdom and to benefit from the knowledge you gain during your quest.

EARLY GRIMOIRES

Originally, a grimoire referred to a book of spells, incantations, invocations, and other practices used to call forth spirits. Grimoires existed in ancient Babylonia and early Middle Eastern civilizations. Later they made their way through Europe during the medieval and Renaissance periods. People have been writing grimoires since the invention of writing, and these works have been connected to three of the world's major religions—Judaism, Christianity, and Islam. They influenced the development of early science and the arts in Europe and parts of Asia. Grimoires thus are an important part of our cultural history.

The word "grimoire" is related to the word "grammar," which pertains to the rules and the relationships of language. Derived from the Middle English *gramere* and the Old French *gramaire*, the root of the word is an alteration of the Latin *grammatica*, which we can trace back to its source from the Greek feminine of *grammatikos*, meaning "of letters." It seems appropriate that this feminine derivative from the language of one of the earliest classical pantheistic civilizations has evolved to describe what many witches now consider a sacred text devoted to practices honoring the Mother Goddess.

Famous Ancient Grimoires

Since ancient times, magicians and mystics have compiled grimoires. These early texts and our knowledge of them are limited, though, mainly because the Church considered them heretical and destroyed those they found. However, some old grimoires managed to survive, and today they give us insight into the magickal thinking and workings of our ancestors.

One of the earliest and most influential grimoires, *The Clavicule of Solomon* or *The Key of Solomon*, was supposedly written by the great King Solomon and is believed to have appeared in the Middle East some 2,000 years ago. By the fifteenth century, copies of the book had found their way into the hands of European scholars and others who sought to learn the secrets of the wise king. The *Clavicule* included spells for summoning demons as well as the spirits of the dead, along with information about using magick tools and lots more. Another ancient spell book, the *Sepher Ha-Razim*—which is said to have passed down through many generations from Noah to King Solomon—contained techniques for divination, healing, and attracting good fortune.

Summoning Spirits Solomon-Style

Back in the old, old days, people put a lot of faith in spirits of all kinds. Some of those spirits, our ancestors believed, wanted to wreak havoc in our lives, whereas others could be called upon to block the malicious nature of the bad guys' curses. Therefore, early grimoires included invocations, rituals, and other practices for eliciting the aid of spiritual allies. Here's a brief excerpt from *The Key of Solomon* designed to conjure the powers of nonphysical beings. You can read the text in its entirety (translated into English) online at *http://hermetic.com* to get an idea of what early magicians believed.

"O ye Spirits, ye I conjure by the Power, Wisdom, and Virtue of the Spirit of God, by the uncreate Divine Knowledge, by the vast Mercy of God, by the Strength of God, by the Greatness of God, by the Unity of God; and by the holy Name of God EHEIEH, which is the root, trunk, source, and origin of all the other Divine Names, whence they all draw their life and their virtue, which Adam having invoked, he acquired the knowledge of all created things. . . ."

—*The Greater Key of Solomon, Book I,*
translated by S. Liddell MacGregor Mathers

Astrological magick played an important role in some early grimoires including the Arabic *Picatrix*, attributed to mathematician Ahmad Al-Majriti and translated into Latin in the mid-thirteenth century. The *Liber Juratus*, supposedly penned by a legendary magus named Honorius of Thebes, also became popular during the medieval era. It contained techniques for gaining visions from God, commanding demons, and avoiding Purgatory, as well as scientific knowledge of the times. A fifteenth-century collection of Kabbalist magick, the *Book of the Sacred Magic of Abra-Melin the Mage*, offered information about love and prosperity magick, plus the secrets of invisibility and flying—pretty heady stuff for any age!

Grimoires in the Age of Enlightenment

Mysticism flourished in the eighteenth century, as spiritual reaction to the Age of Enlightenment's emphasis on logic and reason. Advanced printing techniques made books cheaper too, which enabled esoteric texts to reach a wider audience than ever before. One of these, a collection of magick symbols and spells for conjuring spirits called *The Sixth and Seventh Books of Moses*, gained prominence in Germany and then in the nineteenth century found its way to the United States. Around the same time, a grimoire known as *Petit Albert*, said to contain spells for invisibility, attracted attention in France as did another called *Le Grand Grimoire ou Dragon Rouge* (although it claimed an older pedigree), which provided instructions for raising demons. In Scandinavia and on the Iberian Peninsula, spell books purported to have been written by St. Cyprian that offered information for finding hidden treasure became popular. For centuries, metaphysicians in Europe and the New World who had kept their views and practices hidden now hungered for knowledge and sought to share it throughout the Western world.

Skeptics might say that this was a period of superstition and fanciful thinking, or that charlatans were trying to dupe gullible people with mystical hocus-pocus. However, the grimoires compiled then—and the much earlier material their authors drew upon—suggest that for centuries magickal workers have been in touch with occult forces. Intuitively we realize, as Shakespeare wrote, "there are more things in heaven and earth . . . than are dreamt of in your philosophy."

Leland's Grimoire

At the end of the nineteenth century, an American folklorist named Charles Godfrey Leland published one of the first grimoires in English. According to Leland, a mysterious Italian witch named Maddalena gave him a collection of magick lore titled *Vangel*, reputedly from a secret group of Goddess worshippers. The document, which Leland claimed Maddalena had written in her own hand, lies at the heart of his book *Aradia, Gospel of the Witches.*

To this day, however, there's a debate about the authenticity of the material. Did it actually come from a secret history of Italian witchcraft? Did Maddalena pass on an account of her own family's mystical practices to Leland, pretending their traditions were more arcane and ancient? Or did Leland make up the whole story, drawing information from various folkloric sources, and insist he'd discovered an early Italian coven's grimoire? Despite questions about the text's origins, Leland's book strongly influenced contemporary Neopaganism and Wicca, and still intrigues witches today.

Some historic grimoires now reside in museums and private collections, and some pricey (and perhaps dubious) books periodically show up for sale online and in auctions internationally. Although many modern witches might find the information contained in these early texts confusing or questionable, it's interesting to examine the rich tradition of grimoires handed down through the ages and to appreciate our ancestors' efforts to preserve esoteric knowledge for future generations, even when doing so might have led to persecution.

THE GRIMOIRE OF GERALD GARDNER AND DOREEN VALIENTE

The most influential book of shadows for contemporary witches is attributed to Gerald Gardner and Doreen Valiente, often considered the Father and Mother of modern witchcraft. Valiente, a prolific English author and poet, began demonstrating her interest in witchcraft and magick at age seven. In 1952—shortly after the 1735 Witchcraft Act was repealed, decriminalizing the practice of witchcraft in England—she met Gerald Gardner. An English witch and noted occultist who owned the Museum of Magic and Witchcraft on the Isle of Man, Gardner initiated Valiente into the Craft on Midsummer's Eve 1953. Their association spawned the modern-day religion we know today as Wicca.

More than a decade prior to meeting Valiente, Gardner discovered fragments of a text that he believed had been written by a group of earlier European witches. He included these findings in his book of shadows—although he didn't call it a "book of shadows" at the time—along with other rituals and practices he'd learned about during his many years of studying esoteric traditions from both the East and the West. His book's contents drew upon the work of Aleister Crowley (perhaps the most notorious magician of the modern era), Celtic folklore, the practices of the Hermetic Order of the Golden Dawn, Tantric yoga, Enochian wisdom, and other sources of mystical and occult knowledge. Valiente revised the material—chucking much of the Crowleyisms, in particular—and added information of her own as well as her poetry. The result was a compilation of inherited rituals from the past blended with original and modern elements. It became the core ethical guide and central spiritual text of the Gardnerian tradition of Wicca (there are several other Wiccan traditions as well).

Today, many witches use a similar method for creating their own grimoires—we draw upon traditional practices and add new ones. Some Wiccans choose to hand-copy material from a book of shadows created by the High Priestess or High Priest who initiated them into the Craft, and then put their personal insights and experiences into their magickal journals. Others prefer to create their own, original grimoires from scratch. Thus, the Craft continues to evolve.

How Did the Term "Book of Shadows" Originate?

According to Doreen Valiente, Gardner stumbled upon a 1949 edition of a magazine called *The Occult Observer* in a Brighton, England, bookstore, which contained an article written by an Indian palmist named Mir Bashir. The article talked about a Sanskrit manuscript, ostensibly thousands of years old, that Bashir had come across in 1941. The document revealed an ancient Hindu technique for divining a person's future by measuring his or her shadow. Bashir titled his article "Book of Shadows" and Gardner latched onto it. Supposedly, the article appeared on the page opposite an ad for Gardner's book *High Magic's Aid*, a fantasy novel about witchcraft in Victorian-era England. Perhaps he saw this as a fortunate sign, but whatever the reason the term "book of shadows" stuck, and witches still use it today.

SHARE IT OR KEEP IT SECRET?

As mentioned already, some witches choose to keep their grimoires completely private, solely for their own use—after all, the spiritual journey is a very personal one and you may not feel you can be totally honest if you know someone else will read the intimate details of your experience. Other witches share their books with magickal partners or members of their covens. Still other witches decide to reveal some of their magick practices publicly—as I've done in *The Modern Guide to Witchcraft* and *The Modern Witchcraft Spell Book* and my other books—in hopes that by doing so we can assist other people on the path.

A History of Secrecy

In earlier times, occult knowledge was passed down orally to neophytes by more experienced practitioners. Most likely, small groups of witches and other magicians met in secret, and they may have possessed little knowledge of the whereabouts or practices of other groups. Few kept written records of their activities. They did this not only because in those days hardly anyone could read or write, but also because they needed to protect themselves. In many parts of the world, for many years, people suspected of practicing witchcraft were imprisoned, tortured, and killed. Even today, witches who reveal their beliefs publicly may suffer ridicule, prejudice, and worse.

Destroy the Evidence

Consider this excerpt from Gerald Gardner and Doreen Valiente's book of shadows:

> *If you would Keep a book let it be in your own hand of write. Let brothers and sisters copy what they will, but never let the book out of your hands, and never keep the writings of another, for if it be found in their hand of write, they well may be taken and enjoined. Each should guard his own writings and destroy it whenever danger threatens. Learn as much as you may by heart, and when danger is past, rewrite your book an it be safe. For this reason, if any die, destroy their book if they have not been able to, for an it be found, 'tis clear proof against them, And our oppressors well know, "Ye may not be a witch alone" So all their kin and friends be*

in danger of torture. So ever destroy anything not necessary. If your book be found on you. 'tis clear proof against you alone. You may be enjoined. Keep all thoughts of the Craft from your mind. Say you had bad dreams; a devil caused you to write it without your knowledge. Think to yourself, "I know nothing. I remember nothing. I have forgotten everything." (For more, see The Gardnerian Book of Shadows, *by Gerald Gardner, at* www.sacred-texts.com.*)*

When witches and practitioners of other magickal arts faced the threat of capture with such dire consequences, it's no wonder they insisted on keeping their grimoires secret. During the Burning Times in Europe, which lasted from the fourteenth until the eighteenth centuries, at least tens of thousands of people were executed as witches. The majority of these were women and girls.

Unfortunately, this fragmented approach has left us severely wanting in the area of verifiable information. It is very difficult to piece together the rites and rituals of an oral tradition when few written records exist and where fear and suspicion force people into hiding. Even today, some of us may worry about reprisals from our families, communities, or religious or political groups. Therefore, use your best judgment as to whether you wish to keep your book of shadows to yourself.

MODERN GRIMOIRES

The term "grimoire" is generic and may be used in place of the title of an actual book that its author chooses to keep secret. Today's grimoires are usually handwritten by individuals for their own personal use, although you can also create an effective and wonderful book of shadows digitally. A grimoire may include information and instructions related to a particular tradition, or it may contain strictly personal records and reminiscences intended only for the use of the author. Sometimes portions of a grimoire are passed down over time, copied by initiates from a master book.

Some Wiccans choose to keep more than a single book of shadows. One of these books contains the rituals upheld and enacted by a particular coven or circle to which the witch belongs. These rituals may have their roots in earlier times and, as such, preserve traditional practices and wisdom. The information in one coven's "core" grimoire will probably differ from that of other covens. Members of a select group are permitted to copy material from this book into their own grimoires for their own purposes. In a separate book a witch might record information of a more personal nature—the intimate thoughts and experiences of her or his sojourn along the road less traveled.

However, some covens share information or make certain practices and beliefs available to other "kindred spirits." The necessary secrecy that once existed when a witch's life depended on hiding her thoughts is loosening in modern-day witchcraft. Still, many people choose to preserve their private practices and ideas by limiting access to their grimoires.

What Should You Include in Your Book?

Every grimoire is essentially a book of shadows, but not every book of shadows conforms to the strict definition of a grimoire. As discussed earlier, what we call a book of shadows today includes elements of the grimoire (such as directions for spells and rituals), but it is not necessarily an exclusively instructive tome. Instead, it's an intimate record of your spiritual journey.

Purists insist that a grimoire should be entirely instructional, full of information, annotation, and practical application. They argue that a book of shadows more closely resembles a journal and that personal musings have no place in the grimoire. Fortunately for our purposes, no officially designated criteria for creating a book of shadows exist, nor is there a correct or incorrect way of building, blessing, and using your personal grimoire. As you read on, you'll see that I use the terms "grimoire" and "book of shadows" interchangeably. That's because I believe a witch's thoughts and feelings cannot be separated from the work she does—each stitch builds upon other stitches to create a whole cloth.

What goes into your book, how you create it, and how you use it will be as unique as you are. The goal is to document physically the spiritual journey of an individual who follows the path of the Goddess and the Craft of the Wise—whatever that means to you.

Online Grimoires

We're fortunate today to have an amazing resource that allows us to share knowledge while remaining anonymous: the Internet. A quick Google search will direct you to lots and lots of Wiccan websites and blogsites, as well as sites that provide historical information about witchcraft, Neopaganism, and various other magickal systems. You'll even find some that interpret early esoteric texts into modern languages and that let you glimpse the thinking and workings of the ancients.

Witchcraft's popularity has grown exponentially in recent years, in part because witches can now disseminate their wisdom widely and safely in the form of e-grimoires. Not only does this protect us from discrimination, it also enables us to gain information from a wider range of sources than ever before.

As you grow in your magickal practice, you may decide to start your own blog to share what you've learned during your spiritual journey in the Craft of the Wise. In doing so, you may meet many fellow travelers from around the world whose knowledge and experiences will enrich your own path. In turn, your wisdom will enhance theirs.

Writing the story of your spiritual awakening and subsequent journey can be an empowering method of self-discovery. You may become passionate about recording your spiritual and psychic progress. In the process, you'll strengthen the connections between divine power and personal power, and open yourself to greater intimacy with the Goddess.

You'll come to see that writing in your grimoire is a ritual in itself—you're creating a sacred tool that contains the chronicle of the magick unfolding within you. As you write, you'll chart your path—like an early seaman using the stars to map his course into previously unknown territory—and look back to see your growth, both as a person and as a witch. You'll forge new perspectives on old traditions and ancient rites, adapting them to your present-day needs and the needs of the world in which you live. You'll rediscover the seasons; you'll honor the passing of time; you'll celebrate life, death, and rebirth—each account recorded in your own hand.

"Magic is believing in yourself, if you can do that you can make anything happen."

—Johann Wolfgang von Goethe

If you so choose, your grimoire can be more than a personal record. Inspired by those who have preceded you, it also can serve as a guide for novices just discovering the Wiccan path. It can remind us of where we came from and how far we still have to go. By writing your story, you take responsibility for the idea that the clearest pathway to the Goddess is through direct experience.

Chapter 2

CRAFTING YOUR GRIMOIRE

Early grimoires were handwritten, usually on parchment (a material made from animal skin) or paper. Depending on the author's ability to procure materials and work with them, the book's binding might have been made of richly tooled leather, carved wood, tapestry or velvet, or engraved metal. A wealthy witch or wizard might have decorated the cover of his or her book of shadows with gemstones, ornate silver hinges, gold leaf accents, or other precious adornments. A poor witch, understandably, would have chosen much more modest materials, perhaps inscribing spells on pieces of tree bark.

As you go about crafting your own grimoire, keep your purpose in mind. Whether elegant or plain, elaborate or simple, your book of shadows is a tool—a very special and personal tool—that you create in order to further your growth as a magick worker. Although you may draw upon the rich tradition that precedes you and let it guide the creation of your personal grimoire, remember there are no rules about what's right or wrong. Each grimoire is as unique as the witch to whom it belongs, and the most important thing is that it serves your objectives.

BEFORE YOU BEGIN

In the coming years, your grimoire will become a close confidant, an intimate account of your personal and spiritual evolution, a valuable reference guide, and, if you so desire, an inspiration for others. You'll keep this precious tool for the extent of your magickal journey on earth. Therefore, you'll want to take some time before you begin in order to determine the design and format that will serve you best.

Ask yourself some questions:

- Does your book need to be portable? If so, size matters. Will you carry your grimoire with you at all times, or only on special occasions?
- How often do you intend to write in your book of shadows? Daily? On new or full moons? After performing a spell? On the sabbats?
- What do you plan to include in your grimoire? Spells and rituals only? Personal musings, insights, and asides? Artwork? Experiences outside those of a magickal nature?
- What intentions do you hold for your grimoire? What role do you envision it playing in your magickal practice? In other areas of your life?
- Will you write in your book of shadows only in the privacy of your own home? In conjunction with a magickal partner or coven members?
- Do you intend to keep the contents of your grimoire completely private, or share them with certain people you trust?
- Will writing in your grimoire be part of a magick ritual, either with other people or solo?
- Where will your book reside? Displayed openly on your altar? In a secret hiding place in your home or office, or perhaps a safe-deposit box? In your backpack?
- Would you consider crafting the book yourself?

- What do you want to happen to your grimoire after you leave the physical world? Will you entrust it to someone else's use, or do you want it destroyed?

Considering these things can aid you in the process of crafting and maintaining your book of shadows. Although many witches have similar reasons for keeping grimoires, your actual practice and your individual objectives may differ from those of other people. My goal in writing *The Modern Witchcraft Grimoire* is to guide you through the process and to provide tips, information, and suggestions along the way.

YOUR GRIMOIRE'S COVER: A REFLECTION OF YOU

Can you judge a book of shadows by its cover? That's up to you. Your grimoire's binding is its outer skin. Each time you take it in hand, even before you begin to write in it, it sparks your magickal thinking and the vision you have of yourself as a witch. Running your fingers over its cover reminds you that you're on a spiritual journey, engaging in an age-old quest for wisdom, evolving as a human being and as a magician. What you hold in your hands is intensely personal, and yet also transcendent, for it draws upon the past and invites input from the spirit realm. Your grimoire is a representation of your deepest and most profound self. What do you want it to say about you?

Choosing Your Book's Cover Imagery

Wicca and witchcraft come in many "flavors": Gardnerian, Alexandrian, Dianic, Saxon, Celtic, and so on. Some witches don't align themselves with any specific group. If you do subscribe to a particular tradition or cultural heritage, you might like to reflect that on your grimoire's cover. For example, because I'm of Irish and Scottish descent, I have a book with a leather cover that features Celtic imagery and fastens with a pewter Celtic knot.

Many witches choose to include magick symbols on the covers of their grimoires: pentagrams, spirals, elemental or alchemical symbols, etc. If you're interested in astrology, you might opt for solar or lunar images, zodiac glyphs, your sun-sign "animal," or stars. If tarot's your thing, you could place a picture of a tarot card that speaks to you on the cover, perhaps The High Priestess or The Magician. Green witches might enjoy enriching their books' covers with botanical imagery. Pictures and symbols that represent the Goddess—or a favorite deity—may appeal to you. Or, you can honor your spirit animal guide by depicting it there. Some people like to use mythological creatures (such as dragons, phoenixes, griffins, or unicorns) on their grimoires; others add angels. The Kabbalah's Tree of Life, the Druids' World Tree, the Egyptian Eye of Horus . . . the list goes on.

Your book's cover may be simple or elaborate, depending on your preference. An online search will turn up lots of intriguing ideas and trigger your imagination. You may also find it helpful to visit a few New Age stores, shops that sell blank journals and scrapbooking materials, or art supply stores that stock sketchbooks. Whatever pleases you, reflects who you are as a person and a witch, and enhances your magickal experience is appropriate. Whatever feels right to you *is.*

Securing Your Grimoire

In order to keep their contents secret, some early grimoires—and some modern ones as well—were kept locked. Spellcasters didn't want the information contained within their books to fall into the wrong hands. Nor could they risk allowing people who might persecute them to gain access to potentially incriminating material. If you feel a need to protect your grimoire's contents from other people, by all means consider placing a lock on the cover.

If you aren't worried about anyone else getting his or her hands on your book of shadows, you can tie it shut with a strip of leather, a silken cord, a string of beads, or whatever strikes your fancy. Additionally, some witches like to slip their grimoires into drawstring pouches or wrap them in silk to protect them from dust and unwanted ambient energies.

INNER BEAUTY

Although the cover of your book of shadows sets the stage for what's inside, the contents matter most. Here's where you will record the story of your journey, chronicle your personal growth, and write down the secrets you hold dear. In a sense, the pages on which you note your thoughts and experiences are like picture frames that display a photo or painting. What "setting" do you feel will best frame your testimony?

Sensory Delights

Spend some time checking out readymade journals and examining scrapbooks/scrapbooking supplies. Some commercial books feature gorgeous, richly textured paper, perhaps embossed with images that resonate with you, or embedded with flowers or other adornments. Others come with lovely patterns and designs. You might also wish to examine books by artisans who have taken the time to fabricate handmade paper pages. (Later in this chapter, I'll give instructions for making your own from scratch.)

The sensory appeal of these journals can help start your creative juices flowing and inspire you to begin recording your steps on the magickal path. In fact, it's a good idea to get all your senses involved in your spellworking, for the more you can enrich the experience, the more power you bring to your spells. Choose a book that you love to look at and touch, one that invites you to grace its pages with your reminiscences. Writing in your grimoire should be a joyful experience.

As you record your spells, rituals, and other activities, consider adding a variety of images and objects that contribute to the beauty, tactile quality, and overall richness of your grimoire: milagros or other charms, feathers, small gemstones, scraps of lace, photographs of special places, pictures from magazines. If you did a candle spell, you might want to drip a bit of molten wax onto a page of your grimoire and engrave it with a symbol to remind you of the experience. If you used an essential oil in a spell, you may wish to dab a little of that fragrant oil on a page to remind you at a later time of your intention and the spell's results.

Keeping It Simple

If you prefer something simpler, that's okay. A loose-leaf binder might suit your purposes, allowing you to easily update your grimoire by adding pages or rearranging them. You can even type your grimoire on your computer or iPad. Although this method lacks the sensory appeal that many witches enjoy, the convenience could be an advantage—especially if you're on the go a lot.

Organizing Your Book of Shadows

How you choose to organize the material in your book of shadows will depend on how you decide to use it. The questions you asked yourself earlier may dictate the flow of your grimoire. No one way is better than any other. A table of contents at the beginning of your book will help you locate your spells easily. Ribbon markers can designate favorite or frequently used spells. If you choose to divide your book into categories, you may want to use tabs to indicate where different sections start. In Chapter 3, I'll discuss some ways you might like to organize your book.

One Book or Many?

If you've selected a design that lets you change or move around your entries, your grimoire can be as large as you like. If you've chosen a book with a fixed binding that doesn't allow you to add pages, however, you're going to fill it up eventually. Therefore, you'll need to continue writing in another book, creating a series. You may decide to use different books for different types of spells, instead of dividing a single grimoire into sections. Whether to keep one book or several is entirely up to you.

CRAFT IT YOURSELF

If you're the crafty type (no pun intended), you may enjoy making your book of shadows from scratch. By doing so, you follow in the footsteps of early spellworkers who fabricated their own grimoires. When you're finished, you'll have a book that is absolutely unique, imbued with your personal energy from the very start. This rewarding project, although time-consuming and (if you make your own paper) rather messy, lets you express your creativity and imagination. Your commitment can also bring you a deep sense of satisfaction.

Fashioning a book from recycled items is not as difficult as you might think and may appeal to ecologically minded witches. If creating the entire book seems too daunting, consider making just a few pages for special incantations and spells to add to your book. Even if you buy your grimoire in a store, you can add herbs and flowers, or sketch in it to customize and personalize the pages.

Make Your Own Paper

The art of papermaking originated in China and ancient Egypt. If you resonate strongly with the goddess Kuan Yin or Isis, this may inspire you. Making your own paper from recycled items does not require any special equipment—you only need simple household products, many of which you may already possess.

The basis of paper is pulp. You can make pulp from almost any kind of paper, but avoid using anything with a glossy surface, such as pages out of magazines, because it is treated with chemicals.

MATERIALS NEEDED

- Paper, such as tissue wrap, computer paper, writing or typing paper, paper bags (about ½ cup paper to 2 cups water; the more pulp you add, the thicker your finished paper will be)
- Plastic bucket
- Warm water
- A piece of mesh (such as window screen) to fit in frames—the finer the mesh, the smoother the paper—or papermaking screen
- 2 wooden frames slightly larger than the size you intend your pages to be. You can use picture frames, but the corners must be tight and secured, or a deckle.
- Staples
- Electric blender (purchase one at a thrift store specifically for this purpose; don't use the one you make smoothies in)
- Food coloring or dyes suitable for cotton fabrics (optional)
- Large spoon or ladle
- Plastic dishpan, large bowl, or other waterproof container big enough to easily accommodate the frames
- Liquid laundry starch
- Palette knife, butter knife, or athame

Absorbent cloths, such as dishtowels (one for each page of paper you intend to make)
Dried or fresh flowers, leaves, or bits of lace (optional)
Plastic wrap or waterproof cloth
Heavy book, cutting board, or brick

1. Tear the paper into postage stamp-sized pieces, stir, and soak the pieces in a plastic bucket of water so that all the pieces are covered. As you tear the paper into bits, focus positive energy into it and make your intentions known by reciting the following: "Goddess, bless this endeavor of art. By my hand, let the transformation begin, for the benefit of all. So mote it be." Let the brew soak overnight.
2. Stretch the mesh over one of the frames and staple it so that it's very taut. This covered frame will pick up the pulp and keep it flat. If the mesh is loose, the paper will be saggy and difficult to remove from the frame. Place the empty frame on top of the mesh frame to keep it taut and give your paper a nice edge. Set the frames aside until step 7. (If you prefer, you can purchase a papermaking screen and deckle at a craft/hobby store.)
3. After your paper has soaked overnight, pour off the excess water and begin transferring the pulp into a blender, spoonful by spoonful.
4. Add water until the pitcher of the blender is no more than three-quarters full. If you plan to color your paper, add food coloring or dye now. Run the blender for about 15 seconds, and then check the pulp to make sure it has broken down evenly. If necessary, stir the pulp, and then run the blender for another 5 seconds or so. The mix should be about the consistency of split-pea soup.
5. Gently pour the pulp into the plastic dishpan. At this point, you can add a spoonful of liquid laundry starch to the pulp. This will make the paper absorb ink better, so it will be less likely to bleed when you're writing in your book.
6. Stir the pulp gently and wait for the movement of the water to cease. At the moment when the water is still—but the pulp has not yet settled—hold the frames securely in your hands with the empty frame on top and the mesh frame with the mesh facing up directly underneath it. Slide the frames under the water in a smooth motion, scooping up a

layer of pulp. It may take some practice to get the pulp evenly distributed over the mesh frame.

7. Keeping the frames steady and flat, lift them out of the water and allow the water to drain away. Remove the top frame. A layer of pulp should cover the mesh screen.

8. While the paper is still wet, but not dripping, gently remove the paper from the screen. This can take some practice—if the paper sticks to the mold, you may need to drain or sponge more water from it. Loosen the edges with a palette knife or butter knife—or if you wish, use your athame, consecrating each page instantaneously as you make it.

9. After you have removed the paper, lay it carefully on one-half of the absorbent cloth.

10. Consider pressing fresh herbs and flowers into the paper surface. Are you thinking about writing a protection spell on this sheet of paper? You might want to add basil leaves or a sprig of rosemary along the edges. Perhaps you have a love spell in mind. Adorn some of your pages with red rose petals.

11. Without bending your page, fold the other half of the cloth over the paper to absorb excess water. (You can even roll it with a rolling pin to squeeze out excess water.) Continue stacking individual pages in this fashion, making sure layers of cloth alternate with sheets of paper.

12. Put something waterproof (such as plastic wrap) at the top of the stack of paper, then place a heavy book, cutting board, or brick on the top. This will weigh the paper down and keep it flat while drying.

13. You can add positive energy to your paper by embossing magickal symbols in it. Emboss the paper by pressing an object, such as a pentagram, into the paper while the paper is still wet, and then remove the object. If you want a well-defined motif, leave the object there while the paper is weighted and don't remove it until the paper has dried completely.

Feel free to experiment. The more personal energy and thought you put into creating your book of shadows, the more you'll enjoy using it. Check out the website *http://paperslurry.com* for good instructions with pictures that show various methods for making paper.

Bind Your Book

Now it's time to bind your book of shadows. Even if you decide not to make your own paper, you can still create your cover, assemble the blank pages, and bind the book yourself. The following steps will explain some finishing options as you complete the construction of your book of shadows.

MATERIALS NEEDED

Binding board or heavy stock paper from a craft store; you can wrap the cover in cloth, securing the cloth with good PVA glue (see end of material list)

Scissors

Ruler

Scoring tool, such as a box cutter or X-Acto knife

Binder clips or similar clamps

Heavy book, cutting board, or brick

Pencil

If you'd rather not use glue to bind, use a cord or ribbon. You'll also need a drill or hole punch and a template for placing the holes.

If you plan to use glue to bind, use a heavy brush and PVA (polyvinyl acetate) glue, which is the most durable. If you want to avoid chemicals, use a natural type of paste or glue, such as fish glue.

1. Choose the material for your cover.
2. Cut two equal-sized pieces that are slightly larger than the pages of the book.
3. Measure about ¼" from the edge of each piece and score lightly so your book will open and close easily.
4. Set aside a strip of the cover material or an extra sheet of paper to use for covering the spine.
5. Assemble all your pages and the front and back covers in a stack. Clamp them together firmly with binder clips or clamps. Put small pieces of wood under the clamps so you don't have clamp marks on your cover. Make sure to stack the pages neatly, for they will be permanently assembled in the configuration you have them in now. Make adjustments at this point or you'll have crooked pages in your book.

6. Line up the pages so that the unclamped edge of the stack hangs slightly over the edge of the table you are working on. This edge will become the spine of the book.

7. Use a heavy book, cutting board, or brick to weigh down the pages and keep them in place.

Note: If you are not going to use glue to make the spine, skip to step 12 for instructions on binding with ribbon.

8. With a brush, spread glue very thickly all along the edges of the pages at the spine. Allow the glue to dry thoroughly.

9. The piece used for the spine should be the same length as the cover of your book and three times the thickness of the book. You can determine the thickness of your book by measuring the total height of the stacked pages. Multiply this number by three, and you will get the correct width of the spine. Draw two parallel lines with a pencil on the inside of the spine (the side you intend to glue onto the book so the pencil marks won't show), dividing the spine into three equal parts. These lines will serve as your scoring guide.

10. Score the cover material along the edge of a metal ruler with your scoring tool. Be careful not to cut through the spine—just score it deep enough so that you can fold it easily.

11. Glue the strip along the edge of the book so that it hides the previously glued area. Allow the spine cover to dry.

12. If you prefer to try a different technique, use cord or ribbon. This method does not require a spine. After you've clamped the pages, punch or drill at least three holes along one side of your book. If you are using a hole punch, first make a template so all the holes will be the same size and distance from the left edge of the pages. Do not attempt to punch holes through the template; use the template to mark in pencil where the holes should be on each page, and then punch them out individually. This will make the holes more accurate, and your finished book will be more attractive. If you're handy with power tools, you can drill very slowly through the clamped stack and achieve the same result in less time. Be sure your pages are securely clamped together so they don't slip while you're drilling.

13. Use a ribbon or cord that is five times the length of your book. Choose a color that pleases you or holds symbolic meaning. Push the ribbon through the first hole at the top of the book, leaving a tail of 2" or more.

14. With the tail in place, weave the ribbon through all the remaining holes. When you reach the end, wrap the ribbon around the bottom and go back again through the hole you just used. Continue weaving the ribbon back through the holes up to the top, envisioning the spiral dance of the Goddess as you go.

15. When you've finished threading the ribbon through the last hole, wrap it tightly around the top, as you did at the bottom, and tie it together with the tail end.

Chapter 3

ORGANIZING YOUR GRIMOIRE

Unless you feel like shuffling through hundreds of pages in your grimoire, you'll need some sort of organizing system so you can find the spell you want when you want it. Just as you organize your kitchen cabinets and your closets for convenience, you'll naturally determine a method that works best for you. Each witch is unique and so is her book of shadows—both the type of book she chooses and the way she puts it together.

How you configure your book depends on your personality, your lifestyle, your individual needs and preferences, the types of spells and rituals you perform, your spiritual path, your goals and objectives, and a whole lot more. Remember the questions you asked yourself at the beginning of Chapter 2? How you answered those questions will guide you as you go about organizing the material in your grimoire.

WHERE TO BEGIN

In the previous chapter, we talked about choosing the style and form for your book of shadows—even the possibility of making your own from scratch. However, the first book you create probably won't be your last. You might even decide to start a new book of shadows each year, on Samhain or another date that holds meaning for you, such as your birthday.

Assess Yourself and Your Objectives

As discussed earlier, old grimoires contained incantations, invocations, and rituals for calling forth spirits. Most witches today don't limit themselves to those practices alone. However, you might decide you only want to record magick spells and rituals in your book of shadows: no poems, no dream scenarios, no doodles in the margins. That's fine. Conversely, you may take an "anything goes" approach and choose to include whatever strikes your fancy. That's fine too. Your grimoire is a sacred tool you create to serve your purposes. Go with whatever facilitates your goal.

- If you're a green witch, your book might emphasize spells that incorporate botanicals and other natural ingredients. Because you have a special relationship with nature, you may find it useful to organize your grimoire according to the seasons.
- If you enjoy drama, you may opt to focus on rituals and ceremonial practices. Arranging your material around the eight sabbats might make sense for you.
- Are you a healer? If so, you could create categories for different healing methods: potions and elixirs, salves and balms, talismans and amulets, etc.
- Do you travel a lot? Perhaps you'll find it useful to keep a small travel journal in which you record some of your favorite spells, in addition to your primary grimoire. You could even keep a selection of spells on your iPad or laptop.

Allow for Updates

As you progress along your spiritual path, you'll continue refining your practice, your techniques, and your objectives. Coven members or other people you work with will influence you. Things you read about the Craft and various magickal traditions will influence you. The outcomes of your spells will influence you. And the world you live in—as well as the nonphysical worlds that interface with our material one—will influence you. Therefore, you can expect to continually update your grimoire as you journey along the course you've chosen.

Your first grimoire might be a three-ring binder or an electronic book. This allows you to experiment with various formats and make adjustments as you see fit—before you invest a lot of time and/or money in a gorgeous grimoire that inspires awe every time you look at it. You can always hand-copy your material into a beautiful bound book later.

METHODS FOR ORGANIZING YOUR GRIMOIRE

As I've said before, each witch's priorities, perspective, and practices are unique; therefore, each book of shadows will reflect its author's individuality. You probably won't configure your book the same way as someone else does, just as you probably don't arrange documents in your computer the same way another person does. The following suggestions for organizing your grimoire are just that: suggestions. If one of them suits your purposes, great. If not, feel free to devise your own system. Or you might start with one method, then later switch to another after you've got more spellcasting experience under your belt.

Keep a Daybook

The easiest way to begin a grimoire is to use a chronological approach, writing in your book on a daily basis, as a sort of journal or daybook of your experiences. This method works well if your book's binding doesn't allow you to add or rearrange the pages. It also enables you to chart your personal and spiritual growth day-by-day. Be sure to date your entries.

Take a Seasonal Approach

Maybe you'd like to align yourself more closely with nature's seasons and organize your book of shadows accordingly. You can designate a section for springtime spells, another for summer spells, another for spells to do in autumn, and another for winter magick. Consider pressing seasonal flowers and leaves between the pages to enhance your appreciation of nature's cycle of growth and decline during the year.

Follow the Moon

In Wicca, the moon represents the Great Goddess and the Divine Feminine. Therefore, many witches tap the moon's energy in spellcraft and time their magickal workings around the moon's phases. You might like to organize your book of shadows according to the movements of the moon through the heavens. We'll take a closer look at this in Chapter 9.

Spell to Protect Your Home

Because the moon rules the home, the moon's phase and sign are especially important in spells you do for your home. If possible, cast this spell while the moon is in Cancer, the moon's sign. Or, perform it 3 days before the new moon.

TOOLS AND INGREDIENTS

An image of your totem animal

Basil leaves (dried or fresh)

1. Do you have a totem animal? Totems serve as guardians and helpers—you can call upon them to aid you in times of need. Your totem is an animal, bird, reptile, or insect with which you feel a strong sense of kinship and which, to you, represents protective power. Select an image of your totem animal—a figurine, illustration, or photograph—and place it near your front door.

2. Say aloud, to your animal guardian:

"Protect this home,
High to low,
Fence to fence,
Door to door,
Light to dense,
Roof to floor."

3. Scatter the basil leaves around the outside of your home, making a big circle. Start in the east and move in a clockwise direction until you've completed the protective circle.
4. If you live in an apartment, you can either scatter the leaves around the entire building or place them in a bowl; set the bowl and your animal image just inside the door to your apartment.

Separate Everyday Spells from Special Occasion Spells

Some witches designate certain spells, rituals, and practices for sabbats and special occasions, such as birthdays or handfastings. Other spells may be performed anytime, or on an as-needed basis. These might include ritual baths, cleansing/clearing practices, and protection or healing spells. Perhaps you'd like to organize your book of shadows this way.

Arrange Your Book by Topic

Some people find it convenient to organize their spells into categories, according to the topic or purpose of the spells. For example, you might have a section for love spells, another for prosperity spells, and so on. Consider using different colored paper for the various types of spells: pink for love spells, green for money spells, etc. In Chapter 10, we'll discuss this method more extensively.

Sort Your Spells by Type

Maybe you'd prefer to sort your spells into categories according to how you create and use them. For instance, you might devote a section to magick potions, another to healing balms and salves, and another to ritual baths. This method can be useful when you're collecting the components you need for your spells or shopping for ingredients. It also lets you see what spells you can do on the spur of the moment, based on the materials you have on hand. In Chapter 14, we'll cover this method in more detail.

The Drink of Love

This magick potion should be shared with a romantic partner to improve the relationship. Perform the spell on a Friday night during the waxing moon, or when the moon is in Libra.

TOOLS AND INGREDIENTS
The Lovers card from a tarot deck
Spring water in a clear glass
A drop of melted honey or a pinch of sugar
A silver (or silver plate) spoon

1. Place the tarot card face-up on a windowsill where the moon will shine on it.
2. Set the glass of water on top of the card and leave it overnight. The image of the card will be imprinted into the water.
3. In the morning, add the honey or sugar to the glass of water.
4. Stir the potion with the silver spoon, using a clockwise motion, to sweeten the water and, symbolically, your relationship.
5. Return the tarot card to your deck.
6. Drink the water with your partner to strengthen the love between you.

Organize Spells by Their Components

Cookbooks often arrange recipes according to their main ingredients—for example, meat, fish, poultry, pasta, vegetables. You can organize your grimoire this way too by setting up sections for herbal spells, gemstone spells, candle spells, and so on. As with sorting your spells by type, this method can simplify things when you're shopping for ingredients or when you need to perform a spell on the spur of the moment using materials you already have on hand.

Gemstone Protection Amulet

This spell provides protection while traveling. Put it in your car's glove compartment to ensure protection on a daily basis, or carry it in your pocket, purse, or suitcase for safety during a long-distance trip.

TOOLS AND INGREDIENTS

1 piece of amber
1 piece of quartz crystal
1 piece of jade
1 piece of turquoise
1 piece of topaz
1 piece of agate
Amber essential oil
1 white pouch, preferably made of silk (or another natural fabric)
1 black ribbon
Saltwater

1. Wash the gemstones with mild soap and water, then set them in the sun for a few minutes to remove any unwanted energies.
2. Rub a little amber essential oil on each of the stones, then slip them into the pouch.
3. Tie the bag closed with the ribbon, making 9 knots.
4. Each time you tie a knot, repeat this affirmation: "This amulet keeps me safe and sound at all times and in all situations."
5. When you've finished, sprinkle the amulet with a little saltwater to charge it.

Have these suggestions started you thinking about how you might organize your own grimoire? In Part II, we'll explore these and other options in greater depth and look at details that can support your journey as a witch and spellworker.

Chapter 4

WHAT TO INCLUDE IN YOUR GRIMOIRE

What does it mean to practice magick? In Wicca, we see "magick" as working harmoniously with the natural forces all around us—in both the material world and beyond—to generate outcomes. A witch uses her attunement and influence to manipulate these forces, in order to elicit a series of controlled coincidences that will achieve a desired result. She seeks to move, bend, or otherwise change the natural flow of energy in the universe to bring about a condition that will benefit herself or someone else, and finally, all other beings as well.

Because your book of shadows will become your personal collection of spells and rituals—as well as an intimate account of your magickal journey—it's important to have a clear idea why you've chosen this path and what you hope to achieve by following the Wiccan Way. Take some time to think about why practicing magick is important to you. Begin to define what you believe. Then write your thoughts in your grimoire. Putting your ideas and desires down on paper helps to clarify them.

What do you consider the dominant aspects of your magickal practice? Are you primarily concerned with affecting your personal life (love, career, money)? Or do you seek to deepen your spiritual connection to the universe and the Divine? Is your magick based in obtaining practical results or enhancing your intuition? Most likely, you will combine all of these, but at various times different motivations will dominate.

Although magick is as limitless as the imagination, it should always be grounded and based in reality. Grounding and centering, as you may know, play a part in many spells and rituals. Effective spells need a structure, and you can best evaluate your structure by recording it. You can only truly observe the results of your work if you write down your spells from conception to outcome. No matter how good your memory is, you can't possibly remember everything—nor can you share your knowledge and experiences with others (if you choose to) unless you create a body of information to pass on.

AT THE BEGINNING

Before you actually start recording spells, incantations, invocations, rituals, etc. in your grimoire, consider writing down the rules, ethics, and principles you choose to follow. These will guide you as you journey on your spiritual path and as you progress in your magickal work. Many witches abide by what's known as the "law of three." This means that whatever intention and energy you send out returns to you like a boomerang, but threefold. As you can see, this serves as a strong deterrent against mischief, manipulation, or other kinds of deceptive practices.

The Wiccan Rede

"Bide the Wiccan law ye must
In perfect love, in perfect trust,
Eight words the Wiccan Rede fulfill:
An' ye harm none, do what ye will.

What ye send forth comes back to thee,
So ever mind the Rule of Three.
Follow this with mind and heart,
And merry ye meet, and merry ye part."

Although your principles may conform to those of a group with which you work or the stated rules of a particular tradition you follow, ultimately they grow out of your individual convictions. Your personal code of ethics may be as simple as "Harm none." In time and with experience, your early beliefs may change, just as your mundane beliefs have likely changed since childhood. Allow your ideas to evolve, as you follow your own truth and inner guidance.

"I think the highest purpose of ritual or magickal work is to seek our gods, to commune with the cosmic 'mirror' and the spirits of nature in order to learn more of the divinity within ourselves and reach evermore toward personal growth in its highest expression."

—Maria Kay Simms, *A Time for Magick*

Begin with a Blessing

You might like to bless what you write in your grimoire by starting each entry with a prayer, poem, or inspirational saying. Many witches call upon the Goddess or another divine being before engaging in magick work and request that entity's protection and guidance. Writing in your grimoire is a magick ritual; therefore, beginning with a blessing makes perfect sense. Use a different blessing for every entry or the same one each time you write. Here's an example:

A Celtic Blessing

"Calm me, Goddess
as you calmed the storm,
Still me, Goddess
keep me from harm.
Let all tumult within me cease.
Enfold me, Goddess, in your peace."

Date Your Entries

I recommend dating each entry you make in your grimoire. This enables you to see how much time elapsed between casting a spell and the manifestation of its outcome. It also helps you place your experiences within a context and lets you witness your personal evolution over time.

RECORD YOUR MAGICKAL WORKINGS

As soon as possible after completing a spell, ritual, or other magickal working, record it in your grimoire. Include any information you consider relevant, such as the following:

- Describe your purpose (intention) for doing what you did. If you performed a spell for another person, you may want to say so (use initials or a pseudonym if you prefer not to mention the person's real name).
- Where did you perform the spell or ritual?
- Did anyone else participate? (Use initials or a pseudonym if you prefer.)
- What tools/ingredients/components did you use?
- What did you actually do? Write down the steps you took, in the order you did them: cleansed the space, cast a circle, called upon deities, lit candles, or whatever you did.
- What did you experience? How did you feel during the process? Did you receive any insights, visions, sensations, etc.? Did anything unexpected occur?
- Describe the results of your spell. How long did it take to manifest? Was the outcome what you intended? What went right or wrong?
- Would you do this spell again? What, if anything, would you do differently next time?

Feel free to adapt this basic list to suit your own needs. Include anything you feel is significant or might be beneficial to your spellworking. You can go back later and add further insights, developments, or information.

Here's an example of what an entry in your book of shadows might look like:

Spell to Get a Raise

December 1, 2016—sun in Sagittarius, waxing moon in Capricorn

TOOLS AND INGREDIENTS

Ballpoint pen

Gold candle

Peppermint essential oil

Candleholder

$20 bill

Matches

1. Cleared the space with sage incense.
2. Cast a circle. (See Chapter 13 for details on how to cast and open circles.)
3. With the pen, inscribed "+ wealth" and three $ signs on the candle.
4. Dressed the candle with peppermint oil and put it in the candleholder.
5. Laid the $20 bill on my altar.
6. Set the candleholder on top of the $20 bill.
7. Lit the candle.
8. Said the following incantation aloud while staring at the flame:

"Element of fire,
Fulfill my desire,
The raise I seek,
I receive this week."

9. Let the candle burn for 20 minutes, then snuffed it out.
10. Opened the circle.
11. Repeated this again on 12/2/16 and 12/3/16, letting the candle burn down completely on the third day. Felt empowered, relaxed, and confident.
12. Success! On 12/8/16, received notice of a forthcoming raise after the first of the year. Thank you, Goddess!

WHAT ELSE GOES IN YOUR GRIMOIRE?

Let's use the kitchen analogy again. If you love to cook, you may keep all sorts of special equipment and cool gadgets in your pantry and cabinets. If you entertain regularly, you may consider it important to have beautiful dishes, sterling silverware, crystal glasses, linen tablecloths, and so on. If you live alone or rely heavily on takeout and frozen meals, your needs will be much simpler. The same holds true for your grimoire. The good news is, you get to choose what to include and what to omit—and you can change that at any time.

When you first begin keeping a grimoire, you may be tempted to put everything you come across within its pages. Over time, however, you'll probably become more selective. Perhaps you'll decide to weed out some material, just as you'd weed your garden to showcase what you consider important. William Morris, a nineteenth-century English textile designer, artist, and poet, said, "Have nothing in your houses that you do not know to be useful, or believe to be beautiful."

I think the same can be said for your book of shadows. Although it can be useful to look back at early entries to track your journey, don't be afraid to discard anything you no longer need.

Keep Track of Celestial Influences

As you record your magickal journey, you may find it helpful to keep track of the cosmic conditions that affect you. In addition to dating each entry in your book of shadows, I suggest you also include the moon's phase, and if you know astrology, note other celestial activity that might be relevant. For instance, Venus's placement could have an impact on love spells. If you're doing a spell for career success, the positions of the sun, Jupiter, and Saturn could factor in. You could even cast a chart for the day, print it out, and add it to your grimoire beside what you write for that day. Many online sites—including *www.astro.com*—offer free charts that you can calculate in a few minutes.

Track Your Health Cycles

Your health can also affect your magickal workings. Therefore, you may want to note any physical or emotional conditions you are experiencing at the time you perform a ritual or spell. Did you feel particularly energized? Tired because the baby kept you awake most of the night before? Did you have a cold or headache when you cast the spell? Women may also find it useful to track menstrual cycles, as these often influence your emotions and, consequently, the magick you do. You may discover that you feel more powerful or more intuitive at certain times of the month.

Note Situations in Your Everyday Life

It's hard to separate our magickal lives from our everyday lives—even for seasoned witches. If something in your mundane world is troubling you and sucking up a lot of your energy, you may not feel as focused or powerful in your spellworking—and you may not achieve the results you desire. Note this in your grimoire. On the other hand, if you're riding the crest of the wave and everything seems right at the moment, note that too. Maybe you've met a new person who shares your path or you started a yoga class or returned from a restful vacation. Occurrences such as these may influence your magick practice, directly or indirectly, so it's a good idea to keep track of them.

"Let my worship be within the heart that rejoices,
for behold: all acts of love and pleasure are my rituals.
And therefore, let there be beauty and strength,
power and compassion, honor and humility,
mirth and reverence within you."

—Doreen Valiente, "The Charge of the Goddess"

Pay Attention to Your Dreams

Many dream researchers and therapists believe your subconscious communicates with you through your dreams. Some metaphysicians suggest that your guides, angels, or other nonphysical entities may also send messages to you via dreams. Record any dreams that seem especially vivid, meaningful, or strange, or that recur again and again—they may provide valuable insights or even glimpses of the future. Also note dreams that have a direct correlation to things you're focusing on in your spiritual or magickal work. In Chapter 18, we'll talk more about dreams and how to work with them creatively.

Record Your Readings

Do you do tarot or rune readings? Consult the *I Ching* or use a pendulum to gain advice? If you work with one or more oracles, you'll probably want to keep a record of your readings. You may designate a separate journal in which to chronicle these, but your grimoire is a good place to write them down too. Date each reading and note the reason you did it or the question you asked. Draw the spread, indicating the positions of the cards, runes, etc. Add your own interpretation—what does the reading mean to you? Later on, you can revisit what you've written and describe how things turned out. You might record your reading like this:

Past, Present, Future Tarot Reading

October 12, 2016

"Please provide insight into my relationship with A"

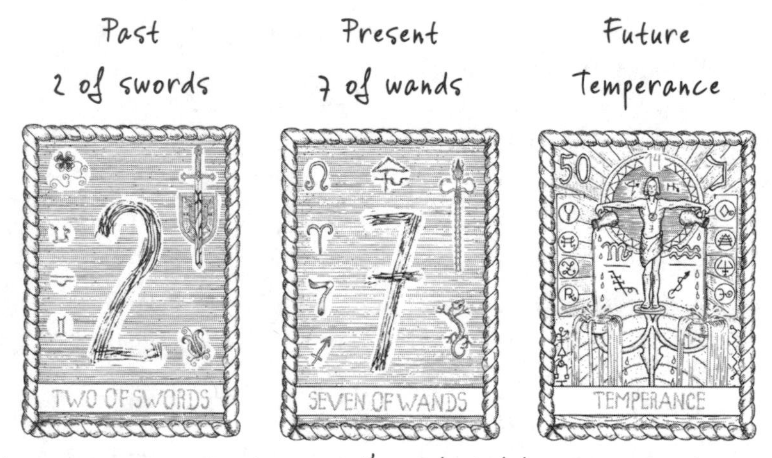

Interpretation: In the past I've felt helpless and confused about what to do. Now, I'm trying to hang in there and be strong; I'm determined to make this relationship work and I'm learning ways to handle problems better, without giving up or giving in. Temperance in the future position suggests things will be more peaceful, and I sense we'll establish a more balanced and harmonious arrangement.

Other Things to Include

Do you have a favorite poem or song that resonates with you at a deep level? Have you just read an inspiring passage in a book? You may wish to jot these down in your book of shadows—especially if they figure into your spiritual and/or magickal path in some way. Musings about things you noticed while walking in the park, comments on what's transpiring in the world around you, thought-provoking ideas raised by a friend—all these, and much more, may have a place in your book of shadows too.

Many witches like to include visuals in their grimoires. Early grimoires often contained drawings of occult symbols and other illustrations as well. Even if you don't consider yourself an artist, you can still sketch images in the margins—you don't have to show them to anyone else, so don't censor yourself. Pictures from print sources or downloaded from the Internet can aid your visualization process. Do you want to take a trip to an exotic land? Why not paste a photo of that place in your book to help you focus on your goal? If you check out online images of grimoires, you'll see that lots of books—both ancient and modern—feature artwork of all kinds. Remember the old saying, a picture's worth a thousand words? This is definitely true in spellcasting.

We've already mentioned affixing dried leaves, herbs, and flowers to your grimoire. Don't limit yourself to these alone, however. Feathers, bits of lovely lace, a scrap of patterned silk, a remnant of an antique Japanese fan, a lock of your lover's hair, tiny seashells, a piece of your favorite sheet music, photos of loved ones, ribbons tied into magick knots . . . the possibilities are endless. What triggers your imagination? The ability to imagine a result, after all, must precede the result you seek to manifest.

Purists might frown on such diversions from tradition, but hey, it's your book, right? Whatever holds meaning for you has the potential to enrich your personal growth and enhance your magickal workings. Your book of shadows is a safe place to explore those parts of yourself that you may never have felt free to unveil before, to face your inner shadow, to acknowledge what holds meaning for you, and to connect with the beautiful being you are in your heart of hearts.

Chapter 5

PREPARING TO USE YOUR GRIMOIRE

You've acquired a book that will become your grimoire—or fabricated your own—and given thought to how you'll organize it. Now it's time to prepare yourself and your book for the ongoing relationship that will develop between you.

Writing in your book of shadows is a magickal act, so you'll want to treat it as such. This means you'll likely do your journaling within a sacred space you've created for your spellwork and other ritual practices. Perhaps you've already established a sacred place in your home. You may also have set up an altar there, where you could display your grimoire. If you haven't done this yet, you can use the following instructions or design your own ritual to create a sacred space for all your magickal workings.

CREATING SACRED SPACE

The purpose of defining and consecrating a sacred space is to give yourself a dedicated realm in which to perform magick and ritual, where you can move beyond your ordinary world when you so choose. You are, in essence, raising a temple (though not necessarily a brick-and-mortar one) for meditation, worship, divination, spellcasting, or any other aspect of magickal practice you wish to do here—including writing in your grimoire. You can create a more or less permanent sacred space or a temporary one, depending on your intentions and circumstances.

The Power of the Circle

In *The Spiral Dance*, Starhawk describes the circle as "the creation of a sacred space . . . Power, the subtle force that shapes reality, is raised through chanting or dancing and may be directed through a symbol or visualization. With the raising of the cone of power comes ecstasy, which may then lead to a trance state in which visions are seen and insights gained."

Cleansing Your Sacred Space

Once you've determined the location of your sacred space, take a broom and sweep the area thoroughly to clear away dust, dirt, and clutter. This is the real reason witches use brooms, not to fly through the sky. After you finish physically sweeping the area, focus on cleansing the psychic space. In this way, you remove unwanted energies or influences—any "bad vibes" that might linger there. Begin in the east and work your way counterclockwise around the area, in a circular fashion. Sweep the air, from the floor up to as high as you can comfortably reach. When you have gone around your area three times, lay the broom on the floor and visualize all the negative energy breaking up and dissolving.

Some spellworkers also like to "smudge" the area with the smoke from burning sage. Light a sage wand/bundle (available at New Age shops and online) or a stick of sage incense. Walk in a circle, starting in the east and moving counterclockwise, letting the smoke waft through the area. Then walk in an X across the space to finish cleansing your space. Now stand in the center of your space and feel the fresh, light, clean energy around you.

Purifying Your Sacred Space

For this next level of cleansing you'll need two chalices or tall glasses. Fill one with spring (or bottled) water. The water should be kinetic, not static, during this process for it is the essence of running water that generates potency. In the other chalice, place four pinches of salt, one to represent each of the four directions.

1. Hold the chalice that contains the water in your left hand and the chalice with the salt crystals in your right.
2. Pour the water into the chalice of salt, combining the two elements of water and earth.
3. Pour the now salted water back into the chalice in your left hand, dissolving the salt crystals so that the two distinct elements mix thoroughly. Continue pouring the water back and forth from hand to hand, as you repeat this intention:

"With salt I purify
With water I cleanse
All things in accord
From beginning to end."

If you prefer, you can create your own original incantation or blessing.

Dedicating Your Sacred Space

The next step is to dedicate your sacred space. You can begin by anointing the area you've chosen with frankincense essential oil (or another oil you prefer). Just put a little dab in each corner, starting in the east and moving clockwise around the space, creating a cross within a circle. This symbol represents the balance of female and male energies, the circle of creation, the four directions, and the four elements.

You may also opt to place a stone or crystal that has meaning for you at each of the four compass directions. (If your sacred space is outdoors, you can bury the stones in the ground.) Or you might like to design symbols that signify peace, holiness, protection, power, etc. and position them in your space. Some people display images of beloved deities in their sacred spaces. If you wish, you can create an elaborate ritual for dedicating your space—the choice is up to you.

Protecting Your Sacred Space

After you've finished setting up your sacred space, you'll want to protect it from intrusive energies. Consider these suggestions:

- Place a stone associated with protection, such as onyx, hematite, or peridot, in the area.
- Lay dried basil leaves in your sacred space.
- Position or draw a pentagram or other protective symbol there.
- Sprinkle some sea salt in the corners.
- Set a clove of garlic in your space.

"As a magician, you use ritual in order to create within yourself a mental state that allows you to give clear and direct instructions to your unconscious mind . . . Ritual is a means to an end, not an end in itself."

—Nancy B. Watson, *Practical Solitary Magic*

CONSECRATE YOUR GRIMOIRE

The next step is to dedicate your book of shadows to its sacred purpose. Now you affirm your intention to do good works in the world and to record what you do so that it may benefit all beings.

1. Light a yellow candle on your altar (or other place where you do your magick work). If you wish, call upon Sophia, goddess of wisdom, or another deity to guide you.
2. Light frankincense incense in an incense burner.
3. Hold your book slightly opened above the rising smoke. Turn the pages slowly and gently, allowing the fragrant smoke to drift through the pages.

4. Speak the following words, or improvise your own:

"Blessed be this instrument of art,
By my hand [or human hands] you were made,
By magick, be now changed.
No more an ordinary book in my eyes but a grimoire dedicated to the Craft of the Wise.
By all the power of three times three
As I will, so mote it be."

5. Hold the book on your right hand and place your left hand on top of the book as you open yourself to the changes and lessons yet to come.
6. Imagine all the witches you know of and admire, both contemporary and historical. Picture yourself in the middle of a growing circle. To your left envision those who are older than you, and the elders who have passed on. To your right see the younger ones and those who will come in the future.
7. Recognize your place in the spiral of time and acknowledge this task that you have chosen. See yourself within the context of humanity and companionship. When the image is clear in your mind, speak these words aloud, or improvise your own:

"Wisdom of the ages, be with me here now.
Sacred book of changes, this promise I vow:
To honor those who have gone before;
To preserve the secrets, legends, and lore;
To hold my place in the spiral of time;
Within this sacred grimoire of mine."

When you've finished, take some time to think about the blessing ceremony you just performed. Did you experience a shift in the energy around you? Did you receive any insights, sensations, visions, or guidance? Do you sense that your book of shadows is now ready to serve as a sacred tool for furthering your purpose as a witch? If you called upon a deity to aid you, thank that deity now. Take some time to record the very first entry in your personal book of shadows—the experience of consecrating your book.

WRITING IN YOUR GRIMOIRE

The authors of secular books often dedicate them to people they love or to those who have assisted them in the writing process. You may choose to dedicate your grimoire to a deity to whom you are devoted, one who has played a special role in your life, or one whom you want to guide you in the magickal work you do—including the process of writing in your book of shadows. Therefore, the very first page of your book might be your dedication page.

Protecting Your Secrets

Consider putting a protection symbol at the beginning of your book to help safeguard it. A pentagram is a frequently used symbol of protection, but you can choose any emblem that holds meaning for you. You might even like to design a special symbol for this purpose. In Chapter 12 you'll learn how to create magick symbols known as *sigils*.

In keeping with the tradition of secrecy, you may want to use your magick name or Craft name when writing in your grimoire. If you mention anyone else within its pages, you'll probably want to disguise that person's identity too, referring to him or her by a pseudonym or initials. The same holds true for the names of private locations, such as the homes of fellow witches. This is a good precaution to take if you're worried that your book might fall into the wrong hands.

Writing in Code

Some witches choose to exercise yet another method for ensuring that the information in their grimoires remains secret. They write in code. Then, if an inappropriate person discovers their books, that individual won't be able to read the contents. You can explore this option if you wish. Or you could consider writing only certain parts of your book in a secret script if you want some portions to remain accessible to others.

SECRET SCRIPTS

Since ancient times, magickal workers and others who sought to protect their knowledge—and themselves—have written in secret scripts. Some authors wrote in languages other than those used in the culture or country where they lived, such as Sanskrit or Coptic, which worked well enough in the days when few people could read or write and even fewer knew the languages spoken in foreign lands. Today, however, with the availability of online translation sites, you'll have to go to greater lengths if you really want to keep what you write secret.

The Theban Alphabet

Although we cannot say for certain what the Theban alphabet's origins are, it is a beautiful and widely used magickal alphabet, especially among Gardnerian Wiccans. The Golden Dawn also adopted it in the nineteenth century. Sometimes referred to as the Witch's Alphabet or the Runes of Honorius, this ceremonial text came into use during the medieval period. Heinrich Cornelius Agrippa mentioned the script in Book III of the *Three Books of Occult Philosophy* published in the 1530s, and attributed it to Honorius of Thebes. Agrippa credited Pietro d'Abano (or Peter of Abano), an Italian writer and magician who lived during the thirteenth century, with preserving the Theban alphabet.

A		B		C		D	
E		F		G		H	
I		J		K		L	
M		N		O		P	
Q		R		S		T	
U		V		W		X	
		Y		Z			

The Futhark Runes

Known as the Older Rune Row or the Elder Futhark, these runes were used by Germanic ceremonial magicians for divination and inspiration, and as inscriptions in talismans and amulets. The word "rune" means a secret or mystery. Although they have phonetic correlations, the Futhark runes never evolved into a spoken language. The name "futhark" derives from the first six characters that appear in this system. According to Nordic legend, the god Odin (or Woden) first spied the runes as he hung from the World Tree, Yggdrasil, for nine days and nights.

The runes can also serve as an oracle for divination; each individual rune contains a specific esoteric message. For 2,000 years, this oracle was used throughout Northern Europe and Scandinavia, until 1639 when the Christian church banned it. Viking and Saxon invaders brought the runes to the British Isles. In the United States, J.R.R. Tolkien's *The Lord of the Rings* introduced many readers to the runes, and Ralph Blum's bestseller *The Book of Runes* taught people how to use the oracle.

FUTHARK RUNES			
Number	**Shape**	**Phonetic Value**	**Name**
1	ᚠ	F	Fehu
2	ᚢ	U	Uruz
3	ᚦ	TH	Thurisaz
4	ᚨ	A	Ansuz
5	ᚱ	R	Raidho
6	ᚲ	K	Kaunaz
7	ᚷ	G	Gebo
8	ᚹ	W	Wunjo

FUTHARK RUNES			
Number	**Shape**	**Phonetic Value**	**Name**
9	ᚺ	H	Hagalaz
10	ᚾ	N	Nauthiz
11	ᛁ	I	Isa
12	ᛃ	J	Jera
13	ᛇ	EI	Eihaw
14	ᛈ	P	Perthro
15	ᛉ	Z	Algiz
16	ᛊ	S	Sowilo
17	ᛏ	T	Teiwaz
18	ᛒ	B	Berkano
19	ᛖ	E	Ehwaz
20	ᛗ	M	Mannaz
21	ᛚ	L	Laguz
22	ᛜ	NG	Ingwaz
23	ᛞ	D	Dagaz
24	ᛟ	O	Othala

The Ogham Runes

The early Celts used an alphabet known as Ogham, based on trees. Because the Celts and Druids considered trees sacred, the Ogham letters also serve as mystical symbols. Each of the twenty letters in this system corresponds to a particular tree. B (Beith), for instance, is linked with the birch; N (Nion) represents the ash tree. The letters are composed of a series of straight and angled lines, or notches, cut along a central line or stave. A word or phrase written in Ogham looks a bit like a tree limb with branches sprouting from it. Throughout Ireland and Britain you can see standing stones engraved with Ogham glyphs. Early Celtic manuscripts also feature Ogham script.

Another unique characteristic of Ogham is that it can be signed with the fingers. Using a part of the body—the torso, nose, or leg—as a center dividing line, you can extend your fingers on either side to form letters.

OGHAM ALPHABET			
Shape	**Letter**	**Name**	**Tree**
ᚁ	B	Beith	Birch
ᚂ	L	Luis	Rowan
ᚃ	F	Fearn	Alder
ᚄ	S	Sail	Willow
ᚅ	N	Nion	Ash
ᚆ	H	hÚath	Hawthorn
ᚇ	D	Dair	Oak

OGHAM ALPHABET			
Shape	**Letter**	**Name**	**Tree**
ᚈ	T	Tinne	Holly
ᚉ	C	Coll	Hazel
ᚊ	Q	Quert	Apple
ᚋ	M	Muin	Vine
ᚌ	G	Gort	Ivy
ᚍ	NG	nGéatal	Reed
ᚎ	Z (st)	Straif	Blackthorn
ᚏ	R	Ruis	Elder
ᚐ	A	Ailm	Silver Fir
ᚑ	O	Onn	Gorse
ᚒ	U	Úr	Heather
ᚓ	E	Eadha	Poplar
ᚔ	I	Iodhadh	Yew

Other Options

The Greek mathematician and philosopher Pythagoras, who lived in the sixth century B.C.E., is usually credited with having developed the system of numerology that we use today. This study of numbers, known as *gematria*, attaches a number equivalent to each letter in a word. Each number has an esoteric meaning as well as a mundane one. Someone who understands the hidden correspondences between letters and numbers can read a word and comprehend a secret meaning behind the obvious one.

TABLE OF NUMBER–LETTER CORRESPONDENCES

1	2	3	4	5	6	7	8	9
A	B	C	D	E	F	G	H	I
J	K	L	M	N	O	P	Q	R
S	T	U	V	W	X	Y	Z	

Various other magickal alphabets exist too, such as the Masonic/Rosicrucian system. In his comprehensive book, *The Magician's Companion*, Bill Whitcomb presents a collection of different secret scripts including an intriguing one based on configurations of daggers. You can even design your very own magick language that only you can interpret.

PREPARING YOURSELF TO WRITE

Before you begin writing in your grimoire, you'll want to prepare your body and your mind. Open yourself to the guidance of the Goddess or a particular deity with whom you've chosen to work. You want to move into a realm beyond the mundane, where you align with Spirit. Begin your preparation by making a conscious decision to enter the time and space we refer to as "between the worlds."

Turn off the TV. Shut down your computer. Silence your phone. Dim the lights. Light a candle or two or three. Do not let the outside world intrude. Invite benevolent forces to assist you. Relax and breathe slowly, deeply. Clear your mind.

One by one, begin to release your distractions, letting them flow further and further away from you.

1. Sit in a comfortable place with your spine straight, facing your altar if you have one. Picture a radiant ball of energy located in the center of your being, your solar plexus, about halfway between your heart and your navel. As you continue to breathe, allow the light to expand. As you inhale, understand that as you take the surrounding air into your body, you transform it into energy. As you exhale, you release your cares and concerns. Get in touch with this cycle of breathing, of energy released and replenished, replenished and released.
2. If you are sitting in a chair, bend down and touch the floor with the palms of your hands as you breathe in, imagining that you are gathering energy from the earth beneath you, beneath your home. Picture the earth. Now send your energy outward so that you can psychically touch things beyond your physical reach. Your reach extends beyond the floorboards, beyond the foundations of your home, deep into the sacred earth.
3. Call up this energy as you breathe in. Sit up straight again, and let the energy flow through you. As you exhale, send it spiraling into your center. Envision it transforming into a glowing light that you hold within the core of your being. When this image becomes very clear, visualize the glowing ball of energy moving slightly, first spiraling within itself, and then traveling up and down a bit. Realize that as you breathe, you are taking in energy from the air and transforming it into living breath. You are also taking in energy from the earth and transforming it into active power.
4. Stay focused and let the rising ball of energy reach your heart. Experience this as an embrace from the Goddess, the power of the earth moving through you according to your will. Envision the ball of energy separating and becoming two distinct spheres. As the spheres separate, they travel to your shoulders. Feel the warmth surrounding your shoulders as you would if you were walking in bright sunlight.
5. Let the spheres of pulsing, glowing light travel slowly down your arms; experience each movement as a distinct sensation. Your shoulders drop and become more relaxed. Any residual tension in

your arms completely dissipates. Your wrists grow limp. You are surrendering to the beauty of this power, even as you are directing it. The energy fills your hands and permeates all the way to your fingertips.

6. Turn your hands over so that your palms face-up. Slowly raise your arms. Imagine sending this energy outward to touch all beings. Extend your arms with your palms facing outward in an invoking gesture. Breathe deeply and feel how this transforming energy changes you.
7. Open your eyes and look around the room. Notice how your perception has changed. Lower your arms slowly and let your hands touch the floor once again. Continue focusing on the cycle of breath, releasing and replenishing energy. As you exhale, send the energy back into the earth from which it came. Breathe deeply.
8. You should feel relaxed, but not the least bit sleepy. Tranquil, but invigorated and alive, in touch with the earth and with the delicate energies to which the intuitive mind is open. Think about how a simple act such as grounding your energy and opening your psychic center can heighten your awareness. Now you are ready to begin writing.

"Magick happens when you step into who you truly are and embrace that which fulfills your soul."

—Dacha Avelin, *Embracing Your Inner Witch*

Set aside time to write in your grimoire on a regular basis. Incorporate writing into your magickal practice and into your regular routine. Find some time to write in the morning, remembering your dreams and delineating your hopes for the day. Write in the evening to reflect on the day's events. A line or two will suffice. Honor the moments in life that could be easily forgotten by jotting down a word or two about the sunrise or the approach of twilight.

Your grimoire can be anything and everything you want it to be. It is the place for you to explore and express your spirituality: a safe place free from other people's judgment, criticism, and skepticism. No one but you need be aware of the secrets kept within its pages. Creating your own grimoire lets you deepen awareness of your magickal life. By writing your story, you may also become an inspiration for others. Your book of shadows will enhance your knowledge of yourself, your aspirations, your dreams, and your personal growth. May it comfort you in times of darkness and bring you joy in times of light. May it keep your secrets as a trusted friend would, protect the stories of your lifetime, and hold your personal mythology securely.

Merry meet, and merry part, and merry meet again. Blessed be.

PART II

Using Your Grimoire

Chapter 6

EVERYDAY MAGICK

Magick isn't something you do, it's what you are. As a witch, you will make magickal workings an integral part of your everyday life. We usually think of the sabbats as times to perform spells and rituals. The sabbats, however, only make up eight days out of 365 each year—what about the rest? Why wait for the next sabbat to cast a spell, communicate with the spirit realm, or engage in a meaningful ritual?

Every day is a magickal day, if you choose to see it that way. Wondrous happenings and amazing revelations occur each day of the year. All we have to do is open our eyes and minds and hearts to these occurrences. Each day also affords unique opportunities for spellworking. By understanding the distinct qualities of the days of the week and the forces behind them, you can attune yourself to their special energies and thus enhance the power of your spells. Of course, you'll want to record your experiences in your grimoire.

"To work magic, I need a basic belief in my ability to do things and cause things to happen. That belief is generated and sustained by my daily actions."

—Starhawk

MORNING RITUALS

You may enjoy writing in your book of shadows as soon as you awaken, thus making it part of your morning routine. This way, the images from your dreams will still be fresh and you can record them in detail. Later on, the busyness of the day will likely cloud your memory. Early morning is also a good time to set out your intentions for the day.

In addition to writing, you may want to design a simple ritual that will start the day on a pleasant note. Anything that you do every day with awareness becomes a ritual, such as taking a refreshing shower or savoring a morning cup of coffee. The challenge is to make the ritual sacred, and to receive the benefits of divine grace. You may only need a few moments to transform your morning experience from mundane to magickal, thus paving the way to a more inspired and productive day.

Use the following suggested ritual to start your day, or design one of your own. Personalize the ritual, if you wish, by inserting the names of other goddesses or deities with whom you feel a special affinity.

1. Begin by sitting or standing before your altar. Place a small quartz crystal, a cup or chalice of water, a candle, a little essential oil that you find pleasing, and some incense on the altar. Light the candle to symbolize the rising sun, and then take a moment to reflect silently on the energies you'd like to call to yourself during the unfolding day. Imagine your perfect day and try to form a clear image of it in your mind. You may want to accomplish something specific. Perhaps you'd like to change something in your regimen, such as eating a healthy breakfast instead of grabbing a doughnut.
2. Picture yourself in a state of attainment. See yourself achieving whatever your heart desires. Imagine doing all the things you mean to do and need to do in a state of joy and satisfaction. When the image of what you intend is clear, speak the following words aloud, or improvise your own: "Rosy-fingered Eos, goddess of the dawn who paints the morning sky with light, I ask for your blessing and rejoice as you set the sky alight. I anoint myself as your child, alive and anew with your radiant energy."

3. Place a small drop of essential oil on your fingertip. Touch your fingertip to your third eye (on your forehead, between your eyebrows). See yourself bathed in the light of the breaking dawn.
4. Light the incense and let its perfume waft over you. Inhale its aroma and speak the following words: "The fires of day have risen. Let my heart's desire rise up to the feet of the Goddess, that she may gather and direct my sacred intention with her wisdom and power. As the sun climbs through the sky, bless me, Lady of the Morning, who bestows abundance to us, her children. So mote it be."
5. Grasp the cup/chalice of water and hold it aloft to toast the day. Bring it down to chest level, near to your heart. Dip your fingers in the water, close your eyes, and place a little water on each eyelid. Say aloud, "Goddess Iris, who adorns the sky with rainbows of light, bring me clarity of vision that I may see the true nature of everything around me. May I be blessed in your eyes."
6. Hold the crystal in your hands, feeling it come alive with your energy. Imbue the stone with the intentions of what you most desire to manifest on this day. As you hold the crystal, speak the following words or improvise your own: "Blessed Mother Earth, I honor you and your unending generosity. May your sacred treasure enrich my existence. May I share the abundance of the Goddess on this day."
7. Extinguish the candle. Carry the crystal with you as a talisman to help you maintain your focus throughout the day.

Note in your grimoire any impressions, sensations, insights, or other experiences that arise during your morning ritual. Quite possibly you'll receive some sort of awareness or guidance now that can help you as the day unfolds.

EVENING RITUALS

Twilight is an utterly magickal time—a liminal zone that's not wholly day or night, but betwixt and between. The sun sinks low in the horizon, painting the sky with brilliant light. Behind the sunset darkness approaches in indigo and violet hues, and finally the black of hidden wisdom descends. At this time of transition, the clarity of light merges with the mysteries of darkness. Celebrate with an evening ritual such as the following, or create your own. Personalize it, if you wish, by inserting the names of other goddesses or deities with whom you feel a special affinity.

1. Begin by reflecting on the day that has just passed. Contemplate what you have experienced. Which things went as you had hoped and which things would you have changed if given the chance?
2. Place a cup or chalice of water, a candle, and a moonstone on your altar. Light some incense as you invoke the mysteries of the night with this charge: "Queen of the Night, radiant goddess Nut who shines forth in her many aspects through the moon and stars, bless this coming darkness. I ask for your blessing as one who honors you and seeks to learn your great mysteries."
3. Hold the incense aloft and say: "As the curling whispers of smoke rise to greet the night sky, so does my mind rise along the rivers of dreamtime to welcome you, beloved Goddess, into my dreams. I invoke you and I invite you to inspire my dreams that I may experience your divine grace."
4. Light the candle and meditate on its softly glowing flame, as you say: "I step between the worlds into a world both in and out of time. The candle lights my path as the moon lights the night sky. I gaze upon your great beauty in wonder, Goddess of the Ages, Lady of Mystery, thou who art brighter than all the stars."
5. Hold your cup or chalice and take a sip of water as you say: "May your abundance flow through me, may dreams and visions come to me. May the unseen be seen and the power of sight granted to me that I may perceive in the night that which is unknowable by day."
6. Pick up your moonstone and hold it to your third eye as you say: "Rare gem of the night, send forth your light to guide me through the darkness. I enter into your starry realm in love and trust, abandoning all fear with the knowledge that you are with me always, in my thoughts and in my dreams. I do not merely sleep, but awaken to your presence."

7. Think about what you would like to glean from your dreams. Inspiration? Prophecy? Self-knowledge? When you're ready, extinguish the candle.

Take a few minutes to write in your grimoire your ideas and intentions, as well as any insights or impressions you may have received during the ritual.

> *"It is only by working the rituals, that any significant degree of understanding can develop. If you wait until you are positive you understand all aspects of the ceremony before beginning to work, you will never begin to work."*
>
> —Lon Milo DuQuette, *The Magick of Aleister Crowley*

POWER DAYS

According to astrology and mythology, each day of the week is ruled by one of the heavenly bodies in our solar system. Each day also has a rich Pagan history of its own. Different days have different qualities and characteristics, therefore some days are better suited than others to specific types of spellwork. By casting a spell on the day that corresponds to your intention—based on the deity who presides over the day—you can increase your potential for success. Most love spells, for instance, should be done on Friday because Venus, the planet of love and relationships, governs that day.

Day of the Week	**Ruling Planet/Deity**
Sunday	Sun
Monday	Moon
Tuesday (*Mardi* in French)	Mars (Tiw in Norse mythology)
Wednesday (*Mercredi* in French)	Mercury
Thursday	Jupiter (Thor in Norse mythology)
Friday (*Vendredi* in French)	Venus (Freya in Norse mythology)
Saturday	Saturn

When you prepare yourself to enact a ritual or cast a spell or a charm, you are agreeing to suspend reality for a time to get in touch with energies greater than your own limited scope of individual perception. By entering the space and time "between the worlds," you make an agreement with yourself and with the spirits. You agree to acknowledge their divine presence by inviting them into your sacred space. You agree to accept physical manifestations of the divine presence. And you agree to suspend your sense of disbelief in order to accept that magick and psychic experiences are indeed possible and desirable. You might not hear a clap of thunder to show that the goddesses and gods have acknowledged your work—but, then again, you just might.

Your Personal Best

When's the best time to cast a spell? On your birthday. On that special day each year, the sun shines brightly on you (even if it's raining outdoors) and spotlights your unique talents and abilities. The day's vibrant energy enhances whatever you undertake. As a result, whatever spells you do on your birthday have a better than usual chance of succeeding.

Sunday

As suggested by its name, the sun rules Sunday. The sun's golden rays brighten everything they touch. The sun's light enables us to clearly distinguish one thing from another, and it nurtures growth on our planet. Therefore, Sunday's energy supports spells that involve creativity, inspiration, self-expression, career success, and public image. This is also a good time for celebration and bringing people together—consider performing group rituals on Sundays. Because witches connect the sun with God energy, you may want to call upon the sun gods such as Ra (Egyptian), Apollo (Greek), or Aidan (Celtic) to lend strength and meaning to your efforts.

Monday

The moon rules Monday. Because we associate the moon with Goddess energy, magickal work planned for a Monday should involve aspects of the Goddess. The changing phases of the moon make Monday a good time to do spells and rituals designed to stimulate change. The moon governs the tides, so spells involving water are also appropriate for this day. Think of purification and cleansing work that you may need to do. Consider consecrating your chalice on a Monday. Astrologers associate the moon with home and family; therefore, it's best to cast spells involving these things on a Monday. Lunar energy enhances fertility spells too. Meditate on the aspects of the Greek moon goddess, Artemis, or on her Roman counterpart, Diana, and request her assistance.

Tuesday

Tuesday is ruled by the planet Mars and named for the Nordic god Tiw (or Tyr), the invincible warrior whose attributes include strength, attainment of desire, and manifestation of the will. Perform spells and rituals for strength, courage, daring, or success in any type of competition on Tuesday. If you're doing a spell to help you stand up to an adversary, overcome an obstacle, or reverse an attack on you, Tuesday would be a good day to perform it. It's also a good time to build your psychic defenses through protection rituals.

Wednesday

The planet Mercury rules Wednesday. In Roman mythology, Mercury is the messenger of the gods. Astrologers connect the planet with communication—both spoken and written—as well as with various types of mental activity and short trips. Rituals and spells for Wednesday involve communication, education, sending and receiving messages, and intellectual pursuits. This is also a good day to connect with spirits or do divination, perhaps by using a pendulum, runes, or the tarot.

Mercury's Retrograde Periods

Every four months, the planet Mercury goes retrograde for approximately three weeks when it appears to be moving backward through the sky. Mercury rules communication and thinking in general, so your mind might not be as clear as usual during retrograde periods. Your ability to communicate with others may be hampered as well. Usually, these aren't good times to do magick, as confusion, lack of clarity, and mistakes can occur.

Thursday

The planet Jupiter rules Thursday, and the day gets its name from the Norse god Thor. In mythology, Thor, the god of thunder, wields a mighty hammer; thus he's sometimes linked with strength, justice, and legal matters. If you are trying to influence the outcome of a legal proceeding or political matter, you may find that enacting a spell on a Thursday gives you an edge. Astrologers connect Jupiter—the largest planet in our solar system—with growth, abundance, and good fortune. Do spells for prosperity, career advancement, or any type of expansion on Thursdays. Because Jupiter also governs the zodiac sign Sagittarius, which astrologers associate with long-distance travel, Thursday is a good time to do travel spells.

Friday

Venus, the goddess of love and relationships, governs Friday. The Nordic goddess Freya, the patroness of powerful women, passion, and love, gave her name to this day. As you might expect, spells, rituals, and charms relating to matters of the heart are best performed on Friday. Venus also rules the arts and beauty, so if you want to stimulate your creativity or make yourself more attractive, do a spell on Friday. Friendships and social occasions can also benefit from Venus's influence—hold group rituals and celebrations on a Friday.

Saturday

As its name indicates, Saturday is ruled by the planet Saturn. Astrologers connect Saturn with limitations, endings, and the past, as well as structure, stability, and the business world. Do spells on Saturday to end an unwanted relationship, to bring a successful close to an endeavor, or to create strong boundaries. Protection spells and banishing rituals can benefit from Saturn's power. Do spells to strengthen a business venture, rein in spending, or encourage stability in any area of your life on this day. Saturday is also a good time for past-life work and rituals to honor those who have left the physical world.

BRING MAGICK INTO EVERYDAY TASKS

We spend most of our daily lives engaged in mundane activities and routine tasks. However, you can enrich ordinary undertakings with magickal energy—and why not? Kitchen and hearth witches embrace this concept; they consider everything in their homes sacred and imbue every household chore with magickal significance. For example, you can view sweeping the floor free of dust and dirt as simultaneously cleansing the space of negative energy.

Nowhere is this practice more evident than in cooking. When you prepare food, you put your personal energy, intention, and love into nourishing those who will eat what you cook. And the herbs you use to season your dishes contain magickal properties—you'll learn about these in Chapter 16. Consider incorporating the following practices into your daily routine:

- As you cook and clean, use affirmations to bless your home and loved ones.
- When you open the kitchen door say: "May only health, love, and joy come through this door into this home."
- While stirring a pot on the stove or a mixture in a bowl say: "Thanks be to all beings who contributed to this meal."
- While serving food say: "May the food I share nourish my loved ones in both body and soul."
- While sweeping or vacuuming say: "May all harmful, disruptive, or unbalanced energy be removed from this place."
- When you turn off the kitchen light at night say: "Bless this kitchen, and keep those of us who use it safe and healthy through the night."

Design your own household rituals and magick practices. You may also enjoy studying the ancient Chinese art known as feng shui, which associates each sector of your home with certain parts of your life. Feng shui teaches you how to magickally manipulate energies and bring about results in your world by making adjustments in your living space.

A Kitchen Witchery Spell

This spell uses "kitchen witchery" to sweeten a frustrating situation. You don't have to be a gourmet cook to carry it off—your intention is what counts.

Piece-of-Cake Spell

Things aren't going as smoothly as you'd hoped. Perhaps a project is taking longer or costing more than expected; a romance has hit a snag; you have to deal with a lot of uncooperative people at work or at home. It's time to use your witchy talents to rectify the unpleasant situation.

TOOLS AND INGREDIENTS

A cake mix (or ingredients for making your favorite cake recipe)
Food coloring
A large bowl
Spoon
Cake pan(s)
Candles
Matches or a lighter

1. Collect the ingredients needed for this spell and preheat the oven.
2. Cast a circle around the area where you will do your spell—in this case, your kitchen.
3. Follow the directions for making the cake, according to the package or your favorite recipe. You may want to choose a flavor that suits your intentions: chocolate or strawberry for love, cinnamon or mint for money, almond or vanilla for peace of mind, anise for protection. As you work, focus on your objective and imagine you are sending your intention into the batter.
4. If you like, add food coloring to tint the batter to match your intention: pink for love, green for money, and so on (see Chapter 12 for information about color symbology).
5. Stir the batter using a clockwise motion if your goal is to attract something or to stimulate growth of some kind. Stir counterclockwise if you want to limit, decrease, or end something.

6. Pour the batter into the pan(s) and bake.

7. When the cake has finished cooking, let it cool, and then ice it with frosting in a color that relates to your intention. You may want to decorate it with symbols, pictures, and/or words that describe your objective.

8. Add candles of an appropriate color. The number of candles should also correspond to your goal: 2 for love, 4 for stability, 5 for change, and so on.

9. Light the candles and concentrate on your wish. Blow out the candles.

10. Share the cake with other people who are involved in the challenging situation, so that everyone benefits. Each person who eats some of the cake takes the intention into him- or herself and becomes a co-creator in the spell's success.

"We come into this world with precious gifts that are meant to be shared, if each one of us takes the time to send healing and love to the world, we truly can change the lives of many and the world around us."

—Jasmeine Moonsong

Treat Your Entire Home As Sacred

The Buddha once said, "Wherever you live is your temple if you treat it like one." Sacredness is more a matter of attitude and behavior than of trappings, and it doesn't require a building or props. Nonetheless, creating a sacred space is an important part of practicing magick, and witches often use tools and processes to establish safe havens in which to work.

We talked about creating sacred space in Chapter 5. You can designate a specific area as the sacred space where you'll perform your spells and rituals, write in your grimoire, meditate, and so on. However, if you prefer, you can see your entire home as sacred. Sacred space is a place of peace and calm, but it is not necessarily "between the worlds" as defined by a magick circle. Sacred space is what goes into the circle, or it can simply exist on its own.

When you're in your sacred space you can still interact with the ordinary world—you don't erect barriers. When you use sacred space, you make the existing environment holy, as opposed to creating a whole new surrounding. You remain open to the good energies in the area instead of sealing yourself away.

Sacred space is a wonderful alternative to a circle if you seek to create a harmonious atmosphere for a gathering of people, particularly if the attendees are of mixed spiritualities. You can create it without anyone else's knowledge by purifying and harmonizing the energy of the area. Envision the area cleansed of all "bad vibes" and project your intention for peace and joy into the space. Thus you remove distracting, harmful, or stale energy and in its place leave a positive, comfortable feeling.

Creating sacred space for other people who may not share your beliefs does not manipulate them in any way, nor does it disrespect their own religions. You are offering them a peaceful and balanced environment in which to study, discuss, eat, or mingle. Try creating sacred space before a dinner gathering during the week, when everyone is tired and stressed out, or before a family get-together where conflicts are likely to arise. Watch how everyone relaxes in the serene energy. That's everyday magick at its best.

Chapter 7

SPECIAL OCCASION SPELLS

For millennia, people on earth have observed the sun's apparent passage through the sky and the seasonal changes that resulted. Ancient structures, such as Stonehenge and Newgrange, Ireland, accurately marked the solstices, indicating that our ancestors carefully tracked the ever-changing relationship between the sun and our planet.

Across many lands and many centuries, myths explained earth's seasons as the Goddess's journey. During summer, she brings life to earth. During winter she descends into the underworld and loses everything—her power, her identity, her true love, or all of the above. Through recognition of her divine essence, her supremacy is restored, and life on earth once again flourishes. In some tellings, the Goddess's consort—the Sun King—undertakes an annual trip through the sky, arriving at significant places at certain times of the year to mark what we call the "sabbats."

Wiccans today divide the sun's annual cycle, known as the Wheel of the Year, into eight periods of approximately six weeks each. Each "spoke" corresponds to a particular holiday (or holy day). These special days or sabbats, based in early agrarian cultures, afford unique opportunities for performing magick spells and rituals.

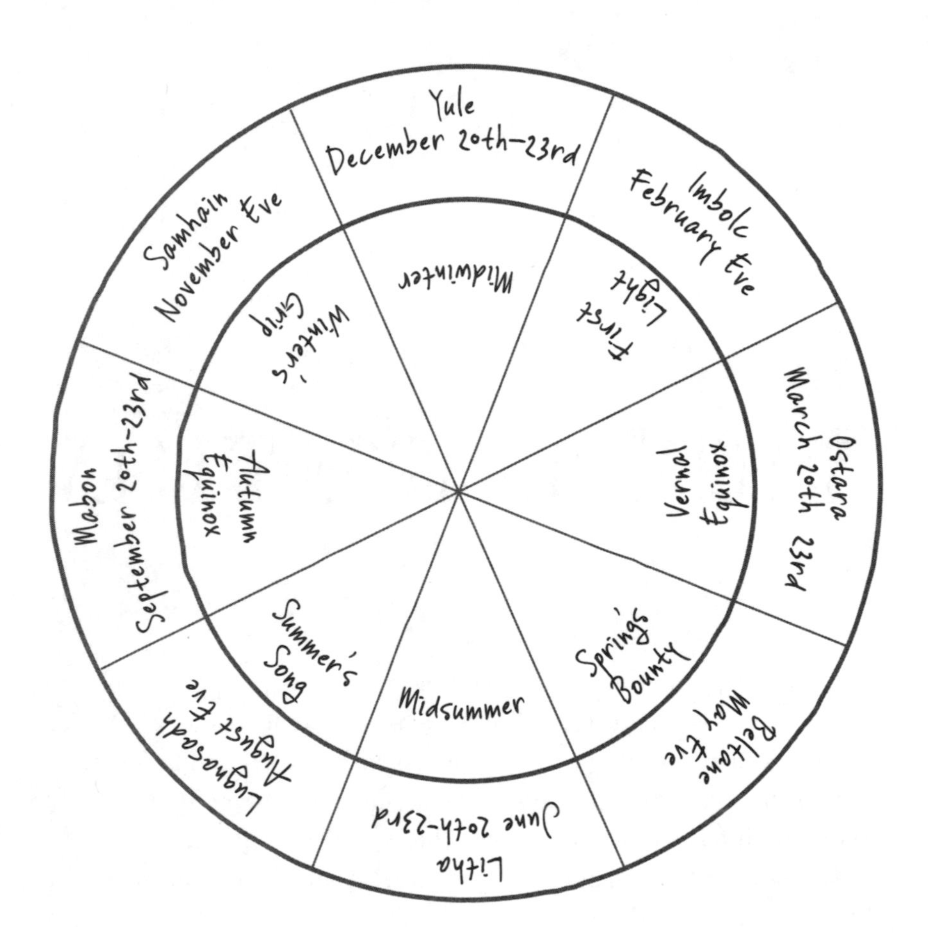

You may choose to organize the sections of your grimoire around these sabbats. Some witches like to start a new book of shadows each year on Samhain. Be sure to record in your book what you experience on these important days—not only the practices in which you engage, but your thoughts, insights, feelings, and dreams as well. Do you celebrate the sabbats with special festivities? If so, describe what you did on each one, with whom, what you ate, what you wore, the results of your spellcasting, and so on.

Song of Amergin

The "Song of Amergin" is one of the earliest examples of Celtic poetic mythology. Dating back to circa 1268 B.C.E., the song is an Irish liturgical hymn and could very well be used as a charge of the god. Consisting of metaphoric statements interspersed with queries, the "Song of Amergin" has been interpreted by Robert Graves to have direct correlations with the ancient Celtic calendar and alphabet. In Graves's translation, the "Song of Amergin" describes a journey through the Wheel of the Year told through the beautiful poetic imagery of a Druidic bard:

"I am a stag: of seven tines,
I am a flood: across a plain,
I am a wind: on a deep lake,
I am a tear: the Sun lets fall,
I am a hawk: above the cliff,
I am a thorn: beneath the nail,
I am a wonder: among flowers,
I am a wizard: who but I
Sets the cool head aflame with smoke?
I am a spear: that roars for blood,
I am a salmon: in a pool,
I am a lure: from paradise,
I am a hill: where poets walk,
I am a boar: ruthless and red,
I am a breaker: threatening doom,
I am a tide: that drags to death,
I am an infant: who but I
Peeps from the unhewn dolmen arch?
I am the womb: of every holt,
I am the blaze: on every hill,
I am the queen: of every hire,
I am the shield: for every head,
I am the tomb: of every hope."

The rich images contained in this verse suggest that the spirits of nature are irrevocably connected to the spirit of the gods and goddesses. Divine grace can be discovered anywhere—in hopes and fears, in achievements and disappointments, in shadow and light, in joy and pain, in life and death. All are valid expressions of Divine Consciousness.

SAMHAIN

The most holy of the sabbats, Samhain (pronounced SOW-een) is observed on the night of October 31, when the sun is in the zodiac sign Scorpio. Better known as Halloween or All Hallows' Eve, this is the holiday people usually associate with witches and magick. Most of the ways the general public marks this sabbat, however, stem from misconceptions—it's a solemn and sacred day for witches, not a time for fear or humor. Some religious groups that don't understand its true meaning feel threatened or offended by Halloween and have even tried to ban it.

The Holiday's Significance

Considered the witches' New Year, Samhain begins the Wheel of the Year. Thus, it is a time of death and rebirth. In many parts of the Northern Hemisphere the land lies barren now; the last of the crops have been plowed under to compost, and the earth rests in preparation for spring.

Witches view Samhain as a time to remember and honor loved ones who have passed over to the other side. That's why Halloween is associated with the dead. No, skeletons don't rise from graves nor do ghosts haunt the living on Samhain, as movies and popular culture tend to portray it—though you may connect with spirits and departed friends on this magickal night.

Samhain Magick

Witches believe the veil that separates the seen and unseen worlds is thinnest at Samhain. Consequently, you may find it easy to contact spirits in other realms of existence or to request guidance from ancestors and guardians. Samhain is also a good time to do divination, because insights and information can flow more easily on this sabbat than at any other time of the year.

In keeping with the concept of an ongoing cycle of destruction and renewal, witches often choose to shed old habits or attitudes at this time, replacing them with new ones. Consider doing a psychological housecleaning on Samhain. On a slip of paper, write whatever you want to leave behind when the old year dies—fear, self-limiting attitudes, bad habits, unwanted relationships, and so on. Then burn the paper in a ritual fire. Samhain is also a good time to perform banishing spells.

Rune Reading
October 31, 2016
"How can I improve my career path?"

Situation	Obstacle	Action	Outcome
ᚾ	ᛁ	ᛟ	ᛒ
Nauthiz	Isa	Othala	Berkano

Interpretation: Nauthiz clearly describes my feelings of being constrained and frustrated in my present job situation. Isa as the obstacle indicates I'm at a standstill and there's no opportunity for advancement where I am now. Othala in the action position suggests I need to leave my current job and seek something else. Berkano as the outcome heralds growth in the future.

WINTER SOLSTICE OR YULE

The Winter Solstice occurs when the sun reaches 0 degrees of the zodiac sign Capricorn, usually around December 21. This is the shortest day of the year in the Northern Hemisphere. Also known as Yule, the holiday marks the turning point in the sun's descent into darkness; from this point, the days grow steadily longer for a period of six months.

The Holiday's Significance

Pagan mythology describes the apparent passage of the sun through the heavens each year as the journey of the Sun King, who drives his bright chariot across the sky. Some tellings describe the Sun King as the Goddess's consort; in other stories he is her son. In pre-Christian Europe and Britain, the Winter Solstice celebrated the Sun King's birth. This beloved deity brought light into the world during the darkest time of all—a theme echoed in Christianity's story of the birth of Jesus in this season of the year. Thus, witches celebrate this sabbat as a time of renewal and hope.

Yule Magick

Decorating our homes at Christmas with ornamented pine trees and holiday greenery dates back to pre-Christian times. Because evergreen trees retain their needles even during the cold winter months, they symbolize the triumph of life over death. Do spells for strength, courage, endurance, and protection now. In a magickal sense, pine is used for its cleansing properties. The crisp, clean scent of pine needles can help eliminate negative energies from your home. You can clear bad vibes from your environment by burning pine-scented incense or candles.

Burning the Yule log is another ancient tradition with which Wiccans mark the Winter Solstice. On the eve of Yule, build a fire from the wood of nine sacred trees. The central element in the Yule fire is an oak log, for the oak tree represents strength and longevity. After the fire burns down, collect the ashes and wrap them in a piece of cloth. If you place the package under your pillow, you'll receive dreams that provide guidance and advice for the coming year. Write about the experience in your grimoire and perhaps paste some pine needles into these pages of your book of shadows.

Yule Greenery

The Druids considered the evergreen holly a sacred plant and valued its incredible hardiness. According to Celtic mythology, holly bushes afforded shelter for the earth elementals during the wintertime. The Druids also valued mistletoe, an herb of fertility and immortality. It has long been used in talismans as an aphrodisiac—perhaps that's the reason people still kiss beneath it today.

IMBOLC OR BRIGID'S DAY

This sabbat honors Brigid, the beloved Celtic goddess of healing, smithcraft, and poetry. A favorite of the Irish people, Brigid was adopted by the Church when Christianity moved into Ireland and was canonized as Saint Brigid. Her holiday is usually celebrated on February 1, though some witches mark it around February 5, when the sun reaches 15 degrees of Aquarius. In the Northern Hemisphere, daylight is increasing and the promise of spring is in the air.

The Holiday's Significance

Brigid is one of the fertility goddesses, and Imbolc means "in the belly." This holiday honors all forms of creativity, of the mind as well as the body. Illustrations of Brigid sometimes show her stirring a great cauldron, the witch's magick tool that symbolizes the womb and the receptive, fertile nature of the Divine Feminine. As goddess of inspiration, Brigid encourages everyone, regardless of gender, to stir the inner cauldron of creativity that exists within.

Although Brigid represents an aspect of the Divine Feminine, her day falls under the zodiac sign Aquarius, a masculine air sign in astrology. Her blazing hearth brings to mind both the metalsmith's forge and the homemaker's cook fire. Thus, she represents mind and body, a blend of yin and yang energies, and the union of polarities necessary for creation.

Imbolc Magick

On Imbolc, the Sun King's chariot ascends in the sky; the sun's rays grow stronger and days grow longer. Witches celebrate this spoke in the Wheel of the Year as a time of hope and renewal, a reaffirmation of life, and a time to plant "seeds" for the future. You may wish to build a fire in a magick cauldron to honor Brigid. On a piece of paper, write wishes you want to materialize during the year, then drop the paper into the cauldron. As the paper burns, the smoke rises toward the heavens carrying your requests to Brigid.

In keeping with the holiday's theme of fire, many people light candles to honor the Goddess. Candles are the most common tool in the witch's magick toolbox, used in all sorts of spells and rituals. Engrave words that represent your wishes—love, prosperity, health, etc.—into the candle's wax. Then light the candle and focus your attention on its flame, while you envision your wishes coming true.

The Name of the Goddess

Brigid goes by many names, including Lady of the Flame, Goddess of the Hearth, and Bright One. Her feast day is sometimes called Candlemas because of her association with fire. In magickal thinking, the fire element fuels inspiration and creativity.

SPRING EQUINOX OR OSTARA

Pagans and witches celebrate Ostara when the sun enters 0 degrees of Aries, around March 21. In the Northern Hemisphere, the Spring Equinox ushers in warmer weather, days that are longer than nights, and the advent of new life. Ostara gets its name from the German fertility goddess Eostre; the word "Easter" derives from the same root. Both holidays celebrate the triumph of life over death.

> *"This is the time of spring's return, the joyful time, the seed time, when life bursts forth from the earth and the chains of winter are broken. Light and dark are equal: It is a time of balance, when all the elements within us must be brought into a new harmony."*
>
> —Starhawk, from an Ostara ritual in *The Spiral Dance*

The Holiday's Significance

The Sun King's chariot continues climbing higher in the sky, reaching the point at which day and night are of equal length on Ostara. The Spring Equinox marks the first day of spring and the start of the busy planting season in agrarian cultures. Farmers till their fields and sow seeds. Trees begin to bud, spring flowers blossom, and baby animals are born. Ostara, therefore, is one of the fertility holidays and a time for planting seeds—literally or figuratively.

Ostara Magick

On Ostara, sow seeds that you want to bear fruit in the coming months. This is an ideal time to cast spells for new beginnings: launch new career ventures, move to a new home, or start a new relationship. If you're a gardener, you'll start preparing the soil and planting flowers, herbs, and/or vegetables now. Consider the magickal properties of botanicals and choose plants that represent your intentions (see Chapter 16 for more information). Even if you don't have space for a garden plot, you could plant seeds in a flowerpot to symbolize wishes you hope will grow to fruition in the coming months.

According to an old German story, a rabbit laid some sacred eggs and decorated them as a gift for the fertility goddess Eostre. The goddess liked the beautiful eggs so much that she asked the rabbit to share them with everyone throughout the world. Eggs represent the promise of new life, and painting them bright colors engages the creative aspect of the sabbat. And rabbits, of course, have long been linked with fertility. You might enjoy decorating eggs with magickal symbols, such as pentagrams and spirals.

BELTANE

Wiccans usually celebrate Beltane on May 1, although some prefer to mark it around May 5, when the sun reaches 15 degrees of Taurus. The sabbat is named for the god Baal or Bel. In Scottish Gaelic, the word *bealltainn* means "fires of Belos" and refers to the bonfires Pagans traditionally light on this sabbat. The joyful festival celebrates the earth's fertility, when flowers bloom and plants begin sprouting in the fields.

The Holiday's Significance

The second fertility holiday in the Wheel of the Year, Beltane coincides with a period of fruitfulness. To ancient and modern Pagans alike, this holiday honors the earth and all of nature. In early agrarian cultures, farmers built fires on Beltane and led livestock between the flames to increase their fertility.

Sexuality is also celebrated on this sabbat—the Great Rite has traditionally been part of the holiday's festivities. In pre-Christian days, Beltane celebrants engaged in sexual intercourse in the fields as a form of symbolic magick to encourage fertility and a bountiful harvest. Children conceived at this time were said to belong to the Goddess.

Beltane Magick

If possible, celebrate Beltane outdoors in order to appreciate nature's fullness. Because Beltane is a fertility holiday, many of its rituals contain sexual symbolism. The Maypole, around which young females dance, is an obvious phallic symbol. You can decorate the Maypole with flowers in recognition of the earth's beauty and fruitfulness. Consider pressing one or two of those flowers between the pages of your grimoire.

Sometimes a woman who seeks a partner will toss a circular garland over the top of the pole, signifying the sex act, as a way of asking the Goddess to send her a lover. Another fertility ritual utilizes the cauldron, a symbol of the womb. Women who wish to become pregnant build a small fire in the cauldron, and then jump over it. If you prefer, you can leap over the cauldron to spark creativity in the mind instead of the body.

Beltane's connection with the earth and fullness makes this sabbat an ideal time to perform prosperity magick. Incorporate peppermint, parsley, cedar, or money plant into your spells. This is also a good time to make offerings to Mother Earth and the nature spirits.

SUMMER SOLSTICE OR MIDSUMMER

In the Northern Hemisphere, the Summer Solstice is the longest day of the year. The Sun King has now reached the highest point in his journey through the heavens. Wiccans celebrate Midsummer around June 21, when the sun enters 0 degrees of the zodiac sign Cancer. This is a time of abundance, when the earth puts forth her bounty.

The Holiday's Significance

In early agrarian cultures, Midsummer marked a period of plenty when food was abundant and life was easy. Our ancestors celebrated this joyful holiday with feasting and revelry. At this point, however, the sun has reached its pinnacle and begins its descent once again. Celtic Pagan mythology depicts this as the end of the Oak King's reign as he is overthrown by the Holly King, who presides over the waning part of the year. This myth sees the two "kings" as two separate aspects of the God. These rivals are the Goddess's lovers, and each has his season.

Folklore says that at Midsummer earth spirits abound—this belief inspired Shakespeare's delightful play *A Midsummer Night's Dream*. Apparently, life on every level rejoices in the fullness of the season. If you wish, you can commune with the elementals and faeries at this time.

Midsummer Magick

Just as we've done for centuries, witches today celebrate the Summer Solstice with feasting, music, dancing, and thanksgiving. Remember to share your bounty with the animals and birds too, and return something to Mother Earth as a sign of gratitude.

Midsummer is also a good time to collect herbs, flowers, and other plants to use in magick spells. Legend says that if you wish to become invisible, you must wear an amulet that includes seeds from forest ferns gathered on Midsummer's Eve. Perform spells for success, recognition, and abundance on the Summer Solstice.

LUGNASADH OR LAMMAS

Named for the Irish Celtic god Lugh (Lew in Wales), this holiday is usually celebrated on August 1, although some witches prefer to mark it around August 5, when the sun reaches 15 degrees of Leo. According to Celtic mythology, Lugh is an older and wiser personification of the god Baal or Bel (for whom Beltane is named). Lugnasadh (pronounced LOO-na-sah) is the first of the harvest festivals. The early Christians dubbed the holiday *Lammas*, meaning loaf-mass, because farmers cut their grain at this time of the year and made it into bread.

The Holiday's Significance

In agrarian cultures, this holiday marked the time to begin preparing for the barren winter months that lay ahead. Our ancestors cut, ground, and stored grain, canned fruits and vegetables, and brewed wine and beer in late summer. The old English song "John Barleycorn Must Die" describes the seasonal ritual of rendering grain into ale.

Early Pagans sold their wares at harvest fairs and held athletic competitions at this time of the year. You can see this age-old tradition carried on today at country fairs throughout rural parts of the United States.

> *"Threshing of the harvest was considered a sacred act and the threshing barn a sacred place. An old fertility custom is still practiced when a new bride is carried over the threshold."*
>
> —Debbie Michaud, *The Healing Traditions & Spiritual Practices of Wicca*

Lugnasadh Magick

Today, Wiccans enjoy sharing bread and beer with friends on Lugnasadh, just as we've done for millennia. You might like to bake fresh bread from scratch or even brew your own beer as part of the celebration. While you're kneading the bread, add a dried bean to the dough. When you serve the bread, tradition says that whoever gets the bean in his or her piece will be granted a wish.

If you like, you can fashion a doll from corn, wheat, or straw to represent the Sun King. To symbolize the time of year when his powers are waning, burn the effigy in a ritual fire as an offering to Mother Earth. The custom of decorating your home with dried corncobs, gourds, nuts, and other fruits of the harvest also has its roots in Lugnasadh.

AUTUMN EQUINOX OR MABON

The Autumn Equinox usually occurs on or about September 22, when the sun reaches 0 degrees of Libra. Once again, day and night are of equal length, signifying a time of balance, equality, and harmony. Mabon is also the second harvest festival, and witches consider it a time for giving thanks for the abundance Mother Earth has provided.

The Holiday's Significance

This sabbat marks the last spoke in the Wheel of the Year. From this day until the Winter Solstice, the Sun King's path arcs downward toward earth. As the days grow shorter in the Northern Hemisphere and the cold, barren winter approaches, reflect on the joys and sorrows, successes and failures of the year that is nearing its conclusion.

Mabon Magick

Mabon is a good time to do magick spells that involve decrease or endings. Do you want to let go of self-destructive beliefs or behaviors? Lose weight? End an unfulfilling relationship? Now is the time to break old habits and patterns that have limited you. Anything you wish to eliminate from your life can now be released safely, before the New Year begins with Samhain.

Because the Equinox signifies a time of equality and balance, try to balance yin and yang, active and passive on this day. Seek rest and activity, solitude and socializing in equal portions. You may also enjoy engaging in creative endeavors to mark the sabbat.

At each turn of the Wheel, note in your grimoire your feelings, insights, and the results of your magickal workings. Each year, you may enjoy rereading what you wrote the previous year. It's interesting to look back over time to reminisce about your sabbat celebrations and compare your experiences as you grow in the Craft.

Chapter 8

SOLAR SPELLS

Without the sun, life on our planet would not exist. As the center of our solar system, the sun plays a central role in our lives. Therefore, you'll want to describe in your grimoire your relationship to the sun and the seasons that result as the earth revolves around it.

Witches understand the close connection between magick and the heavenly bodies. The positions of the sun, moon, planets, and stars influence our personal cycles, plant growth, animal behavior, weather patterns, the secular and sacred rituals we enact, and the spells we perform. The Wheel of the Year bases the eight Wiccan holidays (known as sabbats) on the sun's movement through the twelve signs of the zodiac, as discussed previously in Chapter 7.

Ancient Observatories

For thousands of years, people have gazed at the sky and considered how the heavenly bodies affected life on earth. Some researchers believe the pyramids were erected as astrological/astronomical observatories. Stonehenge, begun more than 5,000 years ago, accurately predicts the solstices, eclipses, and other celestial events.

If you're like many people, you notice that your emotions and energies shift with the seasons. You may feel more physically vital, sociable, or adventurous during some months and more introspective, imaginative, or sensitive during others. Most likely, you're reacting to the natural energies of the zodiac signs and the movements of the heavenly bodies. By keeping track of your reactions in your grimoire, you'll discover the most auspicious times to do magick work and when to perform certain types of spells for best results.

ASTROLOGY AND MAGICK

When doing magick spells, it's a good idea to take celestial influences into account in order to choose the most auspicious times to perform spells and rituals. The sun and moon, and their ever-changing relationships to our planet, have fascinated human beings since the beginning of time. Our ancestors noticed that the sun's apparent movement brought about the seasons and that the moon's phases altered the tides and affected fertility in both humans and animals. Even today, we can easily see how solar and lunar forces operate in everyday life.

The ancients believed gods and goddesses inhabited the heavenly bodies. From their celestial abodes, the deities governed every facet of life on earth. Each deity—and each planet—possessed certain characteristics and powers. Modern astrologers don't usually think of the planets as the actual homes of gods and goddesses; however, we still connect each of the celestial spheres with specific properties, influences, and powers that affect human and earthly existence.

Planetary Powers

Aligning yourself with planetary powers that support the nature of your spells can improve the effectiveness of your magickal workings. The following table shows each planet's areas of influence. (Note: For convenience, astrologers often lump the sun and moon under the broad heading of "planets" although, of course, we know they're not.)

Planet	Areas of Influence
Sun	Sense of self/identity, public image, career, creativity, leadership, well-being, masculine power
Moon	Emotions, intuition, dreams, home/domestic life, family/children, feminine power
Mercury	Communication, mental skill/activity, learning, travel, commerce
Venus	Love, relationships, social interactions, art, creativity, beauty, women
Mars	Action, vitality/strength, competition, courage, men
Jupiter	Growth/expansion, good luck, knowledge, travel
Saturn	Limitations, responsibility, work/business, stability/permanence
Uranus	Change, independence, sudden or unexpected situations, unconventional ideas or behavior
Neptune	Intuition, dreams, imagination/creativity, the spirit realm
Pluto	Hidden power/forces, transformation, death and rebirth

When you're doing spells, you may want to refer to this table. Venus's energy, for instance, can enhance love spells. Jupiter's expansive power can be an asset when you're doing spells for career success or financial growth. You can use the planets' symbols on candles, in talismans and amulets, and lots of other ways. You may also wish to consult an astrologer or check an ephemeris (tables of daily planetary movements) to determine when the celestial energies are favorable for your magickal workings.

TRACKING SOLAR CYCLES IN YOUR GRIMOIRE

Consider organizing your grimoire around the solar cycles. Each month write down your spells, rituals, and experiences along your magickal journey. Astrologers begin the solar year with the Spring Equinox, when the sun enters the zodiac sign Aries on about March 21. In the witches' Wheel of the Year, this is the sabbat of Ostara. During each solar month, record how you feel, what you see happening around you in nature, what you experience (especially in terms of your magickal and spiritual development), significant dreams and insights, and, of course, the spells you do. You may also enjoy pressing seasonal flowers, leaves, and other botanicals between the pages of your grimoire to mark the beauty of the changing seasons. Some witches begin a new book of shadows every year, and you may choose to do this at the Spring Equinox instead of on Samhain. If you prefer, you could annually revisit the sections designated for each solar month and add updates.

Planets and Signs

Each planet rules one or more signs of the zodiac. You probably know your birth sign—that's the astrological sign in which the sun was positioned on the day you were born. What you may not know, though, is that the moon and all the planets in our solar system also spend periods of time in each of the twelve signs of the zodiac and they continually move through these signs/sectors of the heavens. These signs affect the energy of the planets. Therefore, it's good to check the positions of the planets when you're doing spells—especially the placements of the sun and moon. In Part II, I frequently advise doing spells when the sun or moon is in a particular astrological sign, in order to tip the scales in your favor. The following table shows the connections between the planets and the signs they govern.

Planet	Zodiac Sign(s)
Sun	Leo
Moon	Cancer
Mercury	Gemini, Virgo
Venus	Taurus, Libra
Mars	Aries
Jupiter	Sagittarius
Saturn	Capricorn
Uranus	Aquarius
Neptune	Pisces
Pluto	Scorpio

Now, refer back to the table presented earlier in this chapter that lists the planets and their areas of influence. When the sun or moon is positioned in a sign, it takes on characteristics of that sign and the planet that rules the sign, which can be important in spellwork. For example, it's usually best to do love spells when the sun or moon is in Taurus or Libra—signs ruled by the planet Venus. If you're doing a travel spell, consider casting it when the sun or moon is in Gemini or Sagittarius.

The moon remains in a sign for about two and a half days and completes a circuit of all twelve zodiac signs each month. Check an ephemeris or an online astrology site to determine which days will support your objectives.

Sun Signs

When someone asks "What's your sign?" he's really asking "Where was the sun positioned in the sky on the day you were born?" Astrology divides the sky into twelve sectors and links them with the signs of the zodiac. From earth, the sun appears to travel through all twelve sectors during the course of a year, spending approximately thirty days in each sign.

Aries

The sun enters Aries at the Spring Equinox, around March 21, and remains in the sign until about April 20, although this can vary a day or so from year to year. In many parts of the Northern Hemisphere, the earth now begins to awaken after a period of slumber. Plants start to sprout; baby animals are born; migrating birds return from their winter habitats. Thus, we consider Aries a time of beginnings and planting seeds, physically or symbolically.

Do you sense something stirring in you now? Do you feel inspired to begin something new, break new ground, or "birth" a part of yourself? Because the war god Mars (Ares in Greek tradition) rules this sign, you may seek out challenges, adventures, and physical activities this month. The fiery energy of the period can help fuel your ambitions and desires.

Taurus

The sun enters Taurus around April 21 and remains in this sign until about May 20, although this can vary a day or so from year to year. In many parts of the Northern Hemisphere, the days now grow warmer and the earth begins to bring forth the first of its bounty. Therefore, we consider Taurus a fruitful sign and connect it with abundance.

Are your creative juices stirring? Do you feel a desire to express yourself or use your talents in a productive way that others can appreciate? The earthy energy of Taurus can help bring your ideas to fruition. Do you feel more sexual than usual? Because Venus, the goddess of love and beauty, rules this sign, you may focus on relationships or devote yourself to sensual pleasures now.

Gemini

The sun enters Gemini around May 21 and remains in this sign until about June 20, although this can vary a day or so from year to year. In many parts of the Northern Hemisphere, flowers blossom profusely now, spreading their pollen far and wide. In a similar way, Gemini's energy spreads ideas far and wide, "pollenating" our minds and cultures.

Do ideas blossom in your head now? Do you seek out people with whom to share your ideas and interests? Are you hungry for knowledge? Because Mercury, the god of communication, rules this sign you might choose to read, write, study, communicate with friends, or engage in other intellectual endeavors now.

Cancer

The sun enters Cancer around June 21, and remains in this sign until about July 21, although this can vary a day or so from year to year. This period of fullness in the Northern Hemisphere begins with the Summer Solstice, the longest day in the year, and the Wiccan sabbat Midsummer. As the earth blossoms with abundance, you may become aware of the abundance in your own life and express gratitude for it.

Do you feel a desire to celebrate your tribe, culture, and/or heritage? Do your loved ones seem dearer to you than usual? Do you experience strong nurturing feelings toward others or long to be nurtured by someone else? Because the moon rules Cancer, which astrologers link with home and family, you may enjoy spending time at home with your family now or reconnecting with your ancestors.

Leo

The sun enters Leo around July 22 and remains in this sign until about August 22, although this can vary a day or so from year to year. In many parts of the Northern Hemisphere, the sun shines brilliantly now and illuminates our world. Likewise, Leo's light shines brightly on each of us, illuminating our special gifts.

Are your creative juices flowing? Do you feel inspired to express your unique talents and seek recognition for your abilities? Now's the time to step out of the shadows, into the spotlight. Leo's fiery energy gives you the confidence and courage to show your stuff, and to make your mark in the world.

Virgo

The sun enters Virgo around August 23 and remains in this sign until about September 22, although this can vary a day or so from year to year. In the Northern Hemisphere, the days are growing shorter and cooler temperatures remind us that winter lurks just around the corner. Now we must work to prepare ourselves for bleaker times ahead.

Do you feel a need to tend to the details in your life, to put things in order? Do you seem busier than usual? If you've taken a break during the summer, you may sense pressure to get back to work. Virgo's practical energy helps you see things in perspective and organize your plans for the future.

Libra

The sun enters Libra around September 23 and remains in this sign until about October 21, although this can vary a day or so from year to year. This is one of the most beautiful times of the year in many parts of the Northern Hemisphere, and it begins with the Fall Equinox—the harvest celebration Wiccans call Mabon.

Do you feel a sense of "gathering" as winter approaches, a desire to collect and store the rich abundance of the period (literally or symbolically) in preparation for the future? Do you experience a heightened appreciation for the beauty around you? Venus, the planet of relationships, rules Libra. It makes you aware of your connection to other people and your need for them, inspiring you to gather your loved ones around you.

Scorpio

The sun enters Scorpio around October 21 and remains in this sign until about November 20, although this can vary a day or so from year to year. As the nights grow longer and colder in the Northern

Hemisphere, we tend to draw into ourselves and shift away from outer-world activities, becoming more introspective. Samhain, the most sacred of the witch's sabbats, occurs during this solar month and recognizes the continuing cycle of death and rebirth as the earth slips into a period of decline and rest.

Do you feel like pulling into yourself to explore your innermost depths? Are you shedding things you no longer need, so something new can emerge? Do you sense a connection with the spirit realm, hidden forces, and a desire to delve into regions beyond the material world? The transformative energy of Pluto, the planet that rules Scorpio, can guide you beyond the mundane into the extraordinary.

Sagittarius

The sun enters Sagittarius around November 21 and remains in this sign until about December 20, although this can vary a day or so from year to year. As winter closes in (in the Northern Hemisphere), we feel an urgency to do all that needs to be done in preparation for the harsh time ahead; therefore, this month is often a busy one.

Astrologers connect this sign with questing for knowledge and experiences that broaden us physically and/or spiritually. In some countries, it coincides with a period of travel, generosity, and social celebrations. Do you seek to expand your horizons through study, travel, or exploring the spiritual realms? Do you reach out to others, offering your time, energy, and material benefits in an expression of gratitude and giving back for the abundance you've enjoyed? Do you feel restless and curious about what lies just beyond your reach? The benevolent energy of Jupiter, the planet that rules Sagittarius, can help you find what you're looking for.

Capricorn

The sun enters Capricorn on the Winter Solstice around December 21—also the Wiccan sabbat Yule—and remains in this sign until about January 20, although this can vary a day or so from year to year. During the darkest time of the year (in the Northern Hemisphere), solar forces withdraw to shelter and renew themselves in preparation for the fruitful times ahead. Early cultures recognized this as a time of courage during a harsh period of cold and scarcity and celebrated humankind's strength when faced with difficulty.

Do you find yourself retreating, regrouping, and repairing in preparation for the future? Are you assessing your resources and using them productively? Are career or financial issues a priority now? It's time to get realistic about your goals and start formulating plans—it's no coincidence that we make New Year's resolutions during Capricorn. Let pragmatic Saturn, which rules this sign, guide you.

Aquarius

The sun enters Aquarius around January 21 and remains in this sign until about February 19, although this can vary a day or so from year to year. Even though this can be the coldest period of the year in many parts of the Northern Hemisphere, the days are growing longer and hope for better times glimmers on the horizon. Change hovers in the air, heralded by Uranus, the planet of change, which rules Aquarius.

Do you feel restless and ready for new adventures? Do you sense a change within yourself and/or see change beginning to happen around you? Are your senses and ideas awakening after a period of withdrawal, leading you to seek out the company of like-minded individuals? Let the energy of Aquarius guide you to express your true self.

Pisces

The sun enters Pisces around February 20 and remains in this sign until about March 20, although this can vary a day or so from year to year. The last sign of the zodiac, Pisces bridges the mundane and the spirit realms, showing us that we are not merely physical beings but sparks of the Divine. Even though the days are growing longer, this can still be a cold, dreary, isolating month in many parts of the Northern Hemisphere, during which we spend time looking within ourselves. Draw upon the wisdom of the hidden dimension now and the knowledge that abides in your own deepest regions.

Is your intuition sharper than usual? Are your dreams more vivid? Do you recognize the presence of the Divine acting through you? Do you feel inspired to express artistically what's being conveyed to you?

The visionary power of Neptune, which rules Pisces, can reveal what lies beyond the material world and connect you with spiritual forces that can guide you on your path.

Celestial Charts

You can look up the exact positions of the sun, moon, and planets on any given day in a book called an ephemeris. These tables of planetary motion list the heavenly bodies according to the signs and degrees in which they're located on every day of the year. Usually the data are arranged by month and grouped into a volume that covers a year, a decade, or even an entire century. You can find ephemerides online too.

SPELLS FOR EVERY SEASON

"To everything there is a season," says Ecclesiastes 3:1. That's certainly true in the art of spellcraft. Aligning yourself with cosmic energies that support the nature of your spells can improve their effectiveness. Keep a record in your grimoire of the spells you do during each solar month and note their outcomes. I like to date the spells I perform, so I can go back later and compare my experiences year after year. This also helps me to better understand how the energies operating at different times of the year influence my magickal workings.

Following you'll find information about the types of spells best suited to each month of the solar year. If, however, you can't wait until the "right" month to cast your spell, perform the spell when the moon passes through that sign (which it does for approximately two and a half days each month)—we'll discuss this more in Chapter 9.

Aries

The strong, activating energy present this month helps jump-start spells for new endeavors. If you're facing a challenge, hope to best an opponent, or need some extra vitality or courage—in an athletic event, for example—consider doing a spell at this time. Want to stimulate movement in a situation or remove an obstacle? Aries's fiery energy can provide zing and speed up the process. Spells cast at this time often manifest quickly, but their results don't always endure long-term. Candle spells can be especially effective now.

Taurus

The fruitful and down-to-earth nature of this sign supports spells to attract material goodies. Now's the time to do magick for wealth, comfort and security, and abundance of all kinds. Taurus's creative energy also encourages fertility, whether you're trying to start a family or birth a great work of art. Love spells can benefit from the cosmic forces at work now too. Tap the power of plants and gemstones this month to enhance your spells.

Gemini

This mentally oriented sign supports the use of affirmations, incantations, and chants in spellwork. During this month, you can also benefit from studying magickal traditions and/or sharing your knowledge with other like-minded people. Your ability to communicate may be sharper now, so try contacting spirit guides or use telepathy to send messages to other people. This is a good time to receive guidance from oracles as well.

Cancer

Now's the time to develop your intuition, for Cancer's energy increases your sensitivity to everything in the cosmos. Spells to protect your home and family, bless a new home, or increase fertility can benefit from Cancer's energy too. You might also consider doing past-life regressions this month or connect with loved ones who've left the physical plane. The Summer Solstice occurs when the sun enters Cancer, making this a good time to do magick to attract abundance and to celebrate your blessings.

Leo

Leo's energy supports spells to strengthen your self-esteem, advance your position in the world, improve your public image, or get the recognition you seek. The creative energy of this sign can also boost your own creative ability—use this period to let the artist in you shine. Enrich all your spells and rituals with an extra dash of drama and imagination now.

Virgo

Virgo's practical energy supports spells to improve your work situation and/or relationships with coworkers, clients, and colleagues. This is also an ideal time to perform healing spells, especially using botanicals. Working with plant/tree magick can be rewarding now—invite the nature spirits known as devas to assist you. Connecting with your spirit animal guides may prove fruitful as well. Consider doing spells to heal the earth this month too.

Libra

This sign, ruled by Venus—the planet of love and relationships—strengthens loves spells and spells to improve relationships of all kinds. Spells to enhance your beauty, expand your social network, or encourage people to view you more favorably can benefit from Libra's power of attraction. If you're seeking more peace and harmony in your life, this is the time to perform magick for that purpose—consider doing spells for world peace now too.

Scorpio

Most types of magick can benefit from Scorpio's energy, for astrologers connect this sign with hidden knowledge and occult forces. Your intuition may grow stronger now and your dreams may provide important insights. Consider shamanic journeying, past-life regression, working with spirits and nonphysical entities, divination, and scrying this month. You may also wish to do spells for financial growth and personal power at this time.

Sagittarius

Use the expansive nature of Sagittarius for travel spells—whether you're traveling in the physical world or the realms beyond. Consider shamanic journeying or engaging in a vision quest now to gain wisdom. This is also a wonderful time to expand your knowledge of the Craft or to study other magickal traditions. Growth spells of all kinds can benefit from Sagittarius's energy—use it to get a raise or a promotion.

Capricorn

The pragmatic nature of this sign can aid spells for business and career endeavors, as well as magick to improve your financial savvy. If you wish to bolster your public image or need to ward off attacks from adversaries, tap Capricorn's energy. Do spells for protection, strength, security, and banishing, and to bring something to a successful close.

Happy Birthday!

Pay special attention to the month in which your birthday falls. Your magickal energies increase on your birthday, so this is usually the ideal day to work spells for your own well-being and empowerment.

Aquarius

If you want to make changes in your life, do magick while the sun is in Aquarius. This stimulating sign can help break up stagnant conditions, sometimes quite quickly. Aquarian energy can also aid spells to encourage new adventures, gain new knowledge, or attract new people. Under its influence, you can acquire amazing insights that advance not only your own way of thinking, but other people's too. Consider doing magick with a group of like-minded people now.

Pisces

Your intuition may improve while the sun is in Pisces, so consider engaging in practices such as divination, telepathy, and psychic healing at this time. You could find it easier to communicate with the spirit realm now too. The imaginative energy of Pisces can aid spells to enhance creativity as well as those that use creative visualization. Because Neptune, the planet that rules liquids, governs this sign, you might enjoy concocting magick potions this month—make sure to record your recipes in your grimoire.

Chapter 9

LUNAR SPELLS

One of the most important connections we have in the magickal universe in which we live—and one of the most obvious—is to earth's closest neighbor: the moon. Earthlings can't help being captivated and mystified by the moon. Poets, artists, musicians, lovers, astrologers, and, of course, witches all find the moon juicy subject matter for study and inspiration. For Wiccans, as you know, the moon symbolizes the Goddess and the archetypal feminine power in the universe.

Since ancient times, cultures around the world have connected the moon with the Divine Feminine. In early agrarian cultures, our forebears sowed crops and bred animals in accordance with the moon's cycles. Even today, despite the many sophisticated scientific developments in modern-day agribusiness, the *Farmers' Almanac* still publishes information about lunar cycles—it's not uncommon for farmers who employ advanced technical methods to also consider the moon when planting and harvesting.

If you're like many people, you experience the moon's ever-changing energy in your everyday life—your emotions, your sleep patterns, your mental alertness, your vitality, and your intuitive power. Wiccans know that the moon also plays a key role in spellwork. In your grimoire, keep track of how you relate to the moon and how it influences your mundane and magickal affairs.

The moon rules the night, affects the tides, and influences women's fertility cycles. In Wicca, the moon's phases represent the three stages of a woman's life and the Triple Goddess:

- The waxing crescent moon symbolizes the maiden aspect of the Goddess.
- The full moon signifies the mother aspect of the Goddess.
- The waning crescent moon represents the crone aspect of the Goddess.

"I have called on the Goddess and found her within myself."

—Marion Zimmer Bradley, *The Mists of Avalon*

Moon Goddesses

- Anunit (Babylonian)
- Arianrhod (Celtic)
- Artemis (Greek)
- Candi (Indian)
- Cerridwen (Celtic)
- Chang-o (Chinese)
- Dae-Soon (Korean)
- Diana (Roman)
- Hecate (Greek)
- Ishtar (Babylonian)
- Isis (Egyptian)
- Ix Chel (Mayan)
- Kuan Yin (Chinese)
- Luna (Roman)
- Mawu (African)
- Sarpandit (Sumerian)
- Selene (Greek)
- Sina (Polynesian)
- Yemaya (African/Caribbean/South American)

Some goddesses depict the maiden, some the mother, and some the crone. We often associate maiden goddesses with purity, independence, and joy. Mother goddesses usually represent fertility and fruitfulness, love and relationships, nurturance, and creativity of all kinds. Crone goddesses epitomize wisdom, courage, power, and sometimes death and destruction.

- Maiden goddesses: Artemis, Diana, Bast, Athena, Rhiannon
- Mother goddesses: Brigid, Isis, Demeter, Astarte, Inanna, Ishtar, Tara, Sekhmet, Yemaya, Oshun
- Crone goddesses: Hecate, Cerridwen, Kali, Sophia

Because the moon holds such significance for witches, you may choose to organize your book of shadows around your esbat rituals.

"'Tis the witching hour of night,
Orbed is the moon and bright,
And the stars they glisten, glisten,
Seeming with bright eyes to listen—
For what listen they?"

—John Keats

In a magickal practice known as "drawing down the moon," a witch goes into a trance and invites the Goddess (or divine feminine energy) to enter her body. While the witch is in the trance, the Goddess speaks through her. Margot Adler wrote in depth about this in her book *Drawing Down the Moon*, and it's usually considered a more advanced technique for working with lunar energy. However, novices can connect with the moon's power in simpler ways:

1. Go outside at night and observe the moon. Let its silvery light wash over you. How do you feel standing in the moonlight, under the dark bowl of the night sky? How is this different from how you feel in the daytime?
2. Follow the moon's passage through the heavens, from new to full and back to new again. Pay attention to how you feel during different phases of the moon. Many people feel more energized during the full moon and less vital during the last three days before the new moon.

3. The moon moves into a different sign of the zodiac approximately every two and a half days. You might notice that your moods and feelings change every time the moon passes through a different astrological sign. For instance, you may feel more impulsive when the moon is in Aries, more sensitive when it's in Cancer.

Keep notes in your grimoire about what you experience, so you can refer back to them later. What you learn from strengthening your connection with the moon will be useful to you when casting spells and doing rituals—and perhaps in other areas of your life too.

THE LUNAR YEAR

The ancient Druids used a lunar calendar with thirteen months, rather than a solar one as we do today. They associated each month of the year with a tree.

THE DRUID LUNAR CALENDAR	
Tree	**Month**
Birch	December 24–January 20
Rowan	January 21–February 17
Ash	February 18–March 17
Alder	March 18–April 14
Willow	April 15–May 12
Hawthorne	May 13–June 9
Oak	June 10–July 7
Holly	July 8–August 4
Hazel	August 5–September 1
Vine	September 2–September 29
Ivy	September 30–October 27
Reed	October 28–November 24
Elder	November 25–December 23

ESBATS

Witches often come together for esbats, usually on full and/or new moons, to enjoy community and fellowship. On the full moon, the radiance of the Goddess illuminates the night sky, and her brilliance dims the brightness of the stars. Her shining body hangs like a voluptuous pearl against the surrounding darkness. The full moon calls witches to gather and honor her divine power.

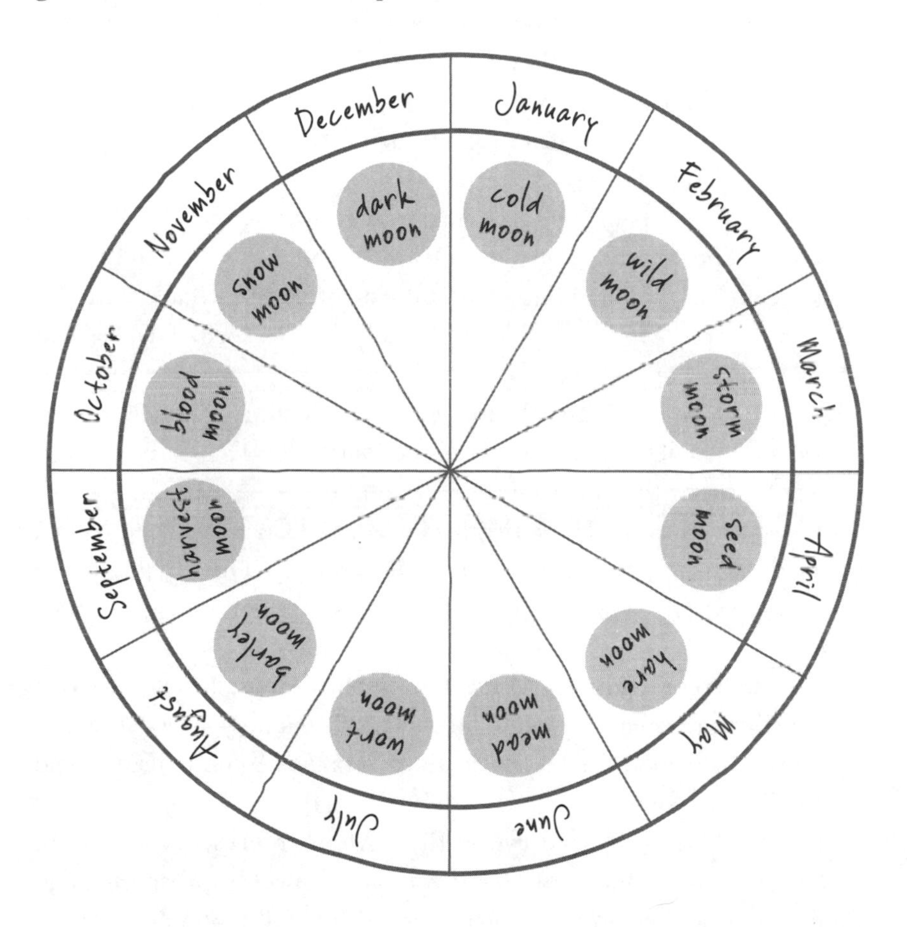

Each full moon has its own unique characteristics, often based on seasonal energies. Use the specific qualities of each full moon to guide you as you create your rituals. Esbat rituals draw upon nature's patterns, as well as mythology, cultural traditions, and astrology. Whether or not your magickal practice involves gathering with a coven or other people, you may wish to mark the full moons with rituals and/or spellwork. The following list briefly describes some of the attributes of each full moon. (Note that different cultures call the moons by different names.)

1. January—Known as the Cold, Frost, Ice, and Quiet Moon, it marks a time for renewal, discovery, resolve, and focusing on your purpose. Now is the time to set goals and to do spells for wealth and prosperity.
2. February—Called the Wild, Snow, Ice, and Starving Moon, it represents a period of healing and purification. Spells that prepare you for initiation, encourage healing or new growth, or foster physical or financial well-being are appropriate at this time.
3. March—The Storm, Wind, or Death Moon ushers in a time of change and awakening after a bleak, dormant period. Goals set under January's Cold Moon now begin to manifest. Do spells for personal growth and change now.
4. April—The Seed, Water, Growing, or Awakening Moon is a time of opening to new opportunities and experiences. Do spells for love, cleansing, growth, and strength at this time.
5. May—Known as the Hare, Bright, Grass, and Corn-planting Moon, it encourages joy, pleasure, sexuality, and fertility. This is a good time to do love spells, as well as spells for healing from emotional trauma and loss.
6. June—During the Honey, Mead, Planting, or Horse Moon, focus on strengthening relationships of all kinds: love, family, friendship, etc. This is also a good time to do spells to enhance communication and domestic harmony.
7. July—The Wort, Raspberry, or Rose Moon represents a time of maturation and fulfillment. Spells for career success, prosperity, and protection can benefit from the energy of this full moon.
8. August—Known as the Barley, Gathering, or Lightning Moon, this marks a time for gathering together all that holds meaning for you. Celebrate your blessings now and show gratitude, which will bring more blessings your way. Work with others of like mind during this time to share ideas, goals, and information.

9. September—The Harvest, Singing, or Spiderweb Moon is another period of reaping rewards for your efforts, and for seeing your dreams come to fruition. Give thanks for goals realized, projects completed, and wisdom gained. Focus on completion and bringing your life into balance.
10. October—During the Blood, Harvest, or Leaf-falling Moon, release old patterns and clear away emotional/psychic debris. Do spells to help you let go of whatever or whoever is standing in the way of your dreams' fulfillment. This is also a time to remember and honor loved ones who have moved on to another realm of existence.
11. November—The Snow, Dark, or Tree Moon is a time to look beyond the mundane world, into the magickal one. Scry to gaze into the future; do divination to gain guidance and wisdom that will aid you in the coming months. Open your mind to receive prophecies of things to come.
12. December—Under the Dark, Cold, or Long Night Moon, release your fears and banish those things in your life that are harmful or no longer useful. This is a time for silence, meditation, and introspection. Do spells to break old bonds, overcome obstacles, and end self-limiting habits/behaviors.

Decorate Your Altar for Esbats

A beautiful way to align yourself with the changing lunar cycles is to decorate your altar in accordance with each esbat. A bowl of pinecones or evergreen branches might grace your altar on the Cold Moon, along with bayberry candles to represent financial stability. In the spring and summer months, place a vase of seasonal flowers on your altar along with candles in a color that harmonizes with the moon's energy. Where you live on Planet Earth will influence what you choose to place on your altar each month. You may also like to display artwork, crystals and gemstones, figurines of deities—and of course, your grimoire—on your altar. Keep notes about what you did. You might also take a picture of your altar on each esbat and include it in your book of shadows.

Whether you belong to a group of magick workers or practice solitary witchcraft, during full-moon nights you will experience the sense of community and fellowship of like-minded individuals. You can be certain that on any full moon, witches around the world are casting circles and performing spells, celebrating and chanting, scrying and meditating. You are an integral part of this global community. By realizing your part in the whole, you will bring yourself into closer connection with your fellow beings and the Divine.

> *"The moon does not fight. It attacks no one. It does not worry. It does not try to crush others. It keeps to its course, but by its very nature, it gently influences. What other body could pull an entire ocean from shore to shore? The moon is faithful to its nature and its power is never diminished."*
>
> —Deng Ming-Dao, *Everyday Tao: Living with Balance and Harmony*

MOON PHASES IN MAGICK

The term *moon phase* refers to the part of the moon's face that you see illuminated in the night sky. The relative positions of the sun, moon, and earth shift as the moon orbits the earth, causing the changing phases. For the purposes of magick, witches are mainly interested in four lunar phases: new, waxing, full, and waning. Astronomically these phases are further defined as the new moon, waxing crescent, first quarter, waxing gibbous, full moon, waning gibbous, third quarter, and waning crescent.

You're more likely to reap the rewards you desire if you do magick during favorable phases of the moon. When casting spells or performing rituals, pay particular attention to the new moon, the full moon, and the waxing and waning phases. Each has its own unique energy that can add to the power of your spells:

- The new moon, as you might expect, encourages beginnings. Are you looking for a new job? A new romance? A new home? The best time to start anything is during the new moon. As the moon grows in light (and seemingly in size), your undertaking will grow too.
- The waxing moon—the two weeks after the new moon and leading up to the full moon—supports growth and expansion. Do you want to boost your income? Turn up the heat in a relationship? Get a promotion at work? Cast your spell while the moon's light is increasing to generate growth in your worldly affairs.

- The full moon marks a time of culmination. It allows you to start seeing the results of whatever you began on the new moon. Want to bring a project to a successful conclusion? Receive rewards, recognition, or payments that are due to you? Perform a spell while the moon is full for best results—its bright glow puts you in the spotlight. If your goal is to attract attention—from a lover, boss, or the public—the full moon illuminates you favorably. The full moon can also shine light on secrets and deception to help you get to the truth of a murky situation.
- The waning moon—the two weeks after the full moon and before the new moon—encourages decrease. Do you want to lose weight? End a bad relationship? Cut your expenses? Reduce your responsibilities at work or home? Cast your spell while the moon is diminishing in light (and size) to diminish the impact of something in your life.

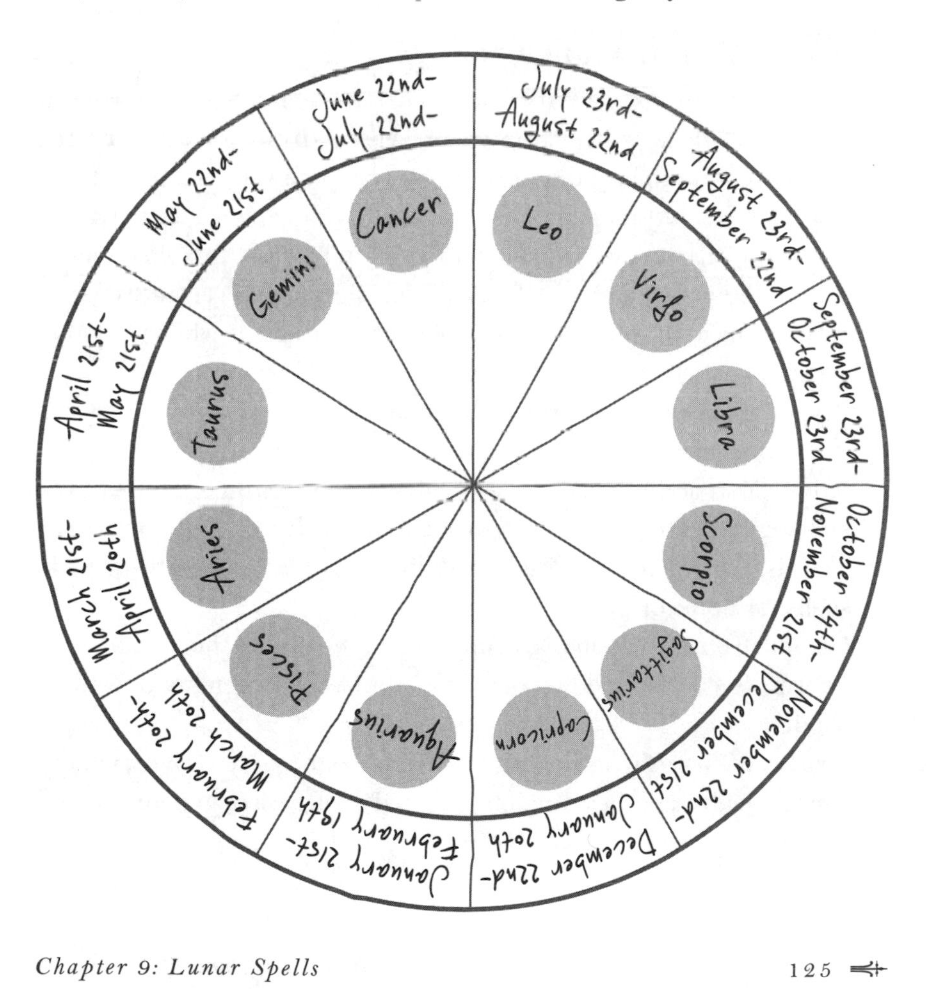

Record in your book of shadows what you experience while working with the energies of the different moon phases. To fine-tune your magick, consider both the moon's phase and its zodiac sign.

Blue Moons and Black Moons

When two full moons occur in the same month, the second is dubbed a blue moon. During the blue moon, you may find you get bigger or better results than on an ordinary full moon, or that you experience a lot more activity or vitality. When two new moons occur in the same month, the second one is called the black moon. This is considerably more powerful than a regular new moon, so any seeding spells you do under a black moon may manifest more quickly.

MOON SIGNS AND MAGICK

Witches have always placed great importance on the moon's role in magick, and astrology helps to explain why. Astrologers associate the moon with emotion, intuition, and creativity—the very things witches rely on when doing magick. As the moon circles the earth, it travels through all twelve zodiac signs in approximately a month, remaining in a sign for about two and a half days. Each sign favors certain types of magick. To make the most of a spell or ritual, perform it while the moon is in a sign that supports your intentions. The following list shows the best types of spells to do during each moon sign:

- Aries: Confronting obstacles and adversaries, courage, competition, starting new ventures, vitality, masculine virility
- Taurus: Abundance, fortitude, fertility, sex, plant or earth magick, spells for home or property
- Gemini: Communication, learning, mental pursuits, short trips
- Cancer: Spells for the home, protection, security, feminine fertility, children
- Leo: Leadership, career success, courage, recognition, creativity, vitality
- Virgo: Health and healing, job-oriented spells, discernment, mental clarity, pets

- Libra: Love, legal matters, peace, artistic endeavors, social situations, balance within and without
- Scorpio: Power, sexuality, psychic pursuits, overcoming obstacles and fears, banishing, transformation
- Sagittarius: Travel, spiritual growth, knowledge, expansion, creating opportunities, good luck
- Capricorn: Firm foundations, self-control, financial stability, career success, public image, manifesting goals, binding or banishing
- Aquarius: Change, new opportunities, adventure, liberation, friendship, group endeavors
- Pisces: Creativity, emotional healing, spiritual pursuits, developing psychic awareness

Let's say, for example, you want to find a better job. Virgo is most closely linked with work and work relationships. But if your main concern is to make more money, do magick while the waxing moon is in Taurus. If financial stability and status are more important, cast your spell while the moon is in Capricorn. If you're seeking fame or recognition, a Leo moon will support your intention. Study the unique properties of each sign to help you choose the right one for your purpose.

Moon Magick Communication Oil

Use this versatile oil to anoint candles, gemstones, ritual tools, and other spell components. It aids all forms of communication, with human beings and nonphysical entities. You can also use it as a massage oil or add it to a ritual bath.

TOOLS AND INGREDIENTS

3 ounces of olive or grape seed oil

A glass jar

3 drops of essential oil of sandalwood

A pinch of cinnamon

3 marigold (calendula) petals

A small quartz crystal

1. Pour the vegetable oil into the jar.
2. Add the essential oil, cinnamon, and marigold petals.
3. Add the quartz crystal.
4. Put a top on the jar and shake it 3 times to charge the mixture.
5. Massage your palms and the soles of your feet with the oil. Put a drop of oil on your throat chakra (the center of communication).

Record the results of your spell in your book of shadows. Also note your experiences, feelings, insights, and sensations while doing the spell, as well as anything that you believe to be relevant.

ECLIPSES

The ancients regarded eclipses with awe and even fear. Astrologers witness the powerful energies produced during eclipses and how these celestial events affect human affairs. Often you'll notice a series of related events occur in connection with a series of eclipses; each eclipse brings further development on what happened at the previous eclipse. You can tap the high-octane energy of solar and lunar eclipses in your magick work too; however, eclipses can sometimes spark unpredictable results, so proceed with caution.

Solar Eclipses

A solar eclipse occurs when the moon is new. At this time, both the sun and moon occupy the same sign and degree in the zodiac. The moon passes between the sun and earth, blocking our vision of the sun. In her book *Lunar Shadows*, Dietrech J. Pessin writes, "This time is filled with a mystery and unseen influences are yet to be developed in our lives . . . it is a time to observe, dream and plan—not to initiate action." Because the moon shadows the sun now, emotion and intuition—things we associate with the moon—tend to take precedence over the solar activities of logic, intellect, and outer world endeavors. Focus on inner growth, dreamwork, and psychic practices during a solar eclipse.

Lunar Eclipses

A lunar eclipse occurs when the moon is full, and the sun and moon are in opposite signs of the zodiac. The earth passes between the two heavenly bodies, blocking the sun's light to the moon. Because the moon is overshadowed, things we associate with the sun—such as logic and intellectual activities—become highlighted. A lunar eclipse brings matters to light that may have lain hidden for some time, but with more force than an ordinary full moon. Pessin calls this a time when "all the cards are on the table." During a lunar eclipse, do magick to bring projects to fruition or to conclude situations in your life.

Familiarizing yourself with the energies of the celestial bodies and their shifting relationships to our earth will benefit not only your spellwork but also your understanding of your place in the cosmos. You'll develop a richer connection with nature and her cycles. You'll witness the meaning of the old axiom "as above, so below" in action. And by studying this information, as recorded in your grimoire, you'll come to a deeper appreciation of the physical expression of the Goddess and the God, as symbolized by the moon and the sun that light up our world.

Chapter 10

SPELLS FOR SPECIFIC PURPOSES

Many cookbooks organize recipes according to types of food: meat, fish, vegetables, bread, pasta, and so on. In a similar way, many witches find it convenient to arrange their grimoires according to the types of spells they do: love, money, health, protection, etc. This method makes it easy to locate the spell you want when you want it. It also lets you see what spells you do most frequently and select some favorite "go-to" spells that you can turn to with confidence.

FIND IT FAST

If you decide to configure your book of shadows in this way, you may want to insert tabs or dividers to mark the various sections of your book. Some people like to "color code" their books, using colored paper to indicate different categories of spells: pink for love spells, green for money, and so on. This works especially well if you're using a book that allows you to shift the pages around, such as a three-ring binder.

If your grimoire has a fixed binding that won't let you add pages, you can demarcate the various "chapters" of your book with bookmarks. Do you have an artsy nature? You may enjoy handcrafting pretty bookmarks to designate the sections of your grimoire. The more personal you make your book and the more imagination you put into it, the better. Try these suggestions:

- Cut strips of posterboard or heavy construction paper, each about 2" wide by 7" long. Onto the strips glue pictures from magazines that represent the topics you've included in your grimoire: happy couples or hearts for love, dollar signs or diamonds for prosperity, airplanes or cruise ships for travel, and so on.
- Dry flowers, herbs, or other botanicals that have magickal connections to the categories you've chosen for your book: roses for love, mint for money spells, etc. (Refer to the charts in Chapter 16 for more information.) Then affix these botanicals to strips of posterboard or heavy construction paper.
- Select posterboard or heavy construction paper in various colors that correspond to the topics in your book. Cut the paper into strips, then draw symbols or other images on the strips to represent the subjects of the spells. You could decorate these strips with magick sigils, which are spells in themselves (see Chapter 12), to mark sections in your grimoire.
- Purchase ribbons in colors that symbolize the topics you've chosen to include in your book. Lay the ribbon markers between the pages to define the different sections. Or, if you opt to craft your own grimoire from scratch, fasten the ribbons in place when you bind your book (see Chapter 2 for instructions). Attach tiny charms, gemstone beads, or other symbolic adornments to the ribbons, if you like.

INVITE DIVINE ASSISTANCE

When you prepare yourself to enact a ritual or cast a spell or a charm, you agree to suspend reality for a time to get in touch with energies greater than your own limited scope of individual perception. By entering the space and time "between the worlds" you make a pact with yourself and with the myriad spirits who share the cosmos with us. You acknowledge their presence by inviting them into your sacred space. You accept them as manifestations of the Divine.

Whether you choose to interact only with the forces of the Divine Feminine and/or the Divine Masculine or to invite assistance from other deities, spirits, and nonphysical beings is up to you. Later in this book, we'll talk more about some of the entities who may assist you in your magickal work.

Devote Each Section of Your Grimoire to a Goddess

Ancient cultures revered certain qualities and characteristics in each goddess, and saw her as having dominion over specific areas of life on earth. Today, many witches and Neopagans continue to honor a pantheon of deities and call upon these deities to aid us in our magickal practice.

As you go about compiling your grimoire, think of the goddesses traditionally associated with the many and diverse parts of your life. Think about the types of spells you intend to perform. Most likely, you'll feel a special attraction to certain goddesses, perhaps based on your own heritage or personal affinities. You may want to dedicate each section of your grimoire to a different goddess and then invoke her power and assistance when you perform spells and rituals in the areas she governs.

Many deities play a number of roles and can be called upon to assist you in numerous areas of your magickal practice. The following list suggests some to consider, but you can find a wealth of additional information online and in other books.

- Love: Venus, Aphrodite, Freya, Hathor, Hera, Juno
- Protection: Tara, Artemis, Tiamat, Frigg, Beset
- Prosperity/Abundance: Venus, Lakshmi, Gaia, Demeter, Ceres, Epona, Renenet

- Healing: Brigid, Isis, Ceres, Freya, Kuan Yin
- Creativity: Brigid, Isis, Venus, Selena
- Wisdom: Sophia, Cerridwen, Hecate, Hestia, Morgan, Saraswati
- Success: Nike, Isis, Cybele, Amaterasu, Cerridwen
- Home: Brigid, Cerridwen, Coatlicue, Beset
- Children/Fertility: Yemaja, Axo Mama, Cybele, Oshun, Demeter, Frigg, Heket
- Happiness: Bast, Hathor, Lilith, Freya
- Strength/Power: Inanna, Artemis, Sekhmet, Tiamat, Pele, Kali, Persephone, Selket

Working with Goddess Energy

Begin by researching various goddesses. Learn all you can about the goddesses with whom you might like to work and to whom you plan to dedicate the different sections of your grimoire. Familiarize yourself with ancient rites of worship and decide how these relate to your modern-day experience. How might you adapt early ideas to your present-day practice?

Next, dedicate each section of your book of shadows to a particular goddess who will help you by lending her powers to your magickal workings. On the first page of each section, write a blessing to the deity who will preside over that portion of your book and the spells and rituals you perform. Let's say, for example, you've devoted the love section of your book of shadows to Venus. Write the following blessing or one of your own creation:

> *"Most beautiful Venus, whose light shines brightest in the night sky, and whose loving energy embraces all humankind, I dedicate the spells and rituals I perform for love and relationships to you. Fill me with the power and perfection of your love, so that I may channel your divine energy into the magick I do. I ask your guidance as I seek to bring more love to myself, other people, and the manifest world. May I and all beings know the blessedness of your divine love that transcends all worldly love, and may it sustain us, uplift us, and bring us joy."*

If you like, add pictures of the deity as you interpret her and other symbols or objects that you attribute to her.

Before you perform a spell or ritual, invite the goddess with humility. Explain your reasons for calling upon her. What, exactly, do you hope to accomplish? Whether you are seeking love, knowledge, protection, or abundance, your invocation must include your statement of intent.

When the Goddess is effectively evoked, she does not merely announce "Here I am!" She will make her true self known to you through images, inspiration, insights, emotions—and often she will have a message to impart. When she speaks through you, you may find that words and visions flow as freely as a wild river, carrying you to places unimaginable heretofore. Remain open to this energy and try to retain the experience of receiving her communication. Record as many details in your grimoire as you can, in order to deepen your understanding of what has transpired.

LOVE SPELLS

Love makes the world go 'round, as the saying goes, and witches cast more spells for matters of the heart than for any other purpose. Therefore, you'll probably want to dedicate a section in your grimoire for love spells. Because emotion is one of the key ingredients in magick, it's logical that love spells would be among the most powerful of all. Usually the best times to perform love spells are during the waxing moon, when the sun or moon is in Libra, or on Fridays—unless you intend to block someone's attention or end an unwanted relationship. In that case, do your spell while the moon is waning, when the sun or moon is in Scorpio or Capricorn, or on Saturday.

Before you begin the spell, cleanse your space, and cast a circle (see Chapter 13 for details on how to cast and open circles). Call upon the goddess who presides over your love spells and ask her to assist you.

Here's a sample love spell you can use if you like:

Light My Fire

Use this spell to spark a new love affair or to fan the flames in an existing romance. You can cast it for yourself or someone else.

TOOLS AND INGREDIENTS

A ballpoint pen

A red candle

Essential oil of jasmine, rose, or patchouli

A ring large enough to slide over the candle

A candleholder

Matches or a lighter

1. With the ballpoint pen, carve the two individuals' names on the candle, so that the letters are alternated and interspersed. For example, you'd write Bill and Sue this way: B S I U L E L.
2. Rub some essential oil on the candle, then slide the ring onto it—the symbolism is obvious.
3. Place the candle in the holder and light it. As you stare into the flame, chant the word created by your joint names (don't worry if it doesn't make any sense or sounds discordant). Envision a union between you and your partner.
4. When you can no longer concentrate on this spell, snuff out the candle and open the circle.
5. Repeat each day until the candle has burned down to the ring.
6. Remove the ring and place it on your altar, or give it to the person for whom you did the spell, to "fire up" a romance.
7. Thank the goddess of love for her assistance.

Be sure to include the date(s) when you performed the spell and record the results. Each time you cast this spell, add more details and experiences in your grimoire, including any changes you may have made from the original.

PROSPERITY AND ABUNDANCE SPELLS

Spells for abundance are probably the second most popular among witches. Of course, prosperity and abundance mean different things to different people, but usually spellcasters perform these spells to attract money and/or material goods. Enact prosperity spells during the waxing moon, when the sun or moon is in Taurus, on a Thursday or Friday—unless your goal is to stabilize finances or cut your expenses. In that case, do your spell when the moon is waning, when the sun or moon is in Capricorn, or on a Saturday.

Before you begin the spell, cleanse your space, and cast a circle. Call upon the goddess who presides over your prosperity spells and ask her to assist you. Here's a sample spell you can use to draw money to you:

Buried Treasure Spell

This spell offers a new twist on the old legends about buried treasure. Instead of hunting for that pirate's hidden chest of gold doubloons or a leprechaun's pot of gold at the end of a rainbow, you symbolically stash treasure in order to "prime the pump" so greater riches can flow to you.

TOOLS AND INGREDIENTS

A small mirror

A tin box with a lid

9 coins (any denomination)

A magnet

A shovel

1. Place the mirror in the bottom of the tin box, with the reflective side up.
2. Lay the coins, one at a time, on top of the mirror while you envision each one multiplying exponentially.
3. Attach the magnet to the inside of the box (on the lid or on a side) and visualize it attracting a multitude of coins to you.
4. Put the lid on the box and open the circle.
5. Take your "treasure chest" and the shovel outside and dig a hole beneath a large tree. Bury the box in the ground near the tree's roots.

6. When you've finished, say this incantation aloud:

"By the luck of three times three
This spell now brings great wealth to me.
The magnet draws prosperity.
The mirror doubles all it sees.
My fortune grows as does this tree
And I shall ever blessed be."

7. Thank the goddess for her assistance.

Be sure to include the date(s) when you performed the spell and record the results. Each time you cast this spell, add more details and experiences in your grimoire, including any changes you made from the original.

Louise Hay's Prescription for Prosperity

In order to become prosperous, bestselling author and publisher Louise Hay in her book *You Can Heal Your Life* says you must:

- Feel deserving.
- Make room for the new.
- Be happy for other people's prosperity.
- Be grateful.

She also explains that "true prosperity begins with feeling good about yourself . . . It is never an amount of money; it is a state of mind. Prosperity or lack of it is an outer expression of the ideas in your head."

PROTECTION SPELLS

Early grimoires contained lots and lots of spells for protection—some of them incredibly complex, and many of which invoked the assistance of spirits. Early spellcasters frequently called upon deities of all sorts to safeguard them, their homes, and their loved ones from both physical and psychic harm. People in many cultures have used evil eyes and hex signs since ancient times and still do today. As in earlier eras, the world presents many dangers today—as a quick glance at the nightly news will confirm—so you'll most likely want to devote a section in your grimoire to protection spells. Usually the best times to perform protection spells are during the waning moon, when the sun or moon is in Capricorn, and/or on a Saturday.

Before you begin the spell, cleanse your space, and cast a circle. Call upon the goddess whom you've chosen to preside over your protection spells and ask her to assist you. Here's a sample spell you can use to create a protection amulet for yourself or someone else:

Protection Amulet

Protection amulets are one of the oldest forms of magick. With this spell you create one to shield you (or someone else) from potential injury or illness.

TOOLS AND INGREDIENTS

A piece of amber (for protection from physical or nonphysical sources)
A piece of bloodstone (for protection from physical injury)
A piece of turquoise (for protection from illness)
Pine incense (for cleansing and purification)
An incense burner
Matches or a lighter
A photo of you (or another person if you're doing this spell for someone else)
A pen with black ink
Essential oil of rosemary
A white pouch, preferably silk
A black ribbon
Saltwater

1. Wash the stones with mild soap and water, then pat them dry.
2. Fit the incense into the burner and light it.
3. Across the photograph write the words "I am safe" as you envision yourself safe and sound, completely surrounded by a sphere of pure white light. If you're doing the spell for someone else, write "[person's name] is safe" and envision her or him protected by white light.

4. Dot each corner of the photo with essential oil. Inhale the scent of the oil and mentally connect it with a feeling of safety.
5. Slip the photo into the pouch (if necessary, fold it so it's small enough to fit).
6. Rub a little essential oil on each of the stones and add them to the pouch.
7. Tie the pouch closed with the black ribbon, making 8 knots. Each time you tie a knot repeat this incantation aloud:

"Anything that could cause harm
Is now repelled by this magick charm."

8. Sprinkle the amulet with saltwater, then hold it in the incense smoke for a few moments to charge it.
9. Open the circle and thank the Goddess for her help.
10. Wear or carry the amulet with you at all times to protect you from harm, or give it to the person you intend to protect.

As you record the spell in your grimoire, be sure to include the date(s) when you performed the spell and describe the results. Each time you cast this spell, add more details and experiences in your book, including any changes you made from the original.

SPELLS FOR HEALTH AND HEALING

In the days before modern medicine and technology, people relied heavily on magick to promote health and healing. Even today, we realize that a patient's attitude and beliefs influence his or her well-being and can have a huge impact on the person's recovery. Like the beneficial nature of prayer, which Dr. Larry Dossey wrote about in his book *Prayer Is Good Medicine*, magick's power can boost all sorts of healing. You may want to dedicate a section of your grimoire to healing spells and rituals. The best times to perform spells for health and healing depend on the nature of the ailment and your intention.

Before you begin the spell, cleanse your space, and cast a circle. Call upon the deity who presides over your health and healing work, and request her assistance. If you're performing a spell for another person, ask his or her permission before you begin. Here's a sample spell you can use yourself or to aid someone else—even at a distance:

Heaven and Earth Healing Spell

This spell draws upon the powers of heaven and earth to help heal any condition. You can perform it anytime.

TOOLS AND INGREDIENTS

A magick wand

1. After casting a circle around yourself, stand in the center of the circle with your feet about shoulder-width apart. (If you're doing the spell for someone else and that person is physically present, cast the circle around both of you.)
2. Hold the wand over your head with both hands, with your arms outstretched and straight, pointing the tip of the wand at the sky.
3. Close your eyes and say aloud: "With this wand I draw down the healing force of the heavens." In your mind's eye see light flowing into the wand, filling it with cosmic energy and making it glow brightly.
4. Open your eyes and point the tip of the wand at the afflicted part of your body (or the other person's body). If the person for whom you are doing this spell is not physically present, aim the wand toward his/her location. Envision the light you collected from the heavens flowing into the injured or ailing body part, filling and embracing it with healing rays.
5. When you sense that all the light has been transferred from the wand to the body, point the wand at the ground.
6. Close your eyes and say aloud: "With this wand I draw up the healing force of Mother Earth." In your mind's eye see light flowing into the wand from the center of the earth, filling it and making it glow brightly.
7. Open your eyes and aim the tip of the wand at the afflicted part of your body (or the other person's body). Envision the light you collected from the earth flowing into the injured or ailing body part, infusing it with healing rays until all the light has been transferred from the wand to the body.
8. When you have finished, thank the Goddess as well as the forces of heaven and earth for assisting you, and then open the circle.

Be sure to include the date(s) when you performed the spell and record the results. Each time you cast this spell, add more details and experiences in your grimoire, including any changes you made from the original.

OTHER SPELLS TO INCLUDE

The other categories you choose to include in your book of shadows will depend on your preferences, your objectives, and the types of spells you do most frequently. If you travel a lot, you might add a section for travel spells. If your career is a primary focus, you may consider devoting a section to spells for success. You could dedicate portions of your grimoire to spells for personal power, spiritual growth, creativity, good luck, peace and harmony, children and pets, or just about anything else that fits your needs. You might want to establish a "Miscellaneous" category for all those great one-off spells you like as well as those that have many potential yet undefined applications.

Over time, as you become more proficient as a magician and collect more and more spells, you may even decide to create an entire book of shadows for each category. Or you could keep a big book that contains all your spells as well as a smaller one that holds some of your favorites.

Each time you perform a particular spell or ritual, note in your book of shadows when you cast the spell, what you actually did, what tools and ingredients you used, what you experienced, and the results you got. How long did it take to see results? What went right and what went wrong? Was anyone else involved in your spellworking? If so, what impact did that person's presence have? If you did a spell for someone else, how did she or he react? Also note anything you changed from your original working. If you did something differently, did this affect the outcome? How? Would you change something in the future? What and why?

CRAFTING YOUR OWN ORIGINAL SPELLS

In the beginning, as a novice witch, you'd probably be wise to stick with tried-and-true spells shared with you by spellworkers you respect. But after a while, when you are more comfortable with your knowledge and powers and have some experience under your magick belt, you'll probably want to try crafting your own spells. That's great! The more personal a spell, the better results it's likely to generate because you invest more emotion in it. Each of us has unique needs, preferences, talents, and strengths—use them to your advantage.

Readers frequently e-mail me and ask me to look at the spells they've designed themselves and to offer suggestions. In nearly every case, the writer has created a fabulous original work of art that shows he or she has invested a great deal of thought, time, and effort into the process. One of the most interesting of these was a woman who'd been nearly blind all her life. She explained that she found it difficult to relate to the visual spells I'd included in my previous books and wanted to adapt the spells to make the best of her other senses. This amazingly creative woman tackled the challenge with enthusiasm and insight. She designed some beautiful spells I could never have imagined that used her individual strengths in very special ways.

Planning Your Spells

Carefully plan your spells before you attempt to cast them. The old adage "Be careful what you ask for, you just might get it" is never more relevant than in spellwork. Consider the implications of every nuance—the color of the candles you choose to place on the altar, the manner in which you have prepared your tools, the conviction with which you consecrate, the spirits you invoke, every word that you speak, and, especially, the intention you hold in your mind and heart.

According to Wiccan theory, the energy you send out via a spell will return to you threefold. Therefore, it's in your best interest to plan carefully before casting your spell into the world, so that you avoid unexpected or undesirable results you didn't intend.

Your Grimoire As a Spellcrafting Companion

When you begin crafting your own original spells, your grimoire becomes an even greater ally than you may have realized earlier. It serves as your workbook while you build the framework of the spells you create. It lets you clearly define your intentions by writing them down—writing is the first step in bringing an idea to fruition in the manifest world. Your book of shadows also enables you to keep track of your steps as you progress on your journey. And it allows you to see whether you've gone astray or could have done something differently to produce a better result.

As you set out to craft a spell of your own design:

- Write down your intention and the ideas you have about what you hope to accomplish.
- Research the implications of the spell you plan to craft. What have other spellcasters experienced? What challenges do you foresee? What outcomes?
- Give your ideas time to settle. During the next few days or weeks, you may gain additional insight, perhaps from your dreams or meditations, into what you could do to enhance or refine your spell.
- Make a list of ingredients and tools you'll need. How will you acquire these? What do you need to do to prepare them for your spellwork?
- Will you include an affirmation or incantation? Practice writing it until it says exactly what you intend. (See the instructions in Chapter 11.)
- Do you plan to ask a deity to assist you? If so, which one? How will you invoke this deity? Write down the invocation you plan to use and study it to make sure it says what you want it to say.
- Determine the best time to cast your spell (see Chapters 6, 8, and 9 for more information).
- Decide where you'll perform your spell, and prepare the space.
- Will anyone else be involved in the process? If so, discuss the details with that person to make sure you're in agreement and clear about your intentions and outcomes, as well as what you plan to do.
- Organize the steps you'll take in casting your spell.
- Try to anticipate what might transpire and how your thoughts, words, and actions may manifest.
- Approach your work with serenity and patience, rather than feeling a need for immediate gratification.

Of course, after you've finished casting your spell, record everything in your book of shadows as soon as possible. Follow up with an explanation of the results and any other experiences related to your magick work. What occurred? How, when, where? In this way, you will gain greater confidence and a more personal understanding of the connections between each aspect of your process. You will be able to observe the results that manifest after you perform your spell. You'll become conscious of your role in what transpires.

In time, you'll notice patterns and synchronicities. You'll learn what works for you and what doesn't. You'll develop your techniques and expand your repertoire. You'll strengthen your magickal muscles and move into the next phase of proficiency. How amazing is that?

Chapter 11
VERBAL SPELLS

When you utter a spell aloud, you create a resonance that begins the process of manifestation. Sounds produce vibrations that echo through the cosmic web that connects everything in our universe. These vibrations stimulate effects in the visible world. Words also act as verbal symbols that convey your intentions. Even a word from a language with which you aren't familiar can serve as a magick symbol. In fact, many spellcasters choose to use words from ancient tongues, such as Sanskrit or Arabic, or from cultures other than their own because for them these words have no mundane associations.

It's safe to say that the earliest spells were most likely spoken ones, intoned by witches and wizards, shamans and sorcerers long before the advent of writing. Verbal spells figured prominently in early grimoires. They owed their popularity, in part, to the fact that the magick worker needed nothing other than a voice to cast the spell. Even if the magician couldn't read or write, he or she could memorize the words and say them at the appropriate time. Our ancestors called upon gods and goddesses, as well as angels, spirits, demons, and other nonphysical entities, via invocations, spoken charms, and incantations.

Witches today still use verbal spells to request the assistance of deities and other beings. Because affirmations, incantations, chants, charms, and blessings continue to play an important role in magickal workings, you may choose to devote a section of your grimoire to spoken and written spells.

Evoking and Invoking

When you *evoke* an entity—a spirit, an elemental, a ghost, or another nonphysical being—you summon it to appear before you and instruct it to do your bidding. When you *invoke* an entity, you invite it to actually enter your body. The entity becomes part of you, temporarily, and works or speaks through you. (Mediums also do this in séances when they channel spirits.) Witches sometimes invoke the Goddess or God in rites, and for the duration of the rite the deity abides within the witch until released. Before you evoke or invoke any being, it's a good idea to learn all you can about that entity so you know what you're getting into. An old saying warns: Don't raise any spirit you can't put down.

CHANTING

What comes to mind when you think of chanting? Medieval monks singing Gregorian chants in European cathedrals? Buddhists dressed in saffron robes sitting in lotus position, uttering the Sanskrit phrase *Om Mani Padme Hum*? Chants are typically phrases or words repeated aloud for a particular purpose. Saying a rosary is a form of chanting. So are the cheers sports fans shout to encourage players on the field.

Some people chant mantras while meditating. A mantra is a group of sacred sounds repeated for spiritual purposes. The mantra not only helps you to focus your mind; it lets you become aware of the spirit housed within your body. Witches sometimes chant in their rituals to raise energy and to unify all the participants in the ritual. Maybe you've heard this popular chant, for instance, or intoned it yourself: "The Goddess is alive, magick is afoot."

The repetitive sounds in a chant—as well as the actual words that compose it—act on your subconscious to generate results. Interestingly, chanting has the power to quiet or enliven. It can help you concentrate, shift your consciousness to an altered state, affect physical processes such as blood pressure and heart rate, connect you to the divine realm, and more.

"She changes everything she touches,
And everything she touches changes!"

Do you have a few favorite chants that help you get into the mood for magick? Some that you recite to calm your mind before meditating? Perhaps you chant to cleanse sacred space or to chase away unwanted energies before spellworking. In your book of shadows, jot down the chants you find valuable. You can use them alone or in conjunction with other magickal processes.

Consider setting some to music or accompanying your chants on a hand drum to boost their power. Although most chants are quite simple, you could add bits of sheet music to accompany the words in your grimoire, or sketch the notes yourself on the pages of your book—this adds both an instructive and an illustrative element. If you are raising magickal children, you may enjoy singing favorite chants to your kids just as you would sing nursery rhymes.

"We all come from the Goddess
And to her we shall return
Like a drop of rain
Flowing to the ocean."

AFFIRMATIONS

In the last few decades, affirmations have gained popularity in psychological and self-help circles, as well as among spellcasters. Affirmations are short positive statements that you formulate to produce a desired result. They express clearly and succinctly what you intend to attract, eliminate, manifest, or change in your life. Whether you write your affirmations or say them aloud, putting your intentions into words helps to focus your mind, clarify your objectives, and empower your spells.

Designing Effective Affirmations

As is true with anything else in life, some ways are better than others when it comes to designing affirmations. These tips will help you to word yours effectively:

- Keep it short.
- Use only positive imagery.
- State your intention in the present tense, as if the condition already exists.

Let's try a couple examples to help you get a feel for creating affirmations.

Right: I am completely healthy in body, mind, and spirit.

Wrong: I don't have any illnesses or injuries.

See the difference? The first sentence affirms what you seek: health. The second makes you think of conditions you don't want: illnesses and injuries.

Right: I now have a job that's perfect for me.

Wrong: I will get the perfect job.

In the first sentence you state that the job you seek is yours *right now.* The second indicates that you'll eventually get the job you want, but doesn't specify when—it could be some time way off in the future. Yes, it may take a while for all the pieces to fall into place, but the first step to achieving success is believing (and affirming) that you already have what you desire and that the situation is already determined in your favor.

Being specific is usually a good thing when creating affirmations. If your goal is to lose twenty-five pounds or you've got your heart set on acquiring a 1965 red Mustang convertible, for instance, list the pertinent details in your affirmation. But sometimes you don't know all the ins and outs of a situation, or you don't want to limit your options—as in the job example we just considered. In such cases, simply state that whatever you achieve is right for you in every way and let the universe work out the fine points.

Consider designing some general, all-purpose affirmations and use them regularly. List these in your book of shadows and, if you like, enrich them with illustrations.

Your list might look something like this:

- My life is rich with abundance of all kinds.
- I have everything I need and desire.
- I am happy, healthy, wealthy, and fulfilled in every way.

You can recite these favorite affirmations first thing in the morning and last thing at night, while driving to work, taking a shower, folding laundry—whenever you have time. In this way, you make magick part of your daily routine and attract good things into your life on a continual basis.

Using Affirmations

The versatility of affirmations makes them the darlings of many modern witches. Each time you read the words of an affirmation you've created, you are reminded of your objective. Seeing the written affirmation makes an imprint on the visual part of your brain; hearing it stated aloud impacts the auditory sense. Together, they provide a one-two punch in spellcasting.

Here are some ways you can use affirmations:

- Say your affirmation aloud several times a day—or at least first thing in the morning—to set your objective into motion.
- Post an affirmation in a place where you'll see it often: near your computer, on your bathroom mirror, on your refrigerator, on the dashboard of your car, and so on.
- Write an affirmation on a slip of paper and add it to a medicine pouch, talisman, or amulet.
- Write an affirmation on a slip of paper and burn it in a cauldron or ritual fire to release something you want to eliminate from your life, such as an unwanted habit or relationship.
- Carve a short affirmation on a candle, and then light the candle to ignite the affirmation.

Once you understand the basics of creating affirmations, you'll probably find lots of original ways to include them in your spells and rituals. Record them in your grimoire, and comment on the results you get from using affirmations. Over time, you may refine the affirmations you've noted in your book of shadows, based on your experiences.

Affirmations and Healing

Bestselling author and publisher Louise Hay, in her book *You Can Heal Your Life*, includes a lengthy section of affirmations intended to aid specific health issues. For example:

Problem	**Affirmation**
Allergies	"The world is safe and friendly. I am safe. I am at peace with life."
Lower back pain	"I love and approve of myself. Life supports and loves me."
Indigestion	"I digest and assimilate all new experiences peacefully and joyously."
Sore throat	"I speak up for myself with ease. I express my creativity."

By repeating an affirmation regularly, you reprogram your thinking process. Your updated perspective enables you to remedy the problem.

INCANTATIONS

One of the oldest known incantations—believed to be more than 3,000 years old—was discovered by archaeologists in the ancient Mesopotamian city of Kish. The author inscribed this ancient love spell in cuneiform on a clay tablet, calling upon Akkadian deities:

"By Ištar and Išhara
I conjure you:
As long as his neck
And your neck
Are not entwined,
You shall find no peace!"

Incantations can be as short as two lines or as long as your imagination and intention dictate (the Mesopotamian one excerpted here, for instance, contains a total of thirty-eight lines). Although early spellcasters used incantations to curse as well as to charm, witches today usually frown on the practice of performing magick to harm or manipulate someone against his or her will.

What's the difference between an affirmation and an incantation? Incantations are usually written as rhymes. The catchy phrasing makes them easy to remember. You don't have to be a poet laureate to create an effective incantation—just follow the same basic rules when writing an incantation as you would when writing an affirmation: keep it simple, use positive imagery, and state it in the present tense. Here's an example of a simple incantation for healing:

"I am healed
In body and mind
Of imbalances
Of any kind."

Although it's perfectly okay to merely write incantations, they become even more effective when spoken aloud. Because incantations feature both rhyme and meter, you may enjoy putting them to music and singing them.

THE FORCES OF THE FOUR DIRECTIONS

Many spells and rituals petition gods, goddesses, and other entities for assistance. You may choose to call upon a deity with whom you feel a particular kinship. Or, if you're performing a ritual on one of the sabbats, you might seek the aid of the deity connected with that day: for example, Brigid on Imbolc, Lugh on Lugnasadh.

Witches often summon the forces associated with the four directions and the four elements. You may envision these as angels, guardians, or other spirits. The archangel Raphael, for instance, is said to oversee the east, Michael the south, Gabriel the west, and Uriel the north.

Here's a simple practice you can use as part of a circle-casting ritual:

1. Stand in the center of the circle, facing east. Outstretch your arms at your sides, with your left palm open and facing down toward the earth and your right palm upturned toward the sky.
2. Say aloud: "Before me Raphael, angel of air, guardian of the east. Please guide, protect, bless, and empower me."
3. Next, say aloud: "Behind me Gabriel, angel of water, guardian of the west. Please guide, protect, bless, and empower me."
4. Next, say aloud: "To my right Michael, angel of fire, guardian of the south. Please guide, protect, bless, and empower me."
5. Next, say aloud: "To my left Uriel, angel of earth, guardian of the north. Please guide, protect, bless, and empower me."
6. Finally say: "About me shines the five-pointed star, and within me the six-rayed star. Blessed be."

While you call to these angelic beings, envision them standing around you and offering their support. Perhaps you'll see Raphael dressed in yellow, Gabriel in blue. Maybe Michael wields his famed sword. See the five-pointed star—the pentagram—overlaid on your body, its points aligned with your head, arms, and legs.

You can design your own ritual, but before you begin calling the quarters, gain as much knowledge as possible about their energies and correspondences. This will enrich your experience and enhance your magickal work.

East, Realm of Dawn

The east corresponds to daybreak. When contemplating the energies of this direction, find an eastern-facing spot and rise early enough that you can see and feel the tranquil transition of the awakening world. This will give you a very real experience of new beginnings, as night surrenders her darkness to the power of the rising sun. Birds emerge from sleep and herald the start of the day. The grass is wet with dew and the world seems fresh and undisturbed. Open yourself to the sensations of dawn and the promises she proffers, then write down your experiences in your book of shadows.

South, Realm of High Noon

Preferably on a bright and sunny day, find a place where you can sit quietly and be undisturbed. Face the south. Do not look directly into the sun overhead, but feel its heat and warmth on your face and shoulders. As you breathe, envision the glowing center of energy contained within you as an internal echo of the sun itself. Notice the heightened activity of the day, when everything seems to be at its very peak. The sun nurtures life on earth, but it can also dangerous, scorching the land and your own skin. Contemplate this duality and other insights or sensations that come to you, and then record your experiences in your book of shadows.

West, Realm of Sunset

In many mythologies, the western lands are seen as a magickal place. To the west lay the Summerlands, the Isle of Apples, Avalon, Tír na nÓg, and the Isle of Man. At the time of the setting sun, when the earth begins to grow quiet again after the day's activities, face the west. Notice the changes in the sky. The sun descends toward the horizon, the temperature cools, and nocturnal creatures emerge from their lairs. Twilight paints the sky with many colors and, on the seacoast, land and ocean appear to be one. As you relax, breathe deeply and observe day surrendering to night. In your grimoire, note your experiences in this place of twilight and mystery.

North, Realm of Midnight

At midnight, when the moon is bright and other humans sleep, begin your contemplation of the north. Gaze at the stars. Find Polaris, the North Star, which has guided sailors and navigators for centuries. Once you find the North Star, you can never truly be lost. The north pulls the compass point to itself, thus its magnetism and power are undeniable. Picture the earth in the sleep of winter, trees bare of their leaves, the earth frozen and solid, icicles dangling from branches and twigs. Feel yourself standing upon the earth, the Great Mother who gave life to us all and who will one day cradle our bones. Turn inward and open yourself to the wisdom and secrets of this direction. Write down your experiences in this time of silence and solitude.

CALLING THE FOUR QUARTERS

When you feel comfortable in your knowledge of the four directions and their energies, you're ready to evoke and/or invoke the deities who reign there. You may do this alone or with other like-minded people, as a ritual in itself or as part of a more extensive ritual or rite. Before performing a spell, you may choose to invite the assistance of the powers and elements of the four directions. Use the following to call the deities who guard the quarters, or better yet, write your own "script."

Call to the East

Start in the east, the realm of new beginnings, of the dawn and of springtime. The east corresponds to the element of air, and represents possibility and awareness. Look to the east when you seek to renew hope and faith. Face east to summon the power inherent there for strength in communication, mental clarity, and wisdom. Call the forces of this direction with this charge:

"I call upon the spirits of air who guard and protect the gateway to the eastern realm. I beckon and call you forth from the far corner of the universe wherein you dwell. Winds of change, strength of tornadoes, bear witness to this ritual and give us your aid. Gentle breeze that carries the seed to fertile soil, descend into this circle and grant us your blessing. Realm of the Dawning Star, bestow upon us your gifts of vision, insight, and song. We seek to know you, we seek to honor you. By the air that is our breath, we charge you, be here now! To the East and the spirits of air, we bid you hail and welcome!"

Call to the South

Proceed clockwise around the circle and face south, the direction of noontime and of summer. The south corresponds to the element of fire, and represents fullness and vitality. Turn to the south when you seek fulfillment of desire, when you need passion, inspiration, or courage. Face the south and call the powers of the direction with this charge:

"I call upon the spirits of fire who guard and protect the gateway to the southern realm. I beckon and call you forth from the far corner of the universe wherein you dwell. Candle flame and hearth fire, come into this circle and warm our hearts.

Strength of wildfire and volcano, descend into this circle and grant us your blessing. Golden orb of the high noon sun, realm of heat and brilliance, bestow upon us your gifts of passion and inspiration. We seek to know you, we seek to honor you. By the fire in our hearts, we charge you, be here now! To the South and the spirits of fire, we bid you hail and welcome!"

Call to the West

Continue around the circle to the western "corner" and face the direction of sunset and of autumn. The west corresponds to the element of water. Turn to the west when you seek to enhance your intuition, uncover mysteries, and balance your emotions. Face the west and call the powers of the direction with this charge:

"I call upon the spirits of water who guard and protect the gateway to the western realm. I beckon and call you forth from the far corner of the universe wherein you dwell. Ocean depths, cradle of life, come into this circle and reveal the truth of our inner visions. Strength of storm, rushing rivers, and rolling tides, descend into this circle and grant us your blessing. Gentle rain that nourishes and cleanses, realm of the setting sun, bestow upon us your gifts of intuition and mystery. We seek to know you, we seek to honor you. By the water in our blood, we charge you, be here now! To the West and the spirits of water, we bid you hail and welcome!"

Call to the North

Finally, you come to the north, the powers of elemental earth, representing both the womb and the grave, the source of all life and that which awaits at the end of life. North corresponds to the season of winter and to midnight. Turn to the north when you wish to manifest outcomes and reveal truth. Face the north and call the powers of the direction with this charge:

"I call upon the spirits of earth who guard and protect the gateway to the northern realm. I beckon and call you forth from the far corner of the universe wherein you dwell. Gaia, Demeter, Earth Mother, come into this circle and manifest the power of your divine law. Strength of earthquake and of mountain, foundation beneath our feet, descend into this circle and grant us your blessing. North Star, navigator's guide, that which calls all other directions unto itself, bestow upon us your gifts of

strength. We seek to know you, we seek to honor you. By the earth that is our body, we charge you, be here now! To the North and the spirits of earth, we bid you hail and welcome!"

Wiccan Words

Wiccans often greet one another with the words "Merry meet." Another phrase, "Blessed be," may be spoken as a welcome, at the end of a ritual, in parting, or any time you want to wish someone well. This simple blessing contains the vibrations of love, and it thus attracts positive energy, dispels harmful vibrations, and confers protection.

ENDING A SPELL OR RITUAL

Spells, like books, have a beginning, middle, and end. Properly concluding a spell or ritual is just as important as the other parts. These final actions seal your spell, activate it, and allow you to step back into your everyday world. Witches do this with actions as well as with words.

Binding a Spell

It's customary to close a spell with a definitive statement. Wiccans often use the phrase "So mote it be" to bind a spell. If you prefer, you can say "So be it now" or "So it is done" or "Amen." The number three represents creativity, form, and manifestation in the three-dimensional world. Therefore, you can end a spell by repeating a statement three times or performing a gesture three times. In her book *The Spiral Dance*, Starhawk offers this closing statement to bind a spell:

"By all the power
Of three times three,
This spell bound around
Shall be.
To cause no harm,
Nor return on me.
As I do will,
So mote it be."

To make sure your spell only generates positive results, say something in conclusion like, "This spell is done for the good of all, harming none." Put the finishing touches on your spell in this way, before you open the circle and allow your intentions to flow out into the manifest world.

Releasing Deities and Spirits

If you've summoned deities, spirits, angels, guardians, or other entities to assist you during your magickal workings, you must release them at the end of the spell or ritual. Do this with gratitude and respect. Just as you called forth these beings with chants, incantations, invocations, or other utterances, you'll say so long to them verbally. You can design a personalized ending ritual or use a "readymade" one from another source. Here's a simple way to release entities, so they can return to their usual realms of existence:

1. Face east, and say aloud: "Guardian of the east, spirit of air, we thank you for your presence here. Depart now and return to your home, harming none, and let there be peace between us. Hail, farewell, and blessed be."
2. Turn to face north, and say aloud: "Guardian of the north, spirit of earth, we thank you for your presence here. Depart now and return to your home, harming none, and let there be peace between us. Hail, farewell, and blessed be."
3. Face west, and say aloud: "Guardian of the west, spirit of water, we thank you for your presence here. Depart now and return to your home, harming none, and let there be peace between us. Hail, farewell, and blessed be."
4. Face south, and say aloud: "Guardian of the south, spirit of fire, we thank you for your presence here. Depart now and return to your home, harming none, and let there be peace between us. Hail, farewell, and blessed be."

If you've asked for assistance from specific beings, include their names in your parting statements. For instance, if you've called upon the four archangels, say something like: "We thank you, Raphael [Uriel, Gabriel, Michael], for your guidance and protection during this ritual/rite."

In this way, you bring your ritual to a close in a pleasant way that honors those who have lent their energies to your joint endeavor. Just as you might say goodnight to valued guests after a dinner gathering, you thank these beings for their participation and wish them a safe return to their homes.

Chapter 12

VISUAL SPELLS

Most of us are visually oriented people, and a vibrant image has the power to strongly impact us. Advertisers know this very well—just watch a commercial for some sort of drug, in which the pictures show happy, healthy people while the voiceover describes all the drug's unpleasant side effects. The viewer's mind reacts to the pictures rather than the words. Because images are so powerful, witches use them to enrich spells and rituals—when you're doing a spell, a picture truly is worth a thousand words.

You may like to add drawings, symbols, and other images to your book of shadows. A quick look at Pinterest will reveal lots of gorgeously illustrated grimoires and may give you some ideas for decorating your own. Many witches sketch in their grimoires. Others affix photos or visuals from magazines. I like to draw Celtic knots in mine because I'm of Irish descent. I also enjoy creating collages that combine pictures, words, fabric, dried flowers and leaves, and all sorts of other objects—the collages serve as spells in themselves.

How about designing what's known as a "vision board" in your book? Write an affirmation that describes your objective, and then decorate the page with pictures that show what you intend to bring about. Look at it in the morning and before going to bed at night to spark your mind's creative power.

CREATIVE VISUALIZATION

In the late 1970s, author Shakti Gawain brought the concept of creative visualization into widespread public awareness. But witches have long known that visualization is the first step in working magick and precedes manifestation. Imagination is at the heart of a spell. If you can't imagine something, you won't be able to attain it. Forming a picture in your mind of the result you intend to manifest begins the process—in so doing, you mentally plant the seeds that will grow into the outcome you desire.

Don't think about the problem or condition you wish to change—instead, focus on the end result you seek. For instance, if your goal is to heal a broken leg, don't think about the injury; instead, envision the leg strong and healthy. If you want to attract prosperity, envision yourself driving an expensive car, living in a luxurious mansion, flying in your own private jet—anything that signifies "wealth" to you. Give yourself permission to dream big! Enrich your mental images with lots of color and action—clear, vivid images generate faster and more satisfactory results than bland ones.

Use Visual Aids

When doing a healing spell for someone you know, paste a photo of the person in your grimoire next to the written spell. This helps you focus your mind and channel the positive energy of the spell to that person.

THE POWER OF COLOR

Most people aren't aware of it, but we are constantly affected by the colors in our environment. Psychological studies show that our responses to color can be measured physically—red stimulates respiration and heart rate, blue lowers body temperature and pulse.

Colors contain myriad symbolic associations too. Blue, for instance, reminds you of the sky; green suggests foliage, grass, and healthy crops; orange is the color of fire and the sun. The Druids considered blue a sacred color that denoted someone who'd achieved the rank of bard (a formally trained storyteller entrusted with the oral history of a group). Early Christians associated blue with peace and compassion, which is why artists often depicted the Virgin Mary wearing blue. The beautiful stained glass windows in European cathedrals drew upon color symbolism to convey information to congregations who were largely illiterate. Because these connections are deeply rooted in our psychology, you can use color to influence the mind in your magickal workings.

The intensity of a color signifies its intensity in spellworking. Bright golden-yellow, for example, brings to mind the sun and fire; therefore it can activate and invigorate a spell. Pastel yellow has a gentler vibration that's usually associated with the air element and ideas. Red denotes sexual passion in a relationship, whereas pink symbolizes a gentler type of love, affection, and friendship.

The Power of Black

Black, a color that witches frequently wear, has many negative connotations to the general public, including death and mourning. To witches, however, black represents mystery and power, for it contains all the colors of the rainbow. It's also reminiscent of the night, the time when witches often gather to work magick.

Color Symbolism

Once you understand the energetic correspondences of colors, you can incorporate them into your spells and rituals. Witches often keep a stash of candles in various colors for spells and rituals. If you fashion medicine pouches or crane bags, use cloth in colors that relate to your objectives. Working with the plant kingdom helps you understand how flower colors can add meaning to spells—even people who know nothing of magick intuitively connect red roses with passion, which is why lovers give them on Valentine's Day. Gemstones, too, come in a wide range of colors that can influence your spells. The clothing you wear during a ritual, how you decorate your altar, and the images you include in your grimoire may also depict your associations with colors. Choose colors carefully in order to bring their energies to the spells.

Consider writing your spells with pens, pencils, markers, or crayons in colors that correspond to your intentions. As mentioned earlier, you may want to include colorful pages in your grimoire to denote specific types of spells: pink for love, green for money, and so on.

Color	**Correspondences**
Red	passion, anger, heat, energy, daring
Orange	confidence, activity, warmth, enthusiasm
Yellow	happiness, creativity, optimism, ideas
Green	health, fertility, growth, wealth
Light blue	peace, clarity, hope
Royal blue	independence, insight, imagination
Indigo	intuition, serenity, mental power
Purple	wisdom, spirituality, connection with higher realms
Pink	love, friendship, sociability
White	purity, clarity, protection
Black	power, wisdom
Brown	stability, practicality, grounding in the physical world

In your book of shadows, describe your responses to colors. What emotions do different colors spark in you? What associations do you have with various colors? Do you find some colors more appealing than others?

Colors and the Elements

In magick work, each of the four elements corresponds to a specific color. So do the four directions, which we discussed in Chapter 11.

Element	Direction	Color Correspondence
Fire	South	Red
Earth	North	Green
Air	East	Yellow
Water	West	Blue

When you cast a circle, you may want to place a yellow object (such as a candle) in the east, a red one in the south, a blue one in the west, and a green one in the north. If you set up altars at each of the four directions, consider decorating each in the appropriate color.

Chakra Colors

Holistic healing links the body's main energy centers, known as the chakras, with the seven colors of the visible spectrum. Red is associated with the root chakra, at the base of the spine; orange with the sacral chakra; yellow with the solar plexus chakra; green with the heart chakra; blue with the throat chakra, indigo with the third eye; and purple with the crown chakra, at the top of the head. Knowledge of these chakra-color connections can help your healing spells.

THE MAGICK OF THE TAROT

The beautiful oracle known as the tarot provides a rich source of magick imagery that you can tap for spells as well as divination. Many tarot decks display colorful palettes, but the colors shown on the cards are not purely decorative—they embody specific symbolic, spiritual, psychological, and physiological properties as well.

You'll find many familiar—and some not so familiar—images on the cards in your deck. Tarot artists intentionally choose symbols from various spiritual, cultural, magickal, and psychological traditions to convey information directly to your subconscious. Like dream imagery, the pictures on the cards speak to us at a deeper level and trigger insights in a more immediate and succinct way than words can.

The cards in the Major Arcana, in particular, offer powerful imagery, although many decks include vivid symbolism on the Minor Arcana cards as well. Some of the symbols are universal in nature, found in many cultures and time periods. Others may reflect the individual designer's intentions or beliefs, rather than holding broader meanings for all users.

The Suits of the Tarot

Each of the four suits in a tarot deck is linked with an element: Wands with the element of fire, Cups with water, Pentacles with earth, and Swords with air. As we discussed earlier, each of the four elements corresponds to a color. Therefore, many tarot artists emphasize red on the cards in the suit of Wands, blue on the Cups cards, green on the Pentacles cards, and yellow on the Swords cards.

Each suit also represents a particular area of life, so in spellwork choose cards from the suit that best relates to your intention. You can use cards from the suit of wands, for instance, in spells for career success or creativity. Choose cards from the suit of cups for love spells, pentacles for money spells, and swords for spells involving communication, intellectual pursuits, and legal matters.

Spellworking with Tarot Cards

Tarot cards make wonderful visual tools for spellcasting. Among the seventy-eight cards in a standard deck, you'll find one or more cards to represent any objective you may have.

I recommend purchasing a deck specifically for spellwork and another for doing readings. Some of the spells you perform require you to leave the cards in place, rather than returning them to the deck afterward. For example, you may wish to slip a card into a talisman or amulet pouch. To do the following spell, you'll need to tape three cards together. Perhaps you'd like to paste some of your favorite cards in your grimoire. I have a miniature deck that's perfect for this purpose.

Tarot Triptych Love Spell

A triptych is an altarpiece or decoration composed of 3 panels joined together. Perform this spell during the waxing moon, when the sun or moon is in Libra, or on a Friday.

TOOLS AND INGREDIENTS

3 tarot cards

Tape

Essential oil of rose, jasmine, patchouli, ylang-ylang, or musk

1. Choose 3 cards from a tarot deck (one you don't use for readings). These cards should depict things you desire in a romantic relationship. For instance, you might select the 10 of Pentacles if financial security is important to you or the Ace of Cups if you want to attract a new partner.
2. Lay the cards face-down, side by side, and tape them together.
3. Dab some essential oil on each card, while you envision yourself enjoying the loving relationship you seek.
4. Stand the triptych up on your altar or in another place where you'll see it often. (If you know feng shui, put it the Relationship Gua of your home.)

If you have a mini deck or a third deck, you can affix three cards from it in your book of shadows when you record the spell. You might also want to dab a bit of essential oil on the page where you write your spell. You can adapt this spell for other intentions too; simply select three cards that symbolize your objective.

RUNE MAGICK

Like tarot cards, runes serve as symbols that you can incorporate into your magick spells. In Chapter 5, we discussed different types of runic alphabets and the significance of these images. If you wish to use runes as a secret code when you write in your grimoire, that's fine, but they also have many other applications in spellcraft. Like the tarot, runes speak directly to your subconscious, bypassing the analytical, left-brain part of your mind. That's one reason why they come in handy in magick work.

Runes in Spellcraft

One of the beauties of runes as visual elements in magick work is their simplicity. You don't have to be a Rembrandt or a Michelangelo to draw runes. Most runes (Norse, Ogham, etc.) can be formed with a few lines, yet their stripped-down imagery doesn't detract from their power. In fact, sometimes a very simple graphic can best convey your meaning. Consider the logos companies choose to represent them—a great logo depicts a company's mission via a strong, uncomplicated, and meaningful design that you can easily remember.

Witches today, like spellcasters centuries ago, use runes in many ways. Divination is one popular practice—see the rune reading example in Chapter 7. However, you can also draw runes on paper, stones, or pieces of wood and add them to talisman and amulet bags. Inscribe them on candles. Decorate your magick tools with runes. Embroider them on ritual clothing or altar cloths. (See the charts in Chapter 5.)

Using Rune Imagery in Your Grimoire

In your grimoire, sketch runes in the margins, alongside your spells and incantations—anywhere you like—to represent your intentions. Not only will these designs dress up a page, they also help you focus on your objectives and imprint your subconscious with their energy. Of course, you'll want to write down the spells you perform using runes, as well as your rune readings. But you can incorporate runes into your book of shadows in other ways too:

- Choose a rune to define the nature of each spell you do and draw that rune on the page where you record that spell. The glyph serves as a visual shortcut for the spell.
- Have you chosen to organize your grimoire according to the types of spells you perform? If so, you could separate the categories with divider pages and draw a rune on each of those pages to signify the subject. The Norse rune Gebo, which looks like an X, could illustrate love spells. Berkano or Fehu could introduce the section where you record spells for abundance.
- Write your intentions in Ogham runes as a decorative border around the pages in your grimoire. Centuries ago, people in Ireland and the

British Isles carved rows of Ogham script on standing stones in this way. Even if you don't comprehend the meanings of the glyphs, your subconscious will understand.

- Drip hot candle wax on a page in your book and imprint a significant rune in the wax.

SIGILS

A sigil is a uniquely personal symbol you draw in order to produce a specific result. The word comes from the Latin *sigillum*, meaning sign. In a sense, a sigil is a way of communicating with yourself via secret code, because no one else can interpret the symbol. Although there are various techniques for designing sigils, the easiest one involves fashioning an image from letters.

Creating Sigils

Start by writing a word or a short affirmation that states your intention. Delete any letters that are repeated. For example, the word SUCCESS contains three Ss and two Cs, but you only need to put one of each into your sigil. Entwine the remaining letters to form an image—this is where you get creative. You can use upper- and/or lower-case letters, block or script. Position them right-side up, upside down, forward, or backward. The end result depicts your objective in a graphic manner that your subconscious understands. You'll instantly recognize its meaning at a deep level, and that reinforces your intention.

The following sigil combines the letters S U C C E S S to create an image. Of course, you could configure the letters in a zillion different ways, according to your own preferences, and each design would be uniquely powerful. That's what makes sigils so special.

Sigils in Spellwork

The processes of creating the sigil and applying it are magick acts. Treat them that way. You may wish to design the sigil as a spell in itself.

Or you can fashion the sigil and then use it later as a component of another spell. In this way you both craft and cast, and both produce effects. You can incorporate sigils into spells in myriad ways. For instance:

- Draw a sigil on a piece of paper and slip it into a talisman or amulet pouch.
- Display a sigil on your altar to remind you of your intention.
- Hang one on the door to your home to provide protection.
- Carve one on a candle, and then burn the candle to activate your objective.
- Draw or embroider a sigil on a dream pillow.
- Add them to paintings, collages, or other artwork you create.
- Paint one on a glass so it can imprint water, wine, or another beverage with your intent.
- Have a jeweler fabricate your sigil as a pendant or pin and wear it as a talisman.
- Get a sigil tattooed on your body.

There's no limit to how many sigils you can draw or how many ways you can use them. Give your imagination free rein.

Creating Sigils on a Magick Square

A magick square is an ancient configuration of smaller, numbered squares arranged in rows and columns in such a way that the numbers in each column and row add up to the same sum. One of the simplest squares, which magick workers associate with the planet Saturn, consists of nine small squares within a larger one.

4	9	2
3	5	7
8	1	6

To design a sigil on a magick square:

1. Decide on a word that represents your intention. Let's say, for example, you want to increase your strength (physically, emotionally, mentally, or spiritually).
2. Refer back to the table of letter and number correspondences in Chapter 5. Write down the numbers that correspond to the letters in STRENGTH: 1 2 9 5 5 7 2 8.
3. Place a sheet of tracing paper over the magick square.
4. Locate the square with the number 1—the number that corresponds to the first letter of your word, the letter S. Draw a small circle on the tracing paper where you see square 1.
5. Next, draw a line on the tracing paper from that circle to the square with the number that relates to the second letter in your word, in this case the square for 2 because that's the number linked with the letter T.
6. The third letter in STRENGTH corresponds to the number 9, so find this square and draw a line to it.
7. If your word contains two letters side by side with the same number value, draw >< on the line where it crosses the box that contains the repeated number.
8. Continue in this manner until your line drawing "spells out" the word. Make a small circle at the end of the last line to denote the end of the word.

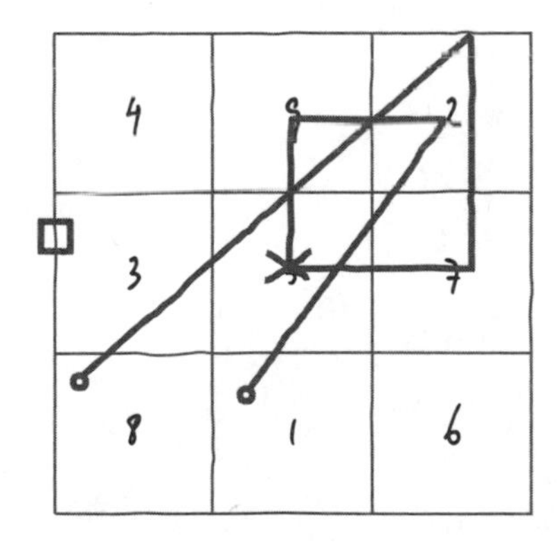

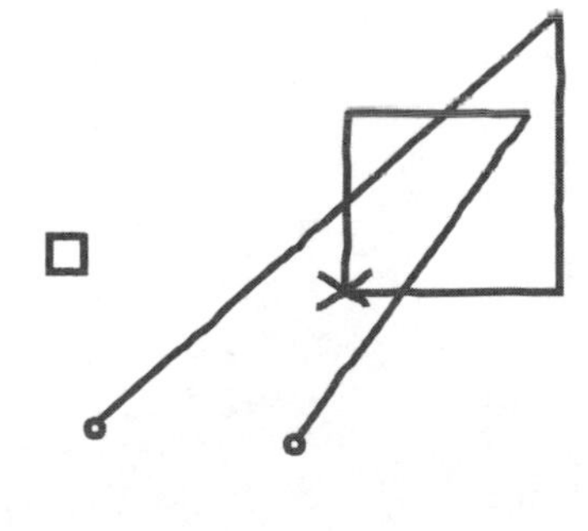

The finished design is your magick sigil. Affix the tracing paper with the image on it into your grimoire. Or, if you prefer, redraw the sigil directly into your book. (If you'd like to learn more about using magick squares, see my book *Magickal Astrology.* You can also see methods for designing sigils on YouTube.)

Add Sigils to Your Grimoire

Not only are sigils the perfect way to encode a spell or anything else you want to keep private, they can be beautiful additions to your grimoire. As with runes, sigils can define the various sections in your book of shadows. They can also stand alone as visual spells. Use them to illustrate the core meaning of an affirmation or incantation. You can even design a sigil that encompasses the entire affirmation. If you like, add other images to a sigil, such as astrological glyphs, runes, stars, spirals, flowers—anything that holds meaning for you.

Chapter 13

ACTIVE SPELLS

Most spells have an active component to them, even if it's just lighting a candle on your altar. The "Buried Treasure Spell" in Chapter 10 is a good example of an active spell. So is the "Spell to Protect Your Home" in Chapter 3. Even writing in your grimoire is an active spell.

Some rituals involve many complex, carefully choreographed steps. When you're doing complicated magickal workings, you may find it necessary to write down the steps in your book of shadows so you can remember them—especially if you don't perform them often. Although you can cast a spell simply by envisioning it in your mind's eye, witches often combine physical movements with words, visualization, and sound. The more you engage your senses in magick work, the more powerful your spells and rituals are likely to be.

CASTING A CIRCLE

Casting a circle is one of the most fundamental and widely used practices in magick work. This circle functions as a shield against any undesirable influences, as well as a container for the energy generated during spells and rituals. It also separates magickal space from mundane space. A circle isn't a flat ring, nor is it a dome over you. Your circle is a sphere surrounding you above and below the place where you do your magick work, as if you were standing in a bubble. You draw a circle, but envision a sphere growing out of the line you draw—it's a circle in three dimensions, a shell that allows the sacred space within the circle to exist between the worlds.

Yes, you can cast a circle by imagining yourself surrounded by a sphere of pure white light—and that circle will work just fine. But many witches enjoy a more active ritual. You'll find lots of suggestions and instructions for circle-casting online and in other books, including many of mine. You can also design your own method. Do whatever you feel inspired to do, whatever engages your senses and your imagination. You may want to try a number of different ways to cast a circle to see which one best suits you. In your grimoire, write what you did, what tools (if any) you used, who else (if anyone) took part, what you felt, and what results you experienced.

Basic Circle-Casting Steps

You can design an elaborate ritual for casting a circle, or you can follow these easy steps:

1. Stand in the center of the space you will define as your circle.
2. Facing east, point your magick wand or athame outward toward where you're going to draw the circle's wall. (If you don't have a wand or athame, you can point your finger. We'll talk more about magick wands, athames, and other tools in Chapter 15.)
3. Center your personal energy within your body. Then ground your energy by envisioning it flowing down through your feet and into the earth, where it connects with the energy of the earth.
4. Draw energy up from the earth, through your body, and out to your hand, into your wand or athame.

5. Allow this energy to flow out to the point where you intend to begin forming your circle.
6. Slowly turn in a clockwise direction until you are again facing the original starting point and the flow of energy joins up with where it started, forming a seamless ring.
7. Visualize the ring thickening and curving inward until it meets above your head and below your feet, forming a perfect sphere of energy.
8. Lower your wand or athame to shut off the energy flow.

You are now ready to enact your magick spell or ritual within the circle you've cast.

Circle-Casting with a Sword

Some witches use a ceremonial sword to cast a circle. Hold the sword with the point facing outward. Beginning in the east, walk clockwise three times around the space where you will work, delineating the outer edge of the circle with the point of the sword. Chant the following incantation (or one you compose yourself) as you walk:

"Thrice around the circle bound
Evil sink into the ground.
This charge I lay by the number three
As is my will, so mote it be."

Circle-Casting with Pentagrams

If you're using a wand or athame to cast your circle, you may want to stop at each of the four directions—east, south, west, and north—to draw a pentagram in the air before you. (You can use your hand if you don't have a wand or athame.) The pentagram represents protection, so this added step in your ritual reinforces the protective nature of the circle.

1. Hold your wand or athame in your hand, with your arm outstretched before and slightly above you, pointing outward.
2. With the tip of your tool, draw a pentagram in the air.

3. Visualize energy flowing from the cosmos into your tool, down your arm, through your body, and into the ground.
4. Repeat this action at each of the four directions.

Calling the Quarters While Casting a Circle

Some witches call the quarters while casting a circle. As you walk around the circle, stop at each of the four directions and call out to the guardians of those directions. You can craft an eloquent incantation or use this simple one:

"Guardian of the eastern sphere
Now we seek your presence here.
Come, East, come.
Be with me (us) tonight."

Repeat this directive at each of the four directions (substituting the name of the specific direction). You may choose to light a candle at each point. Select a color that corresponds to each direction, as discussed in Chapter 12.

The Four Elements Technique

This technique combines the four elements—earth, air, fire, and water—to cast a circle.

1. Fill a bowl with saltwater, which symbolizes the elements of earth and water.
2. Beginning in the east, walk in a clockwise direction, sprinkling the saltwater on the ground to define a circle as you say: "With earth and water I cast this magick circle."
3. Next, light a stick of incense, which represents fire and air (smoke).
4. Again, start in the east and walk clockwise around the circle, trailing the fragrant smoke behind you while you say: "With fire and air I cast this magick circle."

If you prefer, two people can perform this circle-casting ritual together. In this case, one person holds the bowl of saltwater and the other carries the stick of burning incense.

"In Witchcraft, we define a new space and a new time whenever we cast a circle to begin a ritual. The circle exists on the boundaries of ordinary space and time; it is 'between the worlds' of the seen and unseen . . . a space within which alternate realities meet, in which the past and future are open to us."

—STARHAWK, *THE SPIRAL DANCE*

Opening the Circle

At the end of your spell or ritual, you must open the circle in order to return to your ordinary realm of existence. Once you've removed the "psychic fence," your magick can flow out into the world and manifest. Additionally, you must release the entities you've called upon (if any). An easy way to do this is to retrace the steps you took while casting the circle, but in reverse order. Instead of walking clockwise, walk counterclockwise. Imagine the circle you erected dissolving behind you as you move.

Did you call upon the guardians of the four directions or invite other nonphysical entities to join you in your spell or ritual? If so, now's the time to thank them for their assistance and bid them adieu until next time. Pause at each direction and say aloud:

"I thank you for your presence here
And for the aid you gave to me.
Until we meet another time,
Hail, farewell, and blessed be."

If you lit candles at the four directions, snuff them out as you release the spirits of each direction.

Ending your spell or ritual is just as important as beginning it. After you finish your working, record all the details in your grimoire. Describe the actions you took during the ritual. Write down the incantations, invocations, or other chants you used. Later, when you see the results of your spell or ritual manifest, note what happened, how the results came about, how long it took for the outcome to materialize, and anything else you consider significant.

"A spell involves words and actions chosen to achieve a certain goal or desire, and is driven by the will of the person performing it. Words, symbols, and tools are combined to produce a ritual. Power is raised and directed out to the Universe to do its work."

—Debbie Michaud, *The Healing Traditions & Spiritual Practices of Wicca*

MAGICK MUDRAS

Mudra is the Sanskrit word for seal or gesture and refers to a special movement used in a spiritual ritual. Perhaps you've seen people employ a familiar mudra during meditation; they press their thumbs and index fingers together while extending the other fingers. Folding your hands in prayer is another example of a mudra. Although we often associate mudras with Eastern religions, witches in all parts of the world use them in spellwork and ritual practices.

In a broader sense, mudras are gestures or postures that depict your intentions. Purists might argue that the term refers only to sacred gestures, but we use "mudras" all the time to convey our intentions—when we wave to a friend, cross our fingers for good luck, or clap our hands to applaud someone. Think of a police officer directing traffic by waving his arms, or a dog trainer using hand signals to instruct her animal. Holding out your hand with your palm facing away from you clearly says: Stop. These and other gestures serve as active symbols. They also enable you to communicate with other people via sign language during a group ritual.

Witches know that where your attention goes, energy flows. When you point your finger, you steer attention (yours or someone else's) in a particular direction. That's what you do when you extend your hand to cast a circle. Mudras may involve only the hands or the entire body. Try some of these mudras to direct energy for magickal purposes:

- With your hand, draw a pentagram in the air for protection.
- Stretch your arms up above your head to draw down energy from the heavens.

- To invoke a deity, hold one arm outstretched above your head, then draw the energy into yourself by pulling your hand down to your heart center.
- Hold your arms up and outward from your body, curving them in the shape of a crescent moon to invoke the blessing of the moon goddesses.
- Clear sacred space by sweeping your arms and hands about the area to disperse unwanted energies.
- Ground energy by bending down and placing your palms flat on the ground (or floor).
- Touch your index finger to your third eye to stimulate intuition.
- Stand with your arms outstretched at your sides with your right palm turned up to draw down the energy of the heavens and your left palm turned down to draw up the energy of the earth. Then cross both palms over your solar plexus to bring both energies into your body.
- Push away unwanted energies by holding your arms outstretched before you, palms open and facing away from you. Then turn in a counterclockwise direction until you've made a complete circle.
- Lay your hand over a body part or chakra to send healing energy.
- Sign Norse or Ogham runes (see Chapter 5 for charts of rune symbols).

In your grimoire, sketch the mudras you enacted. Describe why and how you used them. How did you feel performing these magickal movements? Could you sense or see energy shifting in connection with your actions? Did you experience anything else? What, if anything, might you do differently to produce a different effect?

You can read about traditional mudras online and in many books. Consider incorporating them into your meditations, yoga, breathwork, healing, and/or other practices. If you like, you can design your own symbolic gestures that have significance for you.

MAGICKAL DANCE

Dancing may be one of the oldest forms of magick. The early Celts incorporated dancing in many of their rituals and festivals. Dancing around the Maypole on Beltane, for instance, symbolized and encouraged fertility. Ancient magicians danced to raise energy, chase away unwanted spirits, petition deities for assistance, align themselves with divine powers, facilitate healing, and more. Today, modern witches still dance for these and other reasons. In group work, dancing stimulates positive energy and unites the individuals participating in the ritual. Besides, dancing is fun!

> *"Dance is the hidden language of the soul, of the body."*
>
> —Martha Graham

Mystical Movements

In classical Indian dance, mudras carry special meanings—the dancer conveys a range of ideas, both mystical and mundane, through hand and body movements. Sufi dancing encourages peace and harmony, in the dancer and in the outer world. In Iran, the Sufi dance samāʿ includes movements that correspond to the planets, the cycle of the seasons, the elements, and humankind's search for union with the Divine. Expressive hand movements also play an important role in Middle Eastern belly dancing.

In Native American traditions, dancing offers a way to connect with Mother Earth and Father Sky. Dancing awakens intuition, inner wisdom, and healing powers as well. A dancer who wishes to invoke a spirit animal's assistance enacts movements similar to those of the flesh-and-blood animal. Shamans may also dance to gain visions or enter trance states.

The Spiral Dance

In a group dance known among Wiccans as the spiral dance, participants weave their energies together to celebrate community and creativity, honor loved ones who have transitioned into the afterlife, and symbolize the cycle of life, death, and rebirth. Starhawk, author of the bestselling book *The Spiral Dance: A Rebirth of the Ancient Religion of the Great Goddess* and a founding member of the Reclaiming Collective, designed the basic movements in the ritual, which was first performed publicly in San Francisco in 1979.

Performed on Samhain, the ritual dance marks the turn of the Wheel and the witches' New Year. Dancers hold hands and twine in both clockwise and counterclockwise directions. Drumming, music, and chanting often accompany the dancers' movements, raising power for ritual work. You can see the dance enacted on YouTube.

Want to participate in a spiral dance? You can. Wiccans and Neopagans in many parts of the world celebrate this uplifting ritual—if you search online you can probably find one being held someplace near you. Or, learn the steps and invite a group of like-minded friends to join you in reenacting this tradition. Record your experiences in your grimoire.

MAGICKAL LABYRINTHS

When you hear the word "labyrinth" what comes to mind? Perhaps you think of the mythical structure in Crete, designed by the architect Daedalus to contain a frightful beast known as the Minotaur, half human and half bull. However, that convoluted prison, rich with psychological symbolism, was really a maze, not a labyrinth. Mazes are puzzles with many blind alleys and dead ends. Labyrinths are magickal, unicursal systems used throughout the world for millennia as tools for spiritual development.

In the mid-1990s, the Reverend Dr. Lauren Artress popularized the thirteenth-century labyrinth on the floor in France's Chartres Cathedral by having it replicated in San Francisco's Grace Cathedral. Labyrinths date back many thousands of years and had mystical and magickal purposes long before the advent of Christianity. This ancient pattern features a single, winding path that leads into the center of the circle and symbolizes the journey to your own center or to the Source.

Walking a Labyrinth

Labyrinths can be found in many different designs in different parts of the world (see Sig Lonegren's *Labyrinths: Ancient Myths and Modern Uses*), but the one many Wiccans and Neopagans favor has seven concentric circuits. Each circuit corresponds to a color, a note on the musical scale, a chakra, and one of the heavenly bodies visible to the naked eye.

You can walk a labyrinth as a form of meditation—the process makes you feel relaxed and centered. A labyrinth can also be a sacred space where you do magickal workings. A potent sending and receiving device, a labyrinth focuses, amplifies, and transmits energies. From its center, you can project intentions with greater power. You can receive messages from deities, spirits, and other entities more easily too.

If you have an outdoor space large enough to allow for a labyrinth, you might like to build one of stone or plantings, or carve the pattern into the ground. Or you can draw one on a large piece of paper or fabric (you'll probably have to tape several pieces together). This portable option allows you to fold up your labyrinth and store it when it's not in use.

Labyrinth Ritual

This active group ritual helps you get in touch with astrological energies and understand how they operate in your own life. It's also a wonderful way to celebrate your connection with the cosmos and nature, as well as with other magickal practitioners.

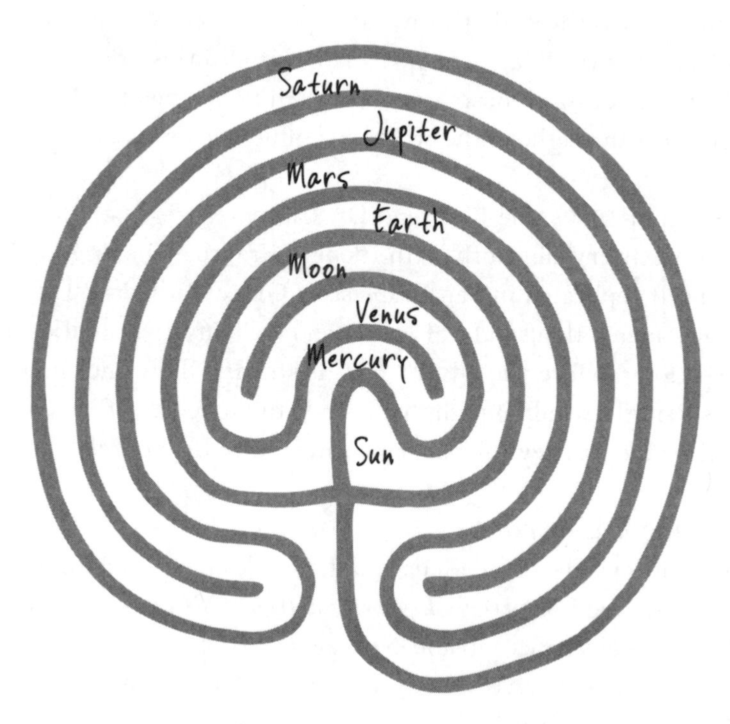

1. Choose eight people to represent the sun, moon, Mercury, Venus, Earth, Mars, Jupiter, and Saturn. It's more fun and dramatic if everyone dresses up in costumes or wears masks that represent the planets' energies. (See Chapter 6 for information about planetary powers.)
2. Each of these people stands at the entrance to the circuit that corresponds to his or her planet or luminary (see illustration).
3. Each participant in the ritual takes a turn walking through the labyrinth. As you come to the entrance of each circuit, the person representing the corresponding planet says a keyword that relates to the planet's nature. For instance, the person representing Venus might say "love" or "beauty."
4. Contemplate the meaning of the keyword(s) associated with each planet while you walk through that planet's circuit.
5. As you move inward toward the center of the labyrinth, reflect on how you respond to each planet's energy. How does it feel to you? How does it affect you personally?
6. Continue in this manner until you have passed through all the circuits and reached the center of the labyrinth.
7. Spend as much time in the center as you wish.
8. As you move back out of the labyrinth, walking through the circuits again but in reverse order, contemplate how you express each planet's energy in the outer world. How does it affect your relationships with other people? How can you handle each planet's challenges better?
9. After everyone has had a chance to walk through the labyrinth, share your experiences.

Be sure to write down in your grimoire what transpired during this ritual. What did you feel? What insights did you gain? Did you have any visions? What reactions did you have to the other participants in the ritual? Did you notice any nonphysical beings in the labyrinth with you? Did you sense a closer or clearer connection with the planets and their powers?

Some people say you can tap the energy of a labyrinth without actually walking it. Draw a labyrinth pattern in your grimoire and then slowly run your finger through the circuits, into the center and back out again. What do you experience?

Chapter 14

MAGICKAL CONCOCTIONS

Let's use our cookbook analogy again. Many cookbooks organize recipes according to the role they play in a meal, how they're prepared, or how they're consumed. You might see a section for appetizers, another for beverages. This method lets the cook quickly locate what's appropriate for her purposes. You can arrange your grimoire in a similar way for convenience.

Most witches do lots of different types of spells. We concoct potions and lotions, salves and balms, talismans and amulets, and so on. Organizing your book of shadows according to this method can be useful when you're collecting the components you need for spells or shopping for ingredients. It also lets you see what spells you can whip up on the spur of the moment, based on the materials you have on hand.

CHOOSING YOUR CATEGORIES

Begin by making a list of the types of spells you do regularly. If you're a healer, your work may focus largely on spells designed to remedy ailments and encourage well-being. If you're a green witch, you'll likely rely heavily on botanicals.

Next, consider what sorts of practices you enjoy most. For instance, I know a woman who agrees with Hippocrates's advice: "The way to health is to have an aromatic bath and a scented massage every day." She formulates all kinds of lovely soaps and bath products with essential oils and other natural substances; the medicinal and magickal properties of her ingredients promote good health. What natural talents do you possess? Maybe you're a great cook and can brew up some fabulous magickal meals. If you have sewing skills, you may lean toward fashioning dream pillows, ritual clothing, or crane bags. A jeweler friend of mine works with gemstones and metals to fashion wonderful magick jewelry.

Where you do your spellwork could influence your choices too. Do you have a designated room or area for magickal activities? Do you live with other people who might not understand or support your beliefs and Craft practices? How much space do you have for storing materials? These considerations may influence the types of spells you do.

Other factors such as your finances, mobility, age, health, availability of ingredients, and so on may dictate the types of spells you choose to perform. If you're new to the Craft, you may want to try a bit of everything in order to discover what you like best and where your strengths lie. After a while, you'll probably emphasize some types and pay less attention to others. Most of us have favorite spells that we do frequently, and you may give those "pride of place" in your grimoire. You might relegate other spells to a back burner—or even toss them out. Remember, your grimoire is your workbook as well as your magick journal. The things you choose to include should be ones you find useful, joyful, interesting, and effective.

POTIONS

Magick potions rank way up there on the list of legendary concoctions. Remember the potion labeled "Drink Me" that shrank Alice down to a height of only ten inches during her adventures in Wonderland? And the one the Little Mermaid quaffed that transformed her fishy tail into legs? Harry Potter and his pals learned to formulate all sorts of potions at Hogwarts, including one to attract good fortune, aptly nicknamed "Liquid Luck."

Of course, love potions are among the most popular of all and people have sought them since ancient times. The first-century Roman philosopher Pliny the Elder recommended making an elixir from hippopotamus snout and hyena eyes. Reportedly, Cleopatra sipped pearls dissolved in vinegar to heighten her sex appeal.

> *"The juice of it on sleeping eye-lids laid*
> *Will make man or woman madly dote*
> *Upon the next live creature that it sees."*
>
> —William Shakespeare, *A Midsummer Night's Dream*

Love Potion #9

This brew calls for 9 components—hence its name. The magickal correspondences of the ingredients give the potion its power.

TOOLS AND INGREDIENTS

- A chalice
- Red wine (or apple juice)
- A drop of honey
- A pinch of ground ginger
- A pinch of cayenne
- A drop of vanilla extract
- Grated chocolate
- ¼ teaspoon ground red rose petals
- A silver spoon

1. If you have a chalice, use it for this spell. If not, wash a pretty glass goblet and substitute it.
2. Cast a circle around your workspace.
3. Pour the wine (or apple juice) into the chalice.
4. Add the honey, ginger, cayenne, and vanilla to the wine.
5. Grate a little chocolate on top of the liquid.
6. Sprinkle the rose petals on the beverage.
7. With the silver spoon, stir the blend 3 times using a clockwise motion to combine the ingredients.
8. Drink the potion to increase the love in your life.
9. Open the circle.

Ingredients for Potions

Usually, we think of magick potions as liquids that a person ingests to produce a desired condition. Because someone consumes these drinks, it's imperative that you use only nontoxic ingredients in your concoctions. The brew needn't taste good, however—many don't. Potions for healing often contain medicinal herbs; other drinks rely mainly on symbolic correspondences, although some potions include substances with recognized physiological properties. Chocolate, for example, stimulates a release of endorphins in the brain, giving you a high similar to being in love, hence its place in love spells.

If you've decided to assign a section in your grimoire to potions, you may want to break it down into additional categories for the types of spells you do most often: love, prosperity, healing, protection, and so on. The following table lists some ingredients you may want to keep on hand for these potions.

COMMON INGREDIENTS FOR MAGICK POTIONS		
Purpose	**Herbs and Spices**	**Other Foods and Beverages**
Love	ginger, cayenne, marjoram, vanilla, cinnamon, rosemary, cardamom, saffron	red wine, apples, apricots, raspberries, strawberries, honey, maple syrup, sugar, chocolate, asparagus, chestnuts, oysters
Prosperity	mint, cinnamon, clove, parsley, dill	champagne, beer, caviar, alfalfa, barley, corn, sunflower seeds, cashews, pecans, hops, spinach, figs
Protection	basil, anise, fennel, parsley, rosemary, sage, cayenne	garlic, pine nuts, witch hazel, salt, mustard, mushrooms, onions, cranberries
Good luck	allspice, bay leaves, cloves, cinnamon, pepper, nutmeg	hazelnuts, cashews, olives, sunflower seeds, coffee, bamboo shoots, bell peppers, cabbage
Healing	chamomile, ginger, yarrow, peppermint, comfrey, calendula	vinegar, aloe, coconut, green tea, molasses, salmon, yogurt, almonds, dandelion greens, bok choy, watercress

LOTIONS, BALMS, AND SALVES

Many lotions, balms, and salves intended for healing purposes contain ingredients with known medicinal properties. Eucalyptus and spearmint, for example, help clear sinus congestion. Aloe soothes burned skin. And although many witches engage in healing practices, we also prepare magickal concoctions for other purposes. In such cases, a spell's power usually comes from the symbolic nature of its components. (In Chapter 16 you'll find charts to guide you.)

If you choose to formulate lotions, balms, or salves, be sure to use nontoxic ingredients that won't cause adverse reactions in the person for whom you've made them. Dilute essential oils in a "carrier oil" such as olive, grape seed, jojoba, or coconut. Ask the person for whom you are doing the spell if he or she is allergic to certain items, such as nuts or wheat. Always test a little bit of the substance on the skin before slathering on a whole lot.

Although many lotions are designed to rub on the body, some may be applied to other objects in spellwork. Witches use oils to dress candles and to anoint magick tools, gemstones, crystals, talismans, and amulets. You may even like to dab a drop of a favorite essential oil on a page in your grimoire.

Prosperity Oil

This versatile magick lotion has many applications—use it alone or in conjunction with other spells to attract money as well as other forms of abundance. Blend it during the waxing moon, preferably on Thursday.

TOOLS AND INGREDIENTS

A green glass bottle with a lid or stopper

4 ounces of olive, almond, or grape seed oil

A few drops of peppermint essential oil

Gold or silver glitter

A small piece of tiger's eye or aventurine

1. Wash the bottle and gemstone with mild soap and water, and then dry them.
2. Cast a circle around your workspace.
3. Pour the olive, almond, or grape seed oil into the bottle.
4. Add the peppermint essential oil and glitter.
5. Drop the tiger's eye or aventurine in the mixture, then put the lid or stopper on the bottle and shake 3 times to charge the potion.
6. Open the circle.

In your grimoire, write down the various ways you use this Prosperity Oil. Of course, you'll also want to note the outcomes you obtain from each use. Did you get better results from rubbing the oil on your body? On candles or gemstones? Did you try dabbing some on your wallet? If you used it in conjunction with other spells, which ones? What happened?

RITUAL BATHS

If you agree with Hippocrates, aromatic healing baths may be your thing. For millennia, people have "taken the waters" for therapeutic reasons—and still do. Spas around the world offer all sorts of delicious treatments that involve immersing yourself in a pool, spring, or tub of water that contains mystical healing properties.

Although witches may embrace the idea of "water cures"—soaking in mineral-rich natural springs or a bathtub to which essential oils have been added—we also bathe for esoteric purposes. A ritual bath not only washes away physical dirt and germs; it also allows you to remove the stress (and outside interferences) of the day, relax, and shift your mood in preparation for magickal work. It's a bit like cleansing your sacred space of bad vibes; in this case, your "temple" is your body. Love spells sometimes call for taking a ritual bath with a partner prior to spellcasting.

As part of your cleansing ritual, consider these additional steps:

- Light candles and/or play soft music.
- Place citrine crystals at each corner of your bathtub. (Golden-colored citrine possesses clearing properties.)

- Add bath salts and/or fragrant essential oils that correspond to your intention: rose for love, mint for prosperity, lavender for peace of mind.
- Sprinkle flower petals that represent your objective into your bathwater.
- Invite the undines or a favorite water deity—Oshun, Mami Wata, Aphrodite, Anuket, Thalassa, Eurybia, Poseidon, Ganga, Nymue—to join you.

Afterward, record your experiences in your grimoire. What did you include in your ritual bath? What did you sense, see, or feel? Did the ritual bath contribute to the magickal work that followed? In what way?

Purifying Ritual Bath Scrub

Try this fragrant purifying scrub before doing a ritual or spell. Use warm—not hot—water. Do not use this scrub on your face. If you have sensitive skin, blend the herbs and essential oils into the oil and omit the salt. Rub the oil gently into your skin prior to your bath, and then rinse it off.

TOOLS AND INGREDIENTS

2 teaspoons lavender flowers (fresh or dry)
2 teaspoons chamomile flowers (fresh or dry)
½ cup sea salt or Epsom salt
A lidded jar
A small glass bowl
½ cup vegetable oil (such as sweet almond, olive, grape seed, or jojoba oil)
3 drops lavender essential oil
3 drops frankincense essential oil
A damp washcloth

1. Purify all the ingredients first. You can do this by visualizing white light around them.
2. Grind the dried flowers finely while you state aloud that they will cleanse and purify your body, mind, and spirit.
3. Put the salt in the jar.
4. In the bowl, mix the oils.
5. Add the oil blend to the salt, then close the jar and shake to combine thoroughly.
6. Open the jar and sprinkle the herbs over the oil and salt blend. Close the jar and shake to blend a final time.
7. Place about a tablespoon of the mixture in the center of a clean, damp washcloth or in the palm of your hand. Gently rub the salts against your skin. Imagine them loosening any negative energy that may cling to you. Feel the purifying ingredients soaking into your body, cleansing your aura and calming your mind.
8. When you feel cleansed, immerse yourself in the bathwater and rinse away the salt scrub along with any negative energy.
9. Step out of the bath and dry yourself gently with a clean towel. If you wish, dress in ritual clothing before engaging in magickal work.

TALISMANS, AMULETS, AND FETISHES

Do you have a special token that you carry to keep you safe or to bring good fortune? If so, you're following a time-honored tradition. The early Egyptians placed good-luck charms in the tombs of royalty to ensure their souls would pass safely into the world beyond. Ancient Greek soldiers carried amulets into battle to protect them. An amulet or talisman may be a single object that has special meaning for its owner, or may be a combination of several items—gemstones, botanicals, magick images, etc.—contained in a charm bag or medicine pouch, designed for a specific purpose. The energies of the ingredients plus your belief in their magickal properties give the talisman or amulet its power.

"Witchcraft is more than just a practice, it is a way of life. A way of looking at the physical and spiritual as a collaborative source of manifestation."

—Dacha Avelin, *Embracing Your Inner Witch*

Amulets

Many people use the words *charm*, *amulet*, and *talisman* interchangeably. However, these three types of portable magick are not the same. Each has its own, distinct purpose and application.

The word "amulet" comes from Latin *amuletum*, which means "a charm"—so it's no wonder people still confuse one with the other. The Greeks called amulets *amylon*, or food. This definition implies that people used food offerings to ask gods and goddesses for protection. They may have even eaten or carried a small bit of that food as an amuletic token. For example, ancient Greeks carried leaves with Athena's name written on them to safeguard themselves from hexes. And, of course, we're all familiar with the idea of hanging garlic to scare away harmful entities.

Witches mainly use amulets for protection. An amulet wards off danger and guards the owner from all manner of harm: illness, assault, accident or injury, theft, natural disasters, evil intent, or black magick. Until something external creates a need for their energy, amulets remain passive. Consequently, an amulet's power might stay latent—but still present—for a very long time.

Amulets and the Moon

Usually it's best to create amulets during the waning moon. You could also consider making an amulet when the sun and/or moon is in Capricorn or on a Saturday.

You can fashion amulets from all sorts of materials: stone, metal, or bundled plant matter. A symbol drawn on a piece of paper will work too. Just make sure whatever you include represents your intention.

Gemstone amulets are perennial favorites—our ancestors prized them, just as people do today. Amulets were sometimes chosen for their shape or where they were found. A stone with a hole through it supposedly protected a person from malicious faeries (who got trapped in the hole). Carrying a crystal found adjacent to a sacred well known for its healthful qualities could encourage well-being. Witches also use plants for protective purposes. Some botanical amulets contain herbs valued for their healing or cleansing properties; others rely on their symbolic nature.

The ancient magi gave precise instructions on how to make amulets. The base components must be organized and measured precisely, and any carving is done in an exact order. Say, for example, you want to create a healing amulet for a sick person. You could use copper as the base material. First you'd apply an emblem for recovery to the copper base, because recovering from the ailment is your primary objective. Afterward, you might choose to add a symbol for ongoing protection to keep sickness from returning.

Protection Amulet

Do you feel a need for some extra protection? This amulet helps to shield you from potential injury or illness. Perform the spell during the waning moon, preferably on a Saturday.

TOOLS AND INGREDIENTS

A piece of turquoise
Black paint or nail polish
Rosemary essential oil
Pine incense
An incense burner
Matches or a lighter
Saltwater

1. Wash the piece of turquoise with mild soap and water, then pat it dry.
2. Cast a circle around the area where you will do your spell.
3. With the paint or nail polish, paint the protection rune Algiz (see Chapter 5) on the stone.
4. Rub a little rosemary essential oil on the other side of the stone.
5. Fit the incense into the burner and light it.
6. Sprinkle the stone with saltwater, then hold it in the incense smoke for a few moments to charge it.
7. Open the circle.
8. Carry the gemstone amulet with you at all times to protect against harm, or give it to the person you wish to protect.

TALISMANS

Talismans serve as active participants in magick work. Unlike amulets, which remain inactive until an outside force stimulates their energy, talismans instigate conditions. Today the word "talisman" refers to any token that has been created specifically to attract or activate a desired result: love, prosperity, success, and so on.

When to Make Talismans

In most cases, talismans should be made or acquired while the moon is waxing. Also consider the position of Venus when fashioning love talismans. Jupiter's placement will affect a talisman for success or abundance.

Unlike amulets, talismans can influence conditions from a distance. For example, a love talisman can attract a partner from all the way on the other side of the world. Although talismans are more potent than amulets—at least in terms of how far their energy extends—their power tends to get used up rapidly because they're constantly projecting it rather than sitting back waiting for a need to arise.

Like amulets, talismans must include materials appropriate to their functions. For example, when making a love talisman you could use rose quartz, rose petals, small heart-shaped tokens, or other components that symbolize love. An effective talisman could be as simple as a single gemstone or quite complex, including numerous carefully chosen ingredients. (See Chapter 16 for lists of correspondences.) As you fashion a talisman, recite affirmations or incantations over it, instructing it to carry out your intentions. Charge it by sprinkling it with saltwater or holding it in the smoke of burning incense.

Aladdin's Lamp

Many old stories tell us that spirits dwelled in talismans and could be commanded by the magician to do specific tasks. Aladdin's lamp, which held a powerful spirit known as a jinni, was a kind of talisman.

How to Use Talismans and Amulets

Most people wear or carry talismans and amulets on their persons, but you can use them in other ways too:

- Display one on your altar.
- Set one on your desk, near your computer.
- Hang one above the entrance to your home.
- If you know feng shui, place them in the sectors of your home that relate to your intentions.
- Slip one under your pillow at night.
- Put one in your car's glove compartment.
- Attach one to your pet's collar.
- Bury them in your yard or garden.
- Put one in the cash register in your place of business.

FETISHES

The word "fetish" probably comes from Latin *facticius* (meaning artificial), by way of Portuguese *feitiço* and French *fétiche.* A fetish can be any object, so long as the person who carries it has a strong emotional connection to the object or regards it as representing a higher authority (such as a spirit or deity).

A fetish represents only one objective—you wouldn't carry a single fetish for love, protection, *and* success. Many fetishes serve as "one shot" magick spells—you need a different one for each instance when help is sought. A witch might make up a bunch of fetishes at the same time, all of them designed for the same purpose. For example, she might fabricate a number of fetishes to stimulate artistic endeavors by wrapping bay leaves (to represent the sun god Apollo) in pieces of yellow cloth (the color of creativity) and empowering those bundles with an incantation. Then whenever she needs a little inspiration, she can use one of the bundles.

You activate the energy of single-use fetishes by carrying them, burning them, burying them, or floating them on moving water. Burning releases your wishes to the heavens and disperses the energy. Burying helps the energy grow. Floating in water transports the energy where it's desired or needed.

In your grimoire, record information about the amulets, talismans, and fetishes you create. When did you fashion them? Did you make them for yourself or someone else? What did you feel, sense, see, or experience during the process? Note the ingredients you included, the steps you took during your spellworking, incantations you recited, and anything else of significance. Be sure to write down your results, how long the outcomes took to manifest, and anything you might consider changing in the future.

Chapter 15

WORKING WITH MAGICK TOOLS

Practitioners in every field of endeavor rely on certain tools to help them do their jobs well. Gardeners work with shovels and hoes, carpenters need hammers and saws, cooks use pots and skillets. Magick workers utilize special tools too. The tools of the Craft speak to the subconscious mind in forms that help support spellwork. A tool's shape, the material from which it's fabricated, and other features provide clues to its symbolism and thus its role in magick.

Of course, you don't really need any equipment to craft and cast spells—the most important "tool" of all is your mind. The implements in a witch's toolbox, however, are good aids to magick work. They serve as centering devices that focus your attention. Wielding magick tools in a spell or ritual also adds drama and excitement, which can kick the magick up a notch.

If you choose to use magick tools in your work—and most witches do—you'll want to discuss them in your grimoire. How did you acquire these tools? Did you purchase them readymade or fabricate your own? Describe the process(es) you used to consecrate and charge them. How do you work with your tools? Record the spells and rituals in which you employ certain tools. How do you feel using them? How do they influence your work? You might even designate a special section in your book of shadows for each tool and the spells and rituals that use it.

"Magic . . . uses all of reality, the world itself, as its medium."

—Bill Whitcomb, *The Magician's Companion*

THE ROLE OF SYMBOLISM

We've talked a lot already about symbols and their role in magick work. When you use a witch's tools, you draw upon their symbolism. If you already own a selection of magick tools, you're probably familiar with their associations. However, if you haven't yet acquired the tools of the Craft, take some time to learn their correspondences and their purposes in spellwork.

Masculine and Feminine Symbolism

Notice that the shapes of the tools of the Craft correspond to the human body. The five points of the pentagram signify the five "points" of the body: head, arms, and legs. The wand and the athame, which symbolize masculine power or yang energy, look distinctly phallic. So do the ritual sword and the rod (or stave). The chalice and cauldron, shaped like the womb, represent feminine or yin energy. So do bells and bowls. Witches often use the wand and athame to project energy, whereas the chalice and cauldron contain and nurture it.

Elemental Symbolism

Additionally, the four primary tools correspond to the four elements: fire, water, air, and earth. The wand represents the element of fire, the chalice signifies the water element, the athame symbolizes air, and the pentagram represents earth. You'll notice that these tools show up in the tarot as the four suits of the Minor Arcana. Usually called Wands (sometimes Rods or Staves), Swords (or Daggers, meaning athames), Cups (or Chalices), and Pentacles (or Pentagrams, sometimes referred to as Coins or Disks), the suits describe fundamental life energies and ways of interacting with the world. It's a good idea to keep these correspondences in mind when you're doing tarot readings as well as when you're performing a spell or ritual.

> *"The four elements . . . are the basic building blocks of all material structures and organic wholes. Each element represents a basic kind of energy and consciousness that operates within each of us."*
>
> — Stephen Arroyo, *Astrology, Psychology, and the Four Elements*

THE WAND

Contrary to popular opinion, witches don't tap people with magick wands to turn them into toads or make them invisible. Witches use wands to direct energy. You can either attract or send energy with your wand. Aim it at the heavens to draw down cosmic power and bring it into the material world. Point it toward a person, place, or thing to project energy toward your goal. You may wish to use your wand to cast a magick circle too.

Choosing or Creating Your Magick Wand

Magick workers traditionally fashioned wands from wood, cut from a living branch of a tree in a single stroke (after asking the tree's permission and making an offering in thanks). The Druids favored yew, hazel, willow, and rowan; however, you may prefer another wood instead for your wand. You don't have to choose wood, if you'd rather use something else—you can find some gorgeous wands made of crystal, metal, or glass rods adorned with gemstones. Perhaps you'd like to mount a quartz crystal at the end of your wand to enhance its power.

You can personalize your wand and enhance your relationship with it by decorating it with elemental symbolism:

- Attach objects to it made of brass, iron, bronze, or gold—metals that correspond to the fire element.
- Paint it fiery colors, such as red, orange, or gold.
- Decorate it with the glyphs for the astrological fire signs Aries, Leo, and Sagittarius, or the elemental symbol for fire (an upward-pointing triangle).
- Engrave it with words of power and/or runes (such as Teiwaz) that signify your intentions.
- Tie red, orange, or gold ribbons onto your wand.
- Affix fiery gemstones to it: ruby, golden topaz, carnelian, bloodstone, tiger's eye.

In your grimoire, describe your relationship with your wand. Did you fashion it yourself? Why did you purchase, fabricate, or otherwise acquire this particular wand? How did you personalize it? Did you imprint it with signs or symbols? What did you experience during the process? How do you plan to work with your wand?

How Long a Wand?

Tradition says a wand should be the length of its owner's forearm from the elbow to the tip of the middle finger. However, that may be unwieldy for some people. Choose a wand that is at least six inches long, but only as long and thick as you find comfortable to handle.

Consecrating and Charging Your Wand

Until you consecrate your wand and charge it with your intention, it's just a stick of wood or an inert rod of metal or glass. The ritual you design to imbue your wand with your own energy can be simple or complex, depending on your personality and your objectives. You may call on a beloved deity to assist you, or invite the fire elementals known as salamanders to join in. You may want to create an incantation or other charge to direct your wand.

Before you begin, cleanse your wand of all unwanted ambient energies. I recommend holding it in the smoke from burning incense or from a ritual fire to purify it. Cast a circle, then proceed with the ritual you've designed. You may want to anoint your wand with essential oil—cinnamon, sandalwood, cedar, and frankincense are good choices. Perhaps you'll want to command your wand to do your bidding with a chant or incantation. Create a poetic directive or say something as simple as "I now consecrate this wand to do the work of the Goddess and God, and charge it to assist me in my magickal work, in harmony with Divine Will, my own true will, and for the good of all concerned."

Match the Tool to the Element

Some witches design rituals that incorporate the element to which the individual tool corresponds. For example, you could charge your chalice by submerging it in a sacred pool of water. Similarly, you could bury a pentagram in the ground beneath a venerable tree or place your wand in the sunshine to let the sun's rays charge it.

After you've finished the ritual and opened the circle, write in your grimoire what you did to consecrate and charge your wand. What steps did you take to infuse it with your energy? Did a god or goddess participate? If you anointed your wand with an essential oil, you may want to dab a bit on the page where you describe your ritual. If you uttered a magickal charge, write it here too. Discuss how you felt during the process. What did you sense, see, intuit, or otherwise experience?

The Pentagram

The tool most often connected with witchcraft, the pentagram symbolizes the element of earth. In magickal work, it's associated with protection, and many Wiccans wear pentagrams as protection amulets. Usually, a pentagram is depicted as a five-pointed star with a circle around it; however you may also see it as a five-pointed star without the circle. (If you visit Texas, where I live, you'll spot pentagrams everywhere—though most people think of them as "Texas stars." The Texas Rangers wore pentagram-shaped badges, and I often wonder how many lives those magick emblems saved.)

Choosing or Creating Your Pentagram

Unless you have metalsmithing talents, you probably won't craft your own pentagram jewelry, but you can purchase some really beautiful pentagram pendants, earrings, and rings. Many witches wear pentagrams made of silver—a metal associated with the Goddess, the moon, and feminine energy—but that's up to you. Perhaps you'd like one decorated with earth-related gemstones, such as jade, moss agate, aventurine, onyx, or turquoise.

In addition to choosing a pentagram to wear, you might acquire another to place on your altar. Consider hanging one near the door of your home for protection, and keeping one in your car as a safety measure. If you're handy at sewing, you could embroider pentagrams on ritual clothing and/or an altar cloth. Some witches even have them tattooed on their bodies.

On one of the beginning pages of your grimoire (or on the cover) draw a pentagram to protect your secrets from prying eyes. Within the pages of your book of shadows, describe how you selected your pentagram. How will you use it? If you purchased a readymade pentagram, did you do anything to personalize it? What did you experience during the process?

Consecrating and Charging Your Pentagram

The ritual you design to consecrate and your pentagram can be simple or complex, depending on your preferences. Before you begin, however, purify your pentagram of all unwanted ambient resonances. The easiest way to do this is to hold it under running water while you envision it cleansed of all harmful, disruptive, or unbalanced energies. Then cast a circle and proceed with the ritual you've planned. If you decide to anoint your pentagram with essential oil, select one that corresponds to the earth element and/or protection such as rosemary, pine, or basil.

Direct your pentagram by saying something as simple as "I now consecrate this pentagram to do the work of the Goddess and God, and charge it to assist me in my magickal work, in harmony with Divine Will, my own true will, and for the good of all concerned." Or write a more elegant and personal incantation. If you wish, invite a favorite deity to join you in performing the ritual.

After you've finished the ritual and opened the circle, write in your grimoire what you did to consecrate and charge your pentagram. How did you infuse it with your energy? Did a god or goddess participate? If you anointed your pentagram with an essential oil, you may want to dab a bit on the page where you describe your ritual. If you uttered a magickal charge, write it here too. Describe how you felt during the process. What did you sense, see, intuit, or otherwise experience?

THE ATHAME

The origins of the word "athame" have been lost to history. Some people speculate that it may have come from *Arthana*, a term for a knife mentioned in the early grimoire *The Clavicule of Solomon*. This ritual dagger is usually a double-edged knife about four to six inches long, although some Wiccans prefer crescent-shaped athames that represent the moon. It needn't be sharp because you're unlikely to cut anything physical with your athame, except perhaps to inscribe symbols on candles. One of its main purposes is to symbolically remove negative energies. You can also use it to slice through obstacles and sever bonds, again symbolically. If you wish, you can cast a circle with an athame instead of a wand—and if someone needs to leave a circle during a ritual, you can "cut" a doorway with your athame to allow passage.

Choosing or Creating Your Athame

Unless you have smithing and carpentry skills you'll probably acquire a readymade athame. Tradition says you should procure your athame yourself, and it should never be used by anyone else. However, if you feel drawn to purchase a vintage dagger for your magick work, make sure it hasn't drawn blood in the past. Some magicians believe that an athame used to physically harm another will never again be functional in magick work, although in ancient times witches often "fed" special ritual knives with blood. Before you use any tool for magick work, you must cleanse it of all energies other than your own.

Like the wand, the phallic-shaped athame represents the masculine force. It corresponds to the element of air too, so you could decorate its handle with symbols such as those for the zodiac signs Gemini, Libra, and

Aquarius or the elemental symbol for air (an upward-pointing triangle with a horizontal line through the center). To personalize it, you may want to:

- Engrave your Craft name on the handle.
- Add runes, sigils, or other images and words that hold meaning for you.
- Decorate it with gemstones that relate to the air element: clear quartz, aquamarine, garnet, or zircon.
- Tie yellow ribbons—the color associated with the air element—to its handle.
- Fasten feathers to its handle.

In your grimoire, describe how you acquired your athame. How do you plan to work with it? How did you personalize it? How did you decorate it? What signs or symbols did you choose (if any) and why? What did you experience during the process?

Consecrating and Charging Your Athame

Before you begin working with your athame, purify it to disperse all unwanted energies. Wash it first with mild soap and warm water, then dry it. Next, hold it in the smoke of burning incense. You can design a complex ritual for consecrating and charging your athame or keep it simple. Call upon deities or spirits to assist you, if you like. Compose a special incantation or affirmation to direct it for your purposes. If you decide to anoint your athame with essential oil, select one that corresponds to the element of air, such as carnation, clove, or ginger.

After you've completed your ritual, write in your grimoire what you did to consecrate and charge your athame. Did a god or goddess participate in the ritual? If you anointed your athame with an essential oil, you may want to dab a bit on the page where you describe your ritual. If you uttered a magickal charge, write it down too. Describe how you felt during the process. What did you sense, see, intuit, or otherwise experience?

THE CHALICE

What's the most famous chalice of all? The Holy Grail, of course. Many people believe it now lies submerged in the sacred Chalice Well in Glastonbury, England. In rituals and rites, witches often drink a ceremonial beverage from a chalice. That's why many chalices feature long stems—so they can be passed easily from hand to hand. Sharing the cup with coven members signifies connectedness and unity of purpose. You may choose to drink magick potions you've concocted from your chalice too, as we discussed earlier.

Choosing or Creating Your Chalice

A symbol of the feminine force, the chalice's shape clearly suggests the womb. Therefore silver, because it's ruled by the moon, is a good material for your magick chalice. Some people prefer crystal, blue or indigo glass, or ceramic chalices, however—the choice is entirely yours. A quick online search will turn up pictures of many fabulous chalices, some dating back more than a thousand years. The chalice also symbolizes the water element, and water is linked with the emotions, intuition, imagination, and dreams. Therefore, you could think of your chalice as the cradle of the emotions, as well as a vessel that holds and nourishes your hopes and dreams.

To personalize your chalice, you may wish to mark it with symbols of the water element, such as those for the astrological signs Cancer, Scorpio, and Pisces, or the elemental glyph for water (a downward-pointing triangle). Or, decorate it with "watery" gems such as moonstones, pearls, or sapphires. Perhaps you'd like to paint your chalice to resemble a flower, such as the blue-and-orange crocus favored by members of The Golden Dawn (be sure to use lead-free paint).

Within the pages of your book of shadows, describe how you selected your chalice and how you plan to work with it. Did you do anything to personalize it? What did you experience during the process? Note anything you consider relevant.

Consecrating and Charging Your Chalice

Wash your chalice in warm water with mild soap (or vinegar and water) before using it for magick work. This removes both dust and unwanted ambient energies that could interfere with your intentions.

The ritual you design to consecrate and charge your chalice may be complex or simple—whatever works for you. A brief blessing may be all you need, but if you feel drawn to plunge your chalice into a sacred well for a lunar month, go for it. Alternately, you could sprinkle it with "holy" water from a spring, sea, or lake that is special to you. Maybe you'd like to invite a particular deity, such as Oshun, Mami Wata, or Poseidon, to join in your ceremony. Chant, sing, or recite a special incantation to dedicate your chalice to the Goddess and to your magickal work. If you decide to anoint your chalice with an essential oil, select one that corresponds to the element of water such as jasmine or ylang-ylang. Make sure the oil you use has no toxic properties.

After you've completed your ritual, write in your grimoire what you did to consecrate and charge your chalice. Did a god or goddess participate in the ritual? If you anointed your chalice with an essential oil, you may want to dab a bit on the page where you describe your ritual. If you uttered a magickal charge, write it here too. Describe how you felt during the process. What did you sense, see, intuit, or otherwise experience?

OTHER TOOLS FOR MAGICKAL WORK

Although the four tools we've already discussed serve as the primary implements of the Craft, you may decide that you'd like to add other items to your collection. If you're new to the Craft, I suggest you start slow and assess your needs, your intentions, and your practice before you go on a magickal shopping spree. Some tools, such as candles, are inexpensive and readily available. Others, such as crystal balls, are not only costly but bring powerful energies into your environment and you must be willing to assume responsibility for them.

Here's a short list of some favorite witchy tools you may want to work with:

- Cauldron—great for brewing magickal concoctions, cooking celebratory meals, and containing small ritual fires
- Sword—use it for circle-casting, to slice through obstacles (symbolically), or in banishing work
- Bell—marks the steps in a ritual or meditation, and may summon a deity or spirit

- Besom (broom)—sweeps unwanted energies from a sacred or ritual space
- Crystals—augment the power of spells, aid scrying and meditation, assist in healing, and much more
- Singing bowls—attune the chakras and attract harmonious cosmic energies for rituals, spellworking, and journeying
- Cords and ribbons—seal spells, bind unwanted entities, and hold energies for future use
- Scrying mirror or crystal ball—lets you gaze into areas beyond your normal range of vision
- Oracles (tarot cards, runes, pendulums, etc.)—predict the future, guide the present, and augment spells and rituals

As you deepen yourself in magickal practice you may find that objects you once considered ordinary now have mystical uses. Treat the tools you bring into your practice as the sacred implements they are. Respect and care for them as you would dear friends, and they will serve you for a lifetime.

No Worries Spell

Worrying never makes things better—in fact, it can exacerbate a troublesome situation. Instead, take out your magick tools and chase those fearful thoughts away. Perform this spell at midnight, during the waning moon.

TOOLS AND INGREDIENTS

A dark blue candle

A candleholder

Matches or a lighter

A hand drum or gong

An athame

A bell

1. Cast a circle around the area where you will do your spell.

2. Fit the candle in its holder, set it on your altar (or other surface where it can burn safely), and light it.

3. Begin playing the drum or gong to break up negative thoughts and vibrations. Feel the sound resonating through you, stirring up your power and confidence. Play for as long as you like.

4. When you feel ready, chant the following incantation aloud. If possible, shout it out—really assert yourself!

"Doubt and fear
Don't come near.
By the dawn
Be you gone.
By this sign [with your athame draw a pentagram in the air in front of you]
And light divine
Peace is mine.
I am strong
All day long.
My worries flee
Magickally.
I ring this bell [ring the bell]
To bind this spell,
And all is well."

5. As you chant, envision your fears receding into the darkness, losing their strength. When you're ready, extinguish the candle and open the circle.

Chapter 16

INGREDIENTS FOR SPELLS

Today, few people use eye of newt and toe of frog in spells. Witches are more likely to choose everyday ingredients we can find in any supermarket or New Age store—or better yet, in the natural environment. Utilizing objects from nature is a wonderful way to enhance your connection with Mother Earth and to increase the power of your spells by adding the energies of plants, stones, and so on.

Since ancient times, witches, shamans, sorcerers, and other magicians have looked to nature for spell materials. They used herbs and flowers to make healing potions, salves, poultices, and tonics. Gemstones and crystals provided protection, augmented personal powers, and attracted blessings. The natural world still provides a cornucopia of plants, minerals, and other treasures that you can incorporate into your own magickal workings.

SYMPATHETIC MAGICK

The basic philosophy of sympathetic magick is simple: like attracts like. This means that in spellwork, an item can serve as a representative or stand-in for another item that's similar to it in some way. It also means that the similarities are not coincidental and that they signify a connection—physical, spiritual, energetic, or otherwise—between the two items. Ginseng root, for example, resembles the human body, a similarity that some healers believe contributes to ginseng's medicinal properties. When you do spells, you can utilize associations between objects in order to make your spells more effective. In some instances, you may be aware of these connections; in other cases, the understanding happens at a subconscious level.

Because similarities exist between items, you can often substitute one ingredient for another in a spell. As we've already discussed, the color pink corresponds to the energy of love. So if you're doing a love spell, you could use a pink rose or a piece of rose quartz—both resonate with loving vibrations. The energy of the flower is quicker, the stone's more enduring.

CANDLES

Early sun-worshipping civilizations considered fire the embodiment of the Divine on earth. The ancient Greek story of Prometheus illustrates this link. Prometheus, one of the race of Titans, stole the sacred fire from Zeus on Mount Olympus and brought it to humankind. For this act, Prometheus suffered horribly—but his gift enabled human beings to enjoy a better existence on earth. Today, witches still associate the sun with the God and the moon with the Goddess, and burn candles to express the power of the fire element.

Candles are probably the most popular component in spells and rituals. The concept of illumination carries both a practical meaning—visible light that enables you to conduct your work—and an esoteric one—an inspiration or awakening that enlivens your spell's energy and expands your understanding. Candles provide a focal point for your attention, helping you to still your mind, and their soft, flickering light creates an ambiance that shifts you out of your ordinary existence.

Light in the Dark

The term "candle" comes from *candere*, a Latin word meaning "to shine." Candles represent hope, a light in the darkness, a beacon that shows the way to safety and comfort. Five thousand years ago, the Egyptians formed beeswax into candles similar to the ones we use today. Beeswax candles with reed wicks have been discovered in the tombs of Egyptian rulers, placed there, perhaps, to light their souls' journey into the realm beyond.

Spellworking with Candles

When you consecrate a candle to a magickal purpose, you infuse it with your intention and thereby transform it from something mundane into something magickal. Lighting the candle links you to the Divine. The burning wick consuming the wax symbolizes the deities infusing the material world with their power, so that a desired outcome may manifest.

Witches usually keep on hand a supply of candles in a range of colors. When you cast spells, it's important to remember these color connections (refer to the table in Chapter 12). If you're doing a love spell, for example, burn a red or pink candle that represents passion, affection, and the heart. Prosperity spells call for green, gold, or silver candles, the colors of money.

Candles can enhance just about any spell. Many magick workers set candles on their altars: white, red, or gold to symbolize male/yang/god; black, blue, or silver to represent female/yin/goddess energies. Some formal rituals involve carefully placing candles in specific spots and moving them according to prescribed patterns, perhaps over a period of days or weeks.

Candle Spell to Increase Your Influence

Begin this spell during the waxing moon, preferably on a Sunday. It increases the light you shine into the world and simultaneously turns the "spotlight" on you.

TOOLS AND INGREDIENTS

A candle (in a candleholder) to represent you

7 candles (in candleholders) each one a different color of the visible spectrum

Matches or a lighter

1. Set the candle that represents you on your altar.
2. Arrange the other candles close together in a circle around "you."
3. Light all the candles and let them burn for several minutes—until your attention starts to wander—then snuff them out.
4. The next day, move the 7 candles out a bit, expanding the circle on your altar and symbolically your circle of influence. Light all the candles and let them burn for several minutes, then snuff them out.
5. Repeat this for 7 days. On the last day, let all the candles burn down completely.

You can also cast a circle with candles in which to perform spells and rituals. Position candles around the space where you plan to do your magick, and then light them in a clockwise manner, beginning at the easternmost point. To open the circle after you've finished your working, snuff out the candles in reverse order.

Engraving Candles

Many spells call for engraving candles with symbols that represent your intentions. Select one or more symbols that resonate with you—runes, sigils, astrological glyphs, names, numbers, etc.—and that depict the purpose of your spell. Practice drawing these images in your book of shadows beforehand. In candle carving, you can't erase a mistake!

When you're ready, hold the candle in your hand and close your eyes. Visualize your thoughts permeating the wax and becoming one with the candle itself. Then, using a ballpoint pen, toothpick, nail, or pin, etch the word or symbol into the wax. (If you're really careful, you can use your athame.) Don't become overly concerned with the artistic renderings of symbols, however. Your intention is the most important aspect of this work, not whether you can draw well. The magick is in performing the task and imbuing the candle with your intention.

When you've finished engraving your candle, you can dress it (see the following) or burn it as is. As the wax burns, your intention is released into the atmosphere where it can begin manifesting.

Dressing Candles

Dressing or anointing candles gives your spell a bit more "octane" by adding the scent (and natural energy) of essential oils. The act of anointing also carries the implication of sanctifying something, making it sacred.

Choose an oil that corresponds to your intention. You could use rose, ylang-ylang, or patchouli for love spells, peppermint oil for money spells, cinnamon or sandalwood for success spells. (For an example, see "Spell to Get a Raise" in Chapter 4.) Start applying the oil to the middle of the candle and then work it gradually in each direction to balance the polarity of the two ends—as above, so below. Think of your request or intention rising into the heavens as you rub oil upward toward the top of the candle. Envision the completed work coming down to reality and materializing on earth as you rub the oil toward the bottom of the candle. Inhale the fragrant aroma and let it trigger impressions in your mind of how your spell will manifest.

Apply a thin, even layer, letting the oil seep into the carvings. Want to dress up your candle even further? Sprinkle a little glitter on the surface—or mix glitter into the oil beforehand. The oil will make the sparkly glitter stick to the candle.

If you wish, you may say an incantation to bind the spell, such as the following. Better yet, improvise your own.

"Blessed be thou creature of wax.
You were made by the art of the hand
And now by magick you are changed.
Thou art no more a candle, but [state your intention].

Blessed by the sweetness of the Goddess,
Consecrated by my will and hand,
You are bound now to this charge,
For strengthening the greater good,
For manifesting intention on earth,
As an agent of the Tripart Goddess.
Charged with the power of three times three
As I will, so mote it be."

How you choose to burn your candle will be determined by the nature of the spell you are doing. Some candles should be burned completely and without interruption—in this case, mini candles and small votives in glass containers are best. Other spells call for burning a candle for a period every day, at a specific time. Pillar candles lend themselves to this. Tapers can set the mood for any spell or ritual, in the same way their lovely soft light enhances a dinner party.

Safety First!

Remember never to leave a burning candle unattended! If you want to burn a candle without interruption but need to leave your altar, consider placing the candle in the fireplace with the screen closed or in the center of your bathtub with the shower curtain removed. But do this only if you don't have rambunctious pets or kids who might be tempted to investigate, knock the candle over, or otherwise interfere.

After you finish your spell, write down what you did in your grimoire. What color candle did you use, and why? What symbols did you engrave on it? What oil(s) did you select to anoint it? Utter an incantation or petition a deity? You may want to drip some of the candle wax on the page where you recorded the spell, and perhaps dot the page with essential oil as a reminiscence. How about inscribing the soft wax with the symbol you carved into the candle? Of course, you'll want to note the results of your spell and any other relevant experiences.

Scrying with Candles

The term "scrying" refers to tapping into your second sight to see what you can't see with your physical eyes. This may mean peeking into the future or glimpsing something that's going on in another place beyond your ordinary range of vision. Often we think of scrying as something a witch does by gazing into a crystal ball. It's not the only way, though. You can look at clouds or into a body of water—or a candle's flame. Here's how:

1. In a dark room, light a candle (set it on your altar or in another place where it can burn safely).
2. Watch its flickering flame, allowing it to gradually quiet your thoughts and bring on a state of relaxation.
3. As you gaze at the flame, allow your vision to "soften"—that is, don't try to focus clearly or intently on the flame. You might even want to let your eyes drift slightly to the side of the flame, rather than staring directly at it.
4. As images begin to arise in the flame, permit them to develop as they will, without trying to direct them. Just observe, as if you were watching a movie.
5. Gaze into the smoke rising from the flame. Do you see images there as well? Allow them to unfold before you, without attempting to control them or even make sense of them.
6. Notice any emotions, sensations, or impressions you experience—prickling on the back of your neck, a fluttering in your heart, or the presence of an unexpected scent, for example.
7. Continue gazing at the candle's flame and smoke for as long as you like, or for as long as the images remain.
8. When you're ready, snuff out the candle and ease yourself back into ordinary reality.

Write in your grimoire what you experienced. What did you see in the flame and/or smoke? Did you recognize any of the images as relating to your everyday life or to the purpose for which you sought visions? What did they mean to you? Describe anything else you sensed or felt. Note details that may seem insignificant at the time—they may turn out to be meaningful. Revisit your grimoire at a later date and record anything that you feel ties into what was revealed to you while scrying. Practicing this technique regularly will strengthen your psychic muscles and enable you to gain insight readily.

Wax Poppets

You can shape candle wax into a human or animal form to create what's known as a "poppet." Typically, a witch creates a poppet to represent someone he or she wishes to send magickal energy to, usually at a distance. Whatever you do to the poppet symbolizes what you intend to do to whomever the poppet represents. For instance, if you fashion a poppet to signify a beloved pet and carefully wrap it in white cloth to protect it, the animal will receive the benefit of that protection.

Wax Heart Spell

This spell is sure to melt your beloved's heart. Perform it during the waxing moon, preferably when the sun or moon is in Libra, or on a Friday.

TOOLS AND INGREDIENTS

A ballpoint pen (or other engraving tool)
1 red candle
1 pink candle
An essential oil that corresponds to love and that you find pleasing
Matches or a lighter
Aluminum foil

1. With the pen carve your name on one candle and your beloved's on the other.
2. Dress both candles with the essential oil.
3. Light both candles, then tilt them so the melting wax drips onto the foil, blending to form a single mound of wax.
4. When you have enough wax to mold, allow it to cool slightly, but don't let it harden. Form a heart out of the wax.
5. Place the wax heart on your bedside table. If you prefer, you can insert a wick into the wax heart while the wax is still pliable and use it as a candle to fire up your romance.

BOTANICALS

It's reasonably safe to say that every plant has probably been used at one time or another in spellcraft. A Greek myth explains that the daughters of Hecate (one of the patronesses of witchcraft) taught witches how to use plants for both healing and magick. The Druids considered trees sacred. According to green witchcraft, all plants contain spirits—to work effectively with plants, you must communicate with them at a spiritual level, not just a physical one. Even the pages of the grimoire in which you are writing come from plant material.

To practice plant magick you'll need to reconnect with nature. You can't honor something you don't feel an intimate connection with, and you certainly can't call on the plant spirits to assist you unless you develop a rapport with plants. If you live in a concrete jungle, this may present some challenges. But even in the heart of the city, you can find parks, botanical gardens, greenhouses, or garden centers where you can commune with plants.

Earth Spirits at Findhorn

In the early 1960s, Eileen and Peter Caddy and their associate Dorothy Maclean began a spiritual community in a wild and windswept area of northern Scotland known as Findhorn. Even though the soil there was mostly sand and the climate inhospitable, Findhorn became famous for its amazing gardens, which produced tropical flowers and forty-two-pound cabbages. How could this happen? According to Dorothy, the spirits of the plants—she described them as "living forces of creative intelligence that work behind the scene"—guided Findhorn's founders in planting and maintaining the incredible gardens. In the book *Faces of Findhorn,* Professor R. Lindsay Robb of the Soil Association writes, "The vigor, health and bloom of the plants in this garden at mid-winter on land which is almost barren, powdery sand cannot be explained . . ." Well, not by ordinary thinking anyway.

Spellworking with Botanicals

Every plant is unique, with its own special energies and applications. Rowan, for instance, hung above a doorway protects your home from harm. Mugwort improves psychic awareness. Healing plays an important role in the work many witches do, and in this work they often draw upon the powers of botanicals. For thousands of years and into the present, people have relied on herbal medicine to heal everything from the common cold to a broken heart. Here are some other ways you might choose to work with the magickal properties of plants:

- Press pretty flowers and herbs in your book of shadows.
- Watch plant behavior for omens and signs.
- Mix leaves and petals into magick potions.
- Use plant matter in amulets and talismans.
- Add plant matter to incense and candles.
- Blend herbs for poultices and healing teas.
- Mix healing plant oils into lotions, salves, and ointments.
- Decorate your altar with flowers.
- Plant flowers in a magick garden to attract nature spirits.
- Make fragrant potpourris to perfume your closets and dresser drawers.
- Place live plants in various parts of your home or yard to encourage personal growth and well-being.

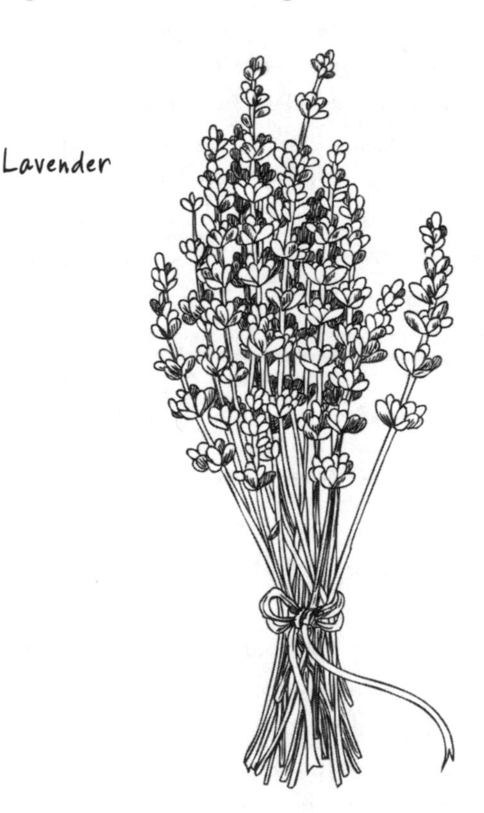

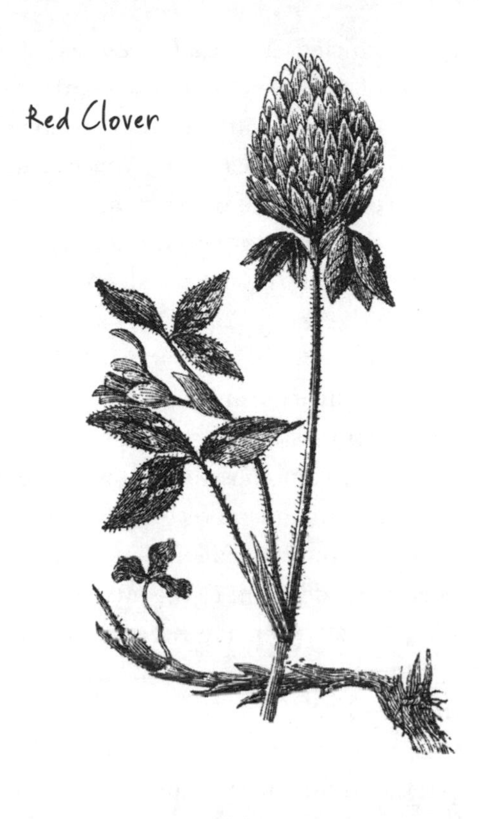
Red Clover

Rosemary

Some plants may be burned in ritual fires, as offerings or for purification. Sage is one of the most popular plants to use for this purpose. Many botanicals also come in the form of incense (sticks, cones, coils) that you can burn in spells and rituals. You can make an herbal infusion by boiling water, removing the water from heat, and then letting the plant material steep in the water for several minutes. If you wish, set flowers in water and leave them in the sun to "steep." The essence of the flowers will be imparted to the water. Add a tiny amount of liquor such as brandy or vodka to the water to preserve it. Mist a room with flower water to purify it or sprinkle a little on an amulet or talisman to charge it.

As any good cook will tell you, the key to great food lies both in the ingredients and how the cook combines them. The same holds true for spells. If you think of a spell as a magickal recipe, you begin to understand why the components (that is, the ingredients) are so important. If you don't measure them correctly, add them to the mix at the right time, and give them enough time to "bake" properly, the magick goes awry.

Choosing Botanicals for Spells

So what constitutes a good spell component? Anything that's essential to the recipe—anything that builds the energy until it's just right. All the ingredients must mesh on a metaphysical level. Of course, the witch herself is the key component of any spell, adding a word, a touch, or a wish.

When selecting botanicals, choose organic plants if possible. You don't want the poisonous vibes of pesticides present in your spellwork! If you are purchasing your herbs and do not know under what conditions they were grown, wash them thoroughly to remove any residual chemicals that may have been used. If you're harvesting a plant that you've grown yourself or found in the wild, ask the plant's permission before picking it, and thank it for its help.

The Magickal Properties of Botanicals

- Acacia: For meditation; to ward off evil; to attract money and love
- Aloe: To soothe burns or skin ailments; for digestion and internal cleansing

- Angelica: For temperance; to guard against evil
- Anise: For protection; burn seeds as a meditation incense
- Balm: To soothe emotional pain, mitigate fears
- Bay: For purification, divination, psychic development, heightened awareness
- Basil: For protection, balance, purification, divination
- Burdock: For purification, protection, psychic awareness; to ward off negativity; aphrodisiac
- Catnip: For insight, love, happiness
- Cayenne: To stimulate courage, sexual desire, or enthusiasm
- Cedar: For wealth, abundance, success
- Chamomile: For relaxation, peace of mind; as a digestive aid; to bless a person, place, or thing
- Cinnamon: For financial and career success, love spells, mental clarity
- Cinquefoil: To stimulate memory, aid communication; for divination or psychic dreams
- Clove: For success, prosperity; to remove negativity; to numb pain
- Clover: For love spells, psychic awareness, luck
- Comfrey: For protection, cleansing, endurance
- Daisy: To attract good luck
- Elder: For protection, healing rituals
- Fennel: For protection
- Foxglove: To heighten sexuality (poisonous)
- Frankincense: To aid meditation, psychic visions, mental expansion, purification
- Garlic: For protection, healing; to lift depression
- Ginger: For love, balance, cleansing; to speed manifestation
- Hawthorne: For success, happiness, fertility, protection
- Jasmine: For love, passion, peace, harmony; to sweeten a situation or relationship
- Kava-kava: To heighten psychic awareness, to calm anxiety
- Laurel: For success and victory
- Lavender: For relaxation, spiritual and psychic development, purification
- Marigold: For happiness, psychic awareness, success in legal matters
- Marjoram: For acceptance of major life changes

- Mint: For prosperity; to speed up results
- Mugwort: For divination, psychic development and awareness; good for washing crystals
- Myrrh: For protection, healing, consecration
- Nettle: To mitigate thorny situations such as gossip and envy
- Parsley: For prosperity, protection, health
- Rosemary: For protection, love, health; to improve memory
- Rue: For protection; to strengthen willpower, to speed recovery from illness and surgery, to expel negativity
- Sandalwood: For consecration, spiritual communication, travel spells, success
- Skullcap: For relaxation before magickal practices
- Thyme: To focus energy and prepare oneself for magickal practice
- Vervain: For protection, divination, creativity, self-confidence; to remove negative energy
- Willow: For love, protection, conjuring of spirits, healing, dowsing
- Wormwood: For spirit communication; to enhance psychic ability (poisonous if burned)
- Yarrow: For divination, love, protection; to enhance psychic ability

"And above all, watch with glittering eyes the whole world around you because the greatest secrets are always hidden in the most unlikely places. Those who don't believe in magic will never find it."

—Roald Dahl, *The Minpins*

GEMSTONES

Today, people wear precious and semiprecious gems mostly because they're so pretty. Witches, however, realize that crystals and gemstones can also be used for spellworking, divination, shamanic journeying, meditation, and dowsing. Stones also play important roles in healing, and each of the body's seven major chakras corresponds to one (or more) gems based on their colors and resonances.

Gemstones and jewelry have long been favored as talismans and amulets. The Chinese, for example, prize jade and wear it to bring health, strength, and good fortune. During the Crusades, ladies gave opals to soldiers to keep them safe in battle. Originally, people wore birthstones to enhance, balance, or moderate their own personal characteristics. Birthstones resonate with the qualities of the zodiac signs to which they correspond. By the way, you should look at your sign, not the month of your birth, to discover your true birthstone. If you're an Aquarian, for example, your birthstone is garnet, regardless of whether you were born in January or February.

> *"When you wear certain gems on your left side you can consciously control and modify stresses from your environment. . . . [W]hen you wear gems on your right side, your gems can aid your productivity."*
>
> —Dorothee L. Mella, *Stone Power*

Spellworking with Gemstones

Like plants, crystals and gemstones are living entities, although they resonate at a rate so slow that most people can't perceive it. However, their slow, concentrated energy enables them to keep working their magick for a long time. You can include gemstones and/or crystals in virtually any spell to increase, focus, stabilize, or fine-tune your spell's potency. Here are some suggestions:

- Wear them to enhance your personal energy field.
- Put them in amulets or talismans to augment your intentions.
- Set them near the windows and doors of your home to provide protection.
- Meditate with them.
- Infuse magick potions with them.
- Dowse with a gemstone or crystal pendulum.
- Display them on your altar to attract positive energy.
- Offer them to deities or nature spirits as gifts in return for assistance.
- Gaze into them to see the past or future.

Choosing Gemstones for Spells

As you might suspect, different stones possess different qualities and serve different functions in spellworking. A general rule of thumb is that clear stones are best for mental and spiritual issues, translucent or milky stones for emotional situations, and opaque stones for physical matters. You can use gems alone or in combination with other substances to produce the results you desire.

A stone's color or pattern can provide clues to its abilities. Pink gems, such as rose quartz and morganite, are perfect for love spells. Jade, aventurine, and other green stones can benefit money spells. Since ancient times, people have valued stones with eye-like markings as protection charms against the "evil eye" and all sorts of misfortune.

The following guidelines offer suggestions for using gems in spellwork. In time, you'll develop your own ideas about which stones you find best for which spells. Be sure to note these in your grimoire.

STONES AND THEIR MAGICKAL PROPERTIES	
Amber	For physical and psychic protection
Amethyst	For meditation, enhancing and remembering dreams, calming emotions, increasing psychic ability
Aquamarine	For clarity and mental awareness, encouraging spiritual insight, stimulating creativity
Aventurine	To attract wealth or abundance
Bloodstone	For healing, strength, and physical protection
Carnelian	To stimulate passion, sexual energy, courage, and initiative
Citrine	For clearing vibrations from other stones and crystals
Coral	To attract love or increase affectionate feelings; to enhance self-esteem; to calm emotions
Diamond	To deepen commitment and trust, especially in a love relationship; to absorb and retain energies and vibrations; for strength and victory

STONES AND THEIR MAGICKAL PROPERTIES	
Emerald	To aid clairvoyance and divination; to promote healing, growth, mental and emotional balance
Hematite	For grounding; to help stabilize emotions
Jade	For prosperity; to enhance beauty and health
Jasper	Red jasper is good in love spells to stir up passions; brown jasper is excellent for healing purposes; poppy jasper breaks up blockages that prevent energy from circulating through the body
Lapis lazuli	For opening psychic channels, dealing with children; to stimulate the upper chakras
Moldavite	To energize psychic talent, to quicken spiritual evolution, to open the upper chakras; moldavite is regarded as an extraterrestrial stone because it resulted from a meteor collision with the earth nearly 15 million years ago
Moonstone	To enhance the vividness of dreams and dream recall; to calm emotions
Onyx	For banishing and absorbing negative energy, grounding and stabilizing; to help break deeply ingrained habits
Opal	For protection; to encourage psychic ability and visions; to attract love
Pearl	To strengthen self-esteem; for balance in love relationships; to increase femininity
Quartz (clear)	To retain information; to amplify the energy of other stones; to transmit ideas and energy; for psychic awareness
Rose quartz	To attract love and friendship; for emotional healing and balance; to amplify psychic energy
Ruby	To stimulate the emotions, passion, love; to open your heart to divine love
Sapphire	To increase spiritual knowledge and connection with the Divine; for wisdom, insight, and prophetic vision; star sapphires provide hope and clarity of purpose

STONES AND THEIR MAGICKAL PROPERTIES	
Smoky quartz	For endurance; to hold problems until you are ready to deal with them
Tiger's eye	For abundance, self-confidence, the freedom to follow your own path
Tourmaline	Green and black tourmaline are good for cleansing, healing, and absorbing negative vibrations; pink and watermelon tourmaline attract friendship, love, and fulfillment; use them to transmit messages and energy
Turquoise	For protection, healing, prosperity; to ease mental tension and emotional anxiety

You can combine several stones to address various aspects of a spell. Let's say your goal is to find a job that pays well and brings you into contact with interesting people—aventurine plus watermelon tourmaline should do the trick. In a love spell, you might seek both passion and affection, in which case you'd choose carnelian and rose quartz. After a while, you'll start to intuit which stones are right for your intentions. Stones play such an important role in magick work that you'll probably want to spend time familiarizing yourself with their many properties. Judy Hall's books provide extensive information about how to use stones for a wide range of purposes.

Caring for Your Stones

Gemstones hold on to thoughts, emotions, and information programmed into them for a long time, even for centuries. You've probably heard of the Hope Diamond, a 45-carat blue diamond that for more than a century supposedly bore a curse that brought death and misfortune to the people who owned it. Although you probably have nothing to fear from the stones you acquire, nonetheless it's a good idea to cleanse and purify them before you use them for magickal work.

Wash them in running water, with mild soap if you like, while you envision them cleansed by pure white light. You can also purify gemstones energetically by gently rubbing them with a piece of golden citrine.

Try one of these other methods for cleansing stones, if you prefer:

- Leave them in sunlight or moonlight for a specific period, say twenty-four hours or a week—it's your call. Do what you feel is necessary.
- Bury them in a small dish of soil or sand for a time.
- Hold the stone in the smoke of burning sage or purifying incense.
- Immerse the stone in water for a time. Holding it in a running stream or the ocean's waves will purify it faster, but leaving the stone in a small bowl of water will work too. Don't worry; you cannot remove the innate energy of a stone, so it's impossible to over-purify or wipe out its powers.

Each time you use a stone for a magickal purpose, it is important to cleanse it before working with it again. You'll also want to purify your stones if someone else handles them—you don't want that person's energy to interfere with your own.

Keep a record in your grimoire of the stones you use in spells. Can you perceive different resonances emanating from different stones? Do you feel an affinity for some more than others? If you combined gems with other ingredients in a spell, how did that work out? Do you sense that certain gems enhance one another's powers? Do you use some stones for healing, others for meditation, others for scrying, and so on? Note any impressions, insights, sensations, or other reactions you experience while working with gemstones and crystals—sometimes these can be pretty amazing. You might even choose to affix small gemstones to the pages of your grimoire, to remind you of spells you did with these gems or because they add a decorative element to your book of shadows—or both.

Chapter 17

SYMBOLS IN SPELLWORK

We've talked a lot about symbols and the importance of symbolic association in spellwork. Symbols are such powerful magickal tools because they speak to us at an unconscious level, evoking hidden truths, archetypes, emotions, and spiritual qualities that lie at the core of our psyches. As a result, we often experience profound feelings in connection with them. Observe the way patriotic people respond to their nation's flag, how Christians relate to the cross, or how the Nazis reacted to the swastika and you'll see the power of symbols at work.

We respond to symbols in collective ways as well as personal ones. Many symbols are universal, appearing in the art and artifacts of numerous cultures from different times and places. The spiral, which represents life energy, is one such symbol. In addition, each of us has a set of individual symbols that have special meanings for us alone. When you use a symbol in spellwork, you draw upon the energy of whatever it represents. Simultaneously, you project your intentions through it to generate a result in the manifest world.

"Witchcraft promotes the advantages of learning and applying new symbolism into one's psyche; this is the Witch's code."

—Gede Parma, *Spirited: Taking Paganism Beyond the Circle*

What symbols speak to you? Keep a record in your grimoire of the symbols with which you feel a special connection—especially the "secret" ones known as sigils that you create yourself. Note your personal symbols and what they mean to you. Draw symbols in your book of shadows and spend time reflecting on them, allowing their secrets to rise into your consciousness. Meditate on various symbols to intuit their deeper meanings. How do you feel when you hold a symbol in your mind's eye? What insights do you gain? Do you see representations of these symbols in the material world? In your own life?

Intricate or Simple?

Intricate shapes strengthen concentration and your ability to perceive detail, beauty, and complexity. Simple shapes free your mind to imagine what lies beyond the pattern.

SHAPES AS SYMBOLS

Remember the saying, "As above, so below"? This means that all things in the spirit realm have some kind of representation here on earth. Spiritual energies manifest themselves as shapes in the mundane world—and because witches understand this we can tap these energies for our own purposes.

Numbers, letters, and geometric shapes are common symbols you see around you every day, usually without giving them a second thought. The average person only recognizes the obvious meanings of these familiar images. To someone versed in occult knowledge, however, symbols reveal something much deeper.

"An idea, in the highest sense of that word, cannot be conveyed but by a symbol."

—Samuel Taylor Coleridge

The Shapes of Things

Geometric shapes contain symbolism that transcends time and place. The cross, for example, isn't unique to Christian belief; it existed in ancient Celtic, Egyptian, and Native American cultures too. This simple yet powerful image represents the union of the archetypal male energy or sky (the vertical line) with female energy or earth (the horizontal line). The intersecting lines also designate the four directions that divide the four quarters we've talked about in earlier chapters.

The star is a common symbol of hope, the circle a well-known symbol of wholeness. Spirals represent life energy in many cultures. Triangles signify trinities, whether Father-Son-Holy Spirit, maiden-mother-crone, past-present-future, or some other threefold concept. The following list gives the symbolic meanings of basic geometric shapes:

Shape	**Meanings**
Arrow	warrior energy, direction, movement, hitting the mark
Circle	union, wholeness, life's cycles, the full moon, containment
Circle with a slash	refusal or banishing
Cross	intersection of male and female/heaven and earth/spirit and matter, the four corners of creation
Spiral	life energy, the spiritual path that leads inward and outward
Square	foundations, stability, permanence, truth and rightness
Star	hope, wishes and dreams, protection
Triangle (point down)	feminine energy, the element of water
Triangle (point up)	masculine energy, the fire element

According to green witches, the shape of a natural item provides a blueprint for how it should be used magickally. If you find a heart-shaped stone or leaf, for example, you can apply it to spells that involve matters of the heart. You see a heart, you think love—and that thought produces positive energy to support your intention.

Elemental Symbols

Alchemy uses triangles to depict the four elements we've talked about in earlier chapters. Triangles that point upward toward the sky and spirit symbolize the masculine force. A simple triangle stands for the element of fire; one with a horizontal line through it signifies the air element. Downward-pointing triangles aim toward the earth and the realm of matter. They represent the feminine force and the elements of water and earth. The emblem for earth has a horizontal line through the center of the triangle, the one for water doesn't.

Historically, symbols have offered one meaning for the masses and another, deeper meaning for initiates. The Star of David is a good example. To most people, the six-pointed star is an image associated with the Jewish faith. However, when you view it as the intersection of two triangles—one pointing up and one pointing down—it depicts the union of masculine and feminine, spirit and matter. The merger of these two energies creates life.

The ancient grimoire known as *The Clavicule of Solomon* or *Key of Solomon* (discussed in Chapter 1) says that the archangel Michael gave King Solomon a magick ring. Its power lay in the symbol engraved on the ring—the Seal of Solomon—which enabled the king to trap demons in jars so they could do no harm. This symbol geometrically depicts the union of all four elements.

Magick Numbers

We usually credit the Greek mathematician and philosopher, Pythagoras, who lived in the sixth century B.C.E., with having developed the system of numerology that's still used today. The study of numbers, known as *gematria,* is also based in esoteric Judaism and the Kabbalah. This practice attaches a number equivalent to each letter in a word (see Chapter 5 for details). Viewed in this way, every word contains a secret meaning based on the number values of its letters, as well as its outer meaning.

Additionally, each number possesses certain characteristics or resonances, as the following list explains:

Number	Meanings
0	wholeness, all and nothing
1	beginnings, individuality, initiative
2	polarity, partnership, duality, balance
3	creativity, self-expression, expansion
4	form, stability, permanence, order
5	change, instability, communication
6	give-and-take, cooperation, beauty, harmony
7	retreat, introspection, rest, spirituality
8	material mastery, manifestation, responsibility, sincerity, practical matters
9	transition, completion, fulfillment, abundance
11	humanitarianism, higher knowledge, insight
22	spiritual power, wisdom, mastery beyond the physical realm

You can tap the qualities inherent in numbers to enhance, activate, bind, or otherwise influence a spell. Witches often use the number three to complete a spell. This number signifies bringing an intention into the realm of form, literally making it three-dimensional.

SHAPES AND NUMBERS IN SPELLS AND RITUALS

Once you understand the symbolism inherent in shapes and numbers, you can utilize them in spells and rituals to emphasize specific energies or intentions. As you know, witches cast circles around a space where a spell or ritual will take place. The circle represents union, wholeness, life's cycles, the full moon, and containment. Tarot cards beautifully depict a smorgasbord of symbols, including numbers. We've talked about carving symbols on candles, using runes and astrological glyphs in talismans and amulets, and creating your own symbols known as sigils.

Let's say you want to do a candle spell to attract a romantic partner. Because two is the number of partnership, you'd light two candles to represent you and your prospective partner. If you're fashioning a prosperity talisman, you could place eight items in a medicine pouch or seal the pouch with a ribbon into which you've tied eight knots. That's because eight is the number of material mastery and manifestation. You can mix and match symbols to customize a spell, as in the one that follows. The important thing is to get your imagination involved. Remember, visualization precedes manifestation.

Candle Spell for Prosperity

This spell incorporates number, image, botanical, shape, and color symbolism to light the way to prosperity and brighten your financial prospects. Start the spell 8 days before the full moon.

TOOLS AND INGREDIENTS

8 green or gold candles
Ballpoint pen (or another sharp instrument)
Peppermint essential oil
8 candleholders
Matches or a lighter

1. On each candle use the pen to inscribe a symbol or word that represents prosperity to you. You can use the same symbol on all 8 candles, or choose several different images.
2. Pour a little essential oil in your palm and rub it on the candles, coating everything except the wicks.

3. Put the candles in the candleholders and position them on your altar, making a square pattern to represent the 4 directions, the 4 quarters, and stability.
4. Light the candles and gaze at the flames.
5. Say aloud: "As these candles burn, prosperity flows to me from all directions, in harmony with Divine Will, my own true will, and with good to all."
6. Let the candles burn for a few minutes, then snuff them out.
7. Repeat this ritual each day for 8 days. Complete the spell on the day of the full moon.

After you've completed the spell, write in your grimoire what transpired. What images did you inscribe on the candles? How did you feel working the spell? Did your experiences change from day to day? What insights did you gain? What results did you get and how long did they take?

Experiment with using symbols in spellwork, trying out different combinations to see which ones you like best. Record the variations you use and describe your experiences in your book of shadows.

THE MAGICK OF DATES

We've talked about the significance of choosing certain days of the week for magickal work, but what about dates? Dates contain numbers and those numbers can be important in spellcasting. The first day of the month, for example, might be a good time to do a spell to launch a new venture.

> *"Those who deepen themselves in what is called in the Pythagorean sense 'the study of numbers' will learn through the symbolism of numbers to understand life and the world."*
>
> —Rudolf Steiner, founder of Anthroposophy and the Waldorf schools

Your Life Path Number

Your birth date forms a very important personal number and its energy influences you throughout your lifetime. Numerologists refer to this as your "life path" number because it indicates your direction or role in this lifetime. To find this powerful number, add the month, date, and year of your birth together. Keep reducing the sum by adding the digits until only a single digit remains. (Note: Usually the double or so-called "master" numbers 11 and 22 are left as is, rather than being reduced to the sum of their digits.) For example, if you were born on August 21, 1986 you would figure your life number this way:

Add $8 + 2 + 1 + 1 + 9 + 8 + 6 = 35$

Reduce the sum to a single digit by adding $3 + 5 = 8$

The following brief interpretations describe the life roles that each number indicates:

Number	Interpretation
1	Leader, initiator, pioneer, a person who breaks new ground
2	Diplomat, mediator, agent, a go-between who assists others
3	Artist, musician, creator, someone who brings beauty into the world
4	Builder, artisan, technician, someone who makes practical, useful things
5	Teacher, writer, communicator, an idea person
6	Caretaker, homemaker, farmer, someone who nurtures and supports others
7	Truth seeker, religious leader, philosopher, mystic, wise wo/man
8	Businessperson, manager, industrialist, a person who uses money and resources in a productive way
9	Humanitarian, social worker, healer, a person who helps improve conditions for everyone
11	Inventor, visionary, avatar, someone who leads by positive example
22	A master builder who organizes people, nations, or institutions on a large scale

Calculate your life path number and note it in your grimoire. Does this describe you? Are you fulfilling the purpose to which you were born? How do you see the characteristics inherent in this number operating in your life? In your spiritual and magick work?

Life Cycles

Our lives are never static. Indeed, change is essential for personal growth. If you understand the influences guiding you, you can align yourself with them and utilize them to your advantage. Numerologists examine what they call "life cycles," which are based on your birthdate, to determine what you're likely to experience in any given year. By working with these cycles you can increase your success and satisfaction in life. You'll be more effective in your magickal work too, because you can harmonize it with the energies influencing you.

Let's look at the numerological cycle known as your "personal year." This changes each year and tells you what forces are operating in your life during a particular twelve-month period. To determine this, add the numbers of your birth month, date, and the year at your last birthday. If you were born on May 16 and you want to know what personal year cycle you will be experiencing from May 16, 2016, through May 15, 2017:

Add 5 + 1 + 6 + 2 + 0 + 1 + 6 = 21

Reduce the sum to a single digit by adding 2 + 1 = 3

Your personal year number for this period is 3. Therefore, you'll want to do things that correspond to a 3 vibration: have fun, enjoy more leisure time, express your creativity, expand your horizons physically and spiritually.

The following table briefly describes the essence of the nine yearly cycles and indicates where you are likely to focus your attention during those years.

Personal Year Cycle	Your Focus for the Year
1	New beginnings, action, independence, self-interest
2	Cooperation, partnerships, balance, developing plans
3	Expansion, travel, creativity, opportunity, personal growth
4	Stability, building, organization, financial matters, security
5	Communication, change, movement, sharing ideas
6	Give and take, balance, domesticity, love, comfort, beauty
7	Rest, retreat, withdrawal, introspection, healing
8	Manifestation, responsibility, power, managing resources
9	Fulfillment, completion, endings, transition, wisdom

In addition to personal year cycles, you also experience personal month cycles. You can tap the energy of these shorter periods in magickal work and in other areas of your life. To find your personal month, add the number of your personal year to the number equivalent of the current month (or any month in the future that you want to know more about). For example, if this year is a "7" for you, and you want to see what March has in store:

Add 7 + 3 (March's number) = 10

Reduce to a single digit by adding 1 + 0 = 1

March is 1 month for you, so during this time plan to do things that correspond to a 1 vibration. Use the table that describes the characteristics of personal years given earlier—the energies for the months are similar, though of shorter duration. This will help you to determine how to tap the power of your personal cycles in your spellwork and your life.

Record in your grimoire what you experience during these monthly and yearly cycles, both in your everyday life and in your magickal practice. Where did you focus your energies? What spells and rituals did you do? What areas of interest called to you? What knowledge and insights did you receive? Write down everything that you consider meaningful: your feelings, ideas, areas of concern, successes and setbacks, interactions with other people, dreams, and so on. In the future, you can compare what you experienced now with what transpires later.

ANIMALS AS SYMBOLS

Animals hold symbolic meaning for us too. A robin serves as a herald of springtime. A lion represents courage; a dog signifies loyalty. Celtic and Old European clans believed that certain animal deities oversaw entire groups of people. Irish clans called their members griffins, wolves, deer, etc., and individuals took their names from these animals. Animal guardians performed numerous functions for a clan, including protecting its warriors in battle.

Many family crests or coats of arms include animals, and those animal symbols convey distinct meanings. The crest of the Rothschild family—one of the most powerful families in the world—features a lion, a phoenix, and a unicorn. We see a version of this symbolism expressed today by our athletic teams. The Denver Broncos, the Boston Bruins, the Miami Dolphins, the St. Louis Cardinals, and the Chicago Bulls are some of the dozens of animal-named teams among the professional leagues.

Both Western and Chinese astrology link zodiac signs with animals. Zodiac means "circle of animals." You likely share some traits with the animal that represents your zodiac sign. If you're a Capricorn with the goat as your symbol, you persevere one step at a time and can climb to great heights. If you're a Leo, you may have regal bearing like the lion and proudly assume your role as a leader.

> *"Animals are sacred. They are living expressions of the divine principle—the Goddess and the God manifest in living form."*
>
> —Timothy Roderick, *The Once Unknown Familiar*

Spellworking with Animals

Perhaps you've heard the term "familiar." In spellwork, a familiar is an animal that works with a witch. Remember Harry Potter's owl? Black cats have long been associated with witchcraft. Ravens, snakes, and other creatures also have special places as wise beings in magick and folklore.

You may want to work with a familiar, but not every animal is intended for this type of relationship. Your beloved Fido or Fluffy may be a wonderful companion, but that doesn't necessarily make him or her your familiar. Often a witch experiences a strong psychic link with her familiar. Your familiar may serve as a guardian, guide, or healer. It can help you connect more deeply with the natural world and your intuition. The witch and her familiar are allies in the work—you don't own your familiar, it is a free being that deserves your utmost respect and gratitude.

Regardless of whether you work with a flesh-and-blood animal, you can incorporate animal symbolism in your magick. Think about various creatures and their distinctive qualities. Cheetahs are known for their speed and hunting skills. Foxes are clever, expert at dodging difficulties. Which animal's characteristics will best serve and guide you now?

Animal Deities

In India, people call upon the elephant-headed deity Ganesh to give them the strength to overcome difficulties. For many indigenous people of North America, the spirit of the bear provides protection.

Spirit Animal Protection Spell

According to shamanic traditions, spirit animal guardians provide protection and guidance in this world and beyond. Think of a creature who symbolizes protection for you. When you've chosen an animal helper, find a photograph, small figurine, or another symbol of that animal.

TOOLS AND INGREDIENTS

A black candle

A white candle

2 candleholders

Matches or a lighter

A photo, figurine, painting, or other image of the animal whose help you are soliciting

1. Cast a circle around the area where you will do your spell.
2. Fit the candles in their holders and set them on your altar (or another surface, such as a tabletop). As you face the altar, the black candle should be at your left and the white one on your right.
3. Light the candles and place the image of the animal between them. Gaze at the animal image. Sense this animal's presence near you, as a spirit being who will accompany you wherever and whenever you need him or her.
4. Breathe slowly and deeply, bringing into yourself the qualities you seek from that animal: strength, courage, speed, cunning, and so on. Feel your fear ebbing away, replaced by the knowledge that your animal guardian is there to take care of you.
5. Ask this animal to share any suggestions that might help you. Listen carefully for an answer—it may come in the form of a vision, insight, sensation, sound, scent, or inner knowing.
6. Commune with your spirit animal guide for as long as you wish. When you feel ready, extinguish the candles, pick up the image of your animal guardian, and open the circle.
7. Carry the image with you for protection and reassurance.

In your grimoire, write down the results of your spell. What animal did you choose and why? How did the animal help you resolve your problem? Also describe your experiences—feelings, thoughts, impressions, insights, and so on.

Animal Divination

Dream researchers believe that when an animal shows up in a dream it bears a message for you. Sometimes you'll see an animal in nature, and if it's a creature you wouldn't ordinarily find in your locale, this could be a sign for you. If you see a ram, for example, think about what it represents to you. Power? Daring? Aggression? Competitiveness? Is it telling you to tackle a matter head on? To engage an adversary forcefully and directly? Are you being too aggressive or not aggressive enough?

Notice your reaction when something like this happens. Record your experiences in your grimoire. When and where did the animal appear to you? How does it relate to what's going on in your life? What message did it convey to you? How can you benefit from drawing upon its traits? Sketch or paste pictures of the animal in your book of shadows. You might even design a sigil that includes the animal's image. To learn more about animal divination and how to understand animals as symbols, see my book *The Secret Power of Spirit Animals.*

Chapter 18

DREAMS AND MAGICK

Some of the greatest moments of inspiration occur while we sleep. In the dark of night, thoughts begin to take form and significance. Shimmering dreams materialize into energy that seems to emanate from an unknowable source. When traveling the river of dreamtime, your mind is unbound, uncensored, and released from ordinary daytime expectations. Images, whether comforting or frightening, flow freely in an endless succession of vivid possibilities. Your grimoire is the perfect place to record your dreams, as dreams often contain guidance and insights. Keeping a log of your dreams also allows you to review them periodically to gain deeper understanding.

Dreams let us explore what lies beneath the surface, the unspoken world of archetypes and mystery that usually lies dormant, ready to rise and make its presence known in our lives—what psychoanalyst Carl Jung called the collective unconscious. The Goddess may visit you in dreams through symbols and signs. She travels from a place beyond, both in and out of time. Enter into her temple with the intention to know her and to open your unconscious mind to her presence, her words, and her teachings.

ONLY A DREAM?

Since the beginning of time, dreams have fascinated and perplexed us. Why do they happen? Where do they come from? What do they mean? Are dreams merely the result of chemical changes in the brain, as some studies suggest, or vehicles for divine communication?

Sources of Wisdom

Dreams figure prominently in the literature and mythology of all cultures. The 4,000-year-old *Epic of Gilgamesh* speaks of temples built to Mamu, who was the ancient goddess of dreams. Early Egyptians believed the gods bestowed dreams on humans, and dedicated many temples in Memphis to Serapis, the Egyptian god of dreams. The ancient Greeks erected temples to Asclepius, the god of healing. People with illnesses spent the night there and received guidance in their dreams from the god; the priests then wrote the cures on the temple walls.

The ancient texts of the Egyptians and Hindus as well as the Old Testament of the Bible discuss dreams, indicating that for millennia people around the world have looked to dreams for guidance, prophecy, wisdom, and inspiration. Muslims believe that a divine source gave the Qu'ran to Muhammad in a dream. Both Native American and Celtic shamanic teachings tell us that the dream realm is a parallel universe, a place we journey to when we sleep—and it is every bit as real as the world we inhabit when we're awake.

In his book *Dreamlife* David Fontana proposes "we sleep partly *in order to dream.* Sleep . . . may be the servant of the dream." You've probably heard of Edgar Cayce, often referred to as the "Sleeping Prophet." Although he had little formal education or medical training, he could go into a sleeplike trance and discover cures for thousands of sick people who sought his aid. He psychically "downloaded" wisdom that great minds before him had placed in the cosmic web (this web is sometimes referred to as the Akashic records).

What secrets and wisdom are your dreams trying to convey to you? Is a spirit or deity attempting to communicate with you via dreams? When you learn to decipher the meanings of your dreams, you can move with greater ease and grace through both the mundane and the magickal worlds.

Recording Your Dreams

Many people keep dream journals to help them remember and understand their dreams. However, you can record your dreams in your book of shadows if you like. Doing so can reveal connections between the realm of dreams and the realm of magick.

As part of your morning ritual, write down your dreams immediately upon waking. You will be better able to capture the fleeting images before they vanish into the ether or get lost in the busyness of the day. You may feel groggy and inarticulate from sleep. Your writing may seem as disjointed and unusual as the dream itself. No problem. This is precisely the point! You don't want your brain fully engaged—you want to capture the images and symbols that linger in the shadowy recesses beyond rational thinking. Don't worry about writing in complete sentences. You're not trying to explain, entertain, or analyze your thought process at this time; you're merely recording what you feel, sense, and recall.

Try a stream-of-consciousness approach to writing and let the images flow freely. Attempt to capture on paper what occurs so easily to your dreaming mind. Don't place value judgments on what you write or censor yourself, just be honest. Record the dominant images, obvious symbols, emotions, or other events that occurred in your dream. Also note little things that might not seem significant at the moment—they may turn out to be important later. As you write, ideas may bubble up to the surface of your consciousness, vying for your attention. Jot down whatever comes to you, even if you don't understand it right away.

As a part of your evening ritual, write a few lines about your day in your grimoire. Did your dream relate to something you encountered during the waking hours? What do you see as significant between what transpired during the day and what you dreamt? Make sure to date your entries and include any other details that may be relevant, such as astrological influences or health issues. When this ritual becomes entrenched in your daily practice, you'll probably notice that your subconscious eagerly presents more and more information to you and you become more facile at working with your dreams.

The Earliest Dream

The earliest known recorded dream, which belonged to King Thutmose IV, is carved upon a granite tablet that rests between the paws of the Sphinx.

DREAM SYMBOLS

No one knows exactly why people dream, yet researchers and psychotherapists generally agree that your dreams are trying to tell you something that can benefit you in your waking life. Usually dream messages are presented in symbolic rather than literal form. Some symbols appear in many people's dreams; others are unique to the dreamer.

Over time, general interpretations have been attached to the most common dream symbols. Personal symbols, though, hold special meaning that only you can comprehend. The following list includes a number of familiar symbols that turn up in most people's dreams at one time or another, along with their usually accepted meanings.

Image	Interpretation
House	you and your life; the basement represents your unconscious, the main floor shows your daily living situation, the attic or upper floors describe your mental or spiritual side
Car	your body and your passage through life; the driver represents who's controlling your life; the car's condition reveals health and physical matters
Water	emotions; the type of water (deep, murky, cold, turbulent, etc.) indicates the quality of your feelings
Sex	merging your masculine and feminine sides, or incorporating another person's qualities into yourself
Death	a transition or change; something is moving out of your life

Image	Interpretation
Birth	a new direction, perspective, or endeavor; creativity; opportunity
School	learning lessons; taking an exam represents being tested in an area of life
Monsters	things you fear or parts of yourself you haven't integrated

---

Dreams about Gems

It's said that when you dream about gemstones you've received a message from the Divine. To understand the message, consider the meanings associated with the particular gem (see Chapter 16).

Keep a list in your grimoire of the symbols you encounter in your dreams and describe what they mean to you. Do some appear frequently? Do they usually turn up in similar scenarios, or in a variety of ways? How do you feel when you encounter a particular symbol in a dream? After a while, you may identify certain symbols that are unique to you, or that hold different meanings for you than those commonly associated with them—pay special attention to these.

INTERPRETING YOUR DREAMS

If we agree that our dreams are trying to tell us something, it behooves us to learn to interpret them. Whether dream insights emerge from the subconscious or are sent to you by entities in the spirit realm, they may provide valuable information you can use in your everyday life and in your magick work. Each night as you enter the dream world, you have an opportunity to delve into areas that may not be available to you while you're awake.

Although dreams rarely play out in logical, easily comprehensible ways, with a little patience you can learn to understand their symbolic language. Think of dreams as your own personal movies, intended solely for you. Therefore, your own impressions are more important than standard textbook interpretations.

The following tips can help you get to the essence of your dreams:

- Try giving your dream a title that relates to what you remember as the most vivid or distinct image. The title could reflect the strongest event that occurred, the main action around which the events of the dream revolved.
- Write down what happened around you, to you, or because of you. These circumstances may be within or outside the realm of your control.
- Look for the crossroads, or the point in the dream at which things began to change, either for positive or negative results. Did your dream spiral up or down, either into delightful pleasure or a nightmare?
- Did some sort of resolution to the situation occur? How did this come about?
- How did you feel during the dream? Happy, sad, frightened, angry, confident, peaceful? How did you feel when you awoke?
- Who was in your dream? Are these characters people you know in your waking life? What associations do you have with them? If you don't know these people in waking life, do they represent something or someone?
- How did you interact with these characters? What transpired between you and them in the dream?
- Did any animals appear in your dream? If so, what associations do you hold with these animals?
- What images, actions, or scenes stood out most?
- Did anything in the dream seem totally fantastic and impossible in earthly terms? Or did the dream scenario play out in a relatively realistic manner?

Words have many meanings, both literal and symbolic, and dreams often play on words to get a point across. Once I dreamt I was in a long-distance race with many other people, and although I wasn't a trained runner I managed to keep up with the leaders in the race. Later, I won a contest and realized the dream had signaled that I was "in the running" for the award. Pay attention to words and phrases in your dreams, and note them in your grimoire—they may contain hidden meanings or puns that can provide insights.

Magick takes you into the secret recesses of the mind and makes you aware of your connections with other levels of reality. Dreams provide access to these realities. Keeping records of your dreams will lead you to a better understanding of your inner dynamics and what goes on beneath the surface of your ordinary mental processes. While in a dream state, you could even tap into the reservoir of knowledge contained in the Akashic records, the great cosmic "Internet" in the universe where many people believe the wisdom of all time is stored.

> *"Your vision will become clear only when you look into your heart. Who looks outside, dreams. Who looks inside, awakens."*
>
> —Carl Jung

Recurring Dreams

Scenarios and images that show up repeatedly in your dreams are especially significant. If you experience recurring dreams, your subconscious may be trying hard to get something across to you. For instance, most of us periodically dream of being in a classroom taking a test for which we feel unprepared. Not surprisingly, we tend to have this dream at turning points in our lives, when we're facing new challenges or moving into a new phase of life.

Pay close attention to your own recurring dreams. Does the dream replay pretty much the same way every time or do you notice variations? Examine any changes in the dream's narrative, setting, or characters—these will tell you how the situation is progressing. Once you comprehend the dream's message and address the situation, you'll probably stop having the dream.

Problem-Solving Dreams

Because dreams take you into a perceptual realm that's different from your waking one, they can provide answers that elude you in your everyday life. Many famous people have used dreams to help them solve problems. Albert Einstein, Thomas Edison, Harry Truman, and Benjamin Franklin were known to "sleep on it" when confronted with a problem or important decision.

One well-known example is Elias Howe, who patented the lock-stitch sewing machine. For ten years Howe had been struggling to perfect his machine. Then one night he dreamt cannibals captured him and told him he would die a horrible death if he didn't solve the problem. As he sat in a large cooking pot, waiting to be boiled alive, he glanced up at their spears and noticed holes near the pointed ends. Howe had his answer. He put the hole near the tip of the needle and the sewing machine was born.

Some researchers, including Michael Newton, PhD, author of *Destiny of Souls*, suggest that spirits or disembodied entities may slip information to you in your dreams. Others believe your subconscious already knows the answer to the conundrum, but the answer hasn't percolated through to your rational mind yet. If you have a dilemma and want help resolving it, write your request on a piece of paper and put it under your pillow at bedtime. Tell yourself you'll receive an answer while you sleep. Ask the Goddess or a favorite deity to assist you. If necessary, repeat the process for a few nights until the solution comes to you.

Healing Dreams

Sometimes dreams suggest cures when we're ill or offer advice about how we can heal ourselves physically and emotionally. They can also illuminate health problems that could develop if we don't take corrective action. Additionally, dreams may tell us that a treatment we're undergoing is right or wrong for us.

If you want your dreams to give you advice about a health situation, use the process described for problem-solving dreams. Also, pay attention to signs and symbols in your dreams that could warn of potential problems. I once dreamed I was driving dangerously fast and wrecked my car. My dream advised that if I didn't stop pushing myself so hard I could damage my health.

Want to help someone else with a health issue? Before you go to bed, hold in your mind an image of the person you wish to help. Ask him or her if it's okay to offer assistance. If you get the go-ahead, envision that person completely healthy, happy, and at peace (don't focus on the ailment or injury). Affirm that while you sleep, you will send healing energy to that person for his or her highest good. You may wish to invite the Goddess, a guide, a guardian, or a deity to aid you. Be confident that the good vibes you project during the dream state will reach your target.

Precognitive Dreams

Sometimes dreams reveal the future. When your perception is loosened during sleep it can range far and wide, even beyond the limitations of time. A dream that lets you see in advance what's coming may help you to prepare yourself or avoid a problem altogether. Some precognitive dreams are laden with poignant images. Others are straightforward and nearly devoid of symbolism. You actually witness an event before it happens in the physical world. For example, three months before his brother died, Mark Twain dreamed of the death and funeral—exactly as it happened, right down to the smallest detail.

The more aware you become of your dreams, the more likely you are to have precognitive dreams and to recognize them when they occur. Often the feeling content of precognitive dreams differs from what you experience during other types of dreams—you may get a sense of heightened clarity, immediacy, or authenticity. Keeping track of your dreams in your grimoire will strengthen your resolve to transcend time and space in order to glimpse the future. Think how useful that could be!

Dreams and Divination

Because dreams erase the boundaries between past, present, and future, you can use this colorful technique to tap the wisdom of your dreams for divination.

- From a sheet of posterboard, cut a dozen or more 4" × 6" rectangles.
- From magazines cut images, words, and/or symbols that represent what you witnessed in one of your dreams.
- Paste the images on one of the posterboard rectangles to create a picture card that depicts the key elements, emotions, actions, etc. in your dream.
- Do the same thing for at least a dozen dreams, until you have at least twelve dream cards. (You don't have to stop at twelve—you can make as many as you like.)
- Use these personal dream cards as you would tarot cards to do readings.
- Record your readings in your book of shadows, along with your interpretations.

Lucid Dreams

In what's known as a lucid dream, you realize you are dreaming. You experience a sense of detachment and clarity as you observe yourself and the action going on in your dream. From this place of clarity, you can guide the dream—like a director controlling the action in a movie. You can transform a nightmare into a sweet dream or make an upsetting scenario turn out the way you want it to. Learning to control your dreams can help you gain better control over situations in your waking life too.

Here's a technique you can try. While you're dreaming, look at your hands. Then give yourself some sort of hand signal, such as pointing or counting on your fingers. This lets you know that you are, indeed, aware and guiding the action. Or, you can say to yourself, "It's only a dream" while you are in the midst of the dream. Once you feel in control, you can guide your dream to help solve problems, peek into the future, journey to other realms, make connections with beings in the spirit world, and more.

Record your dreams in your grimoire. Also note how your experiences in the dream state influenced your waking life. The more you practice lucid dreaming, the better you'll get at taking charge of your dreams and their outcomes.

Herbal Dream Pillow

Crafty witches sometimes sew dream pillows to help them sleep better and/or to inspire meaningful dreams. You can too.

TOOLS AND INGREDIENTS

- 2 rectangular pieces of blue or purple cotton cloth, about 4" × 6" (or whatever size you choose)
- Needle and thread
- Dried mugwort leaves
- Dried lavender blossoms
- Pinch of mint
- Flaxseeds

1. Sew the 2 rectangular pieces of cloth together on 3 sides.
2. Turn the cloth inside out and fill with the dried herbs. The mugwort induces psychic dreams and lavender has a calming effect. The touch of mint aids mental clarity.
3. Fill the remainder of the pillow with the flaxseeds.
4. Sew up the fourth side.
5. Sleep with the pillow and allow it to influence your dreams.

Write any significant results in your book of shadows.

Mugwort (*Artemisia vulgaris*), nicknamed cronewort, is considered sacred to the moon goddess Artemis because of the silvery color of the underside of its leaves. Mugwort symbolizes the gifts of vitality and freedom from repression. You can also use it for centering, grounding, and renewing strength. When burned in small bundles, mugwort can enhance psychic visions.

Chapter 19

DEITIES, ANGELS, AND OTHER NONPHYSICAL ENTITIES

Although ordinarily we can't see them, many beings share our world with us. Perhaps you're aware of nonphysical entities around you—you may see or hear them, or simply sense their presence. Some of them reside on earth, others exist in what is often thought of as heaven. These distinctions, however, are a bit misleading, as the various levels of existence aren't really separate—they interact with and permeate one another.

How you choose to view nonphysical beings is up to you. Most witches believe in at least some of these entities, although our conceptions may differ. In the magickal view of the world, all forces—physical and nonphysical—are linked energetically. When you improve your relationships with gods and goddesses, angels, faeries, elementals, and others in the spirit realms, everything in the universe benefits.

THE GOD

Wiccans, as we've already discussed, believe that instead of one Divine Source (as patriarchal religions teach) there are two distinct powers: Goddess and God. We often think of the God as the Goddess's consort and recognize that both feminine and masculine forces are essential for existence. But the concept of dual forces operating in the universe isn't limited to Wiccans. Many cultures speak of both principles existing in and around us. The Chinese refer to these two energies as *yin* (feminine) and *yang* (masculine). Native Americans respect Mother Earth and Father Sky. These two polarities function in tandem to balance one another and create wholeness.

Throughout this book, we've talked about the Goddess. In Chapters 9 and 10, you'll find lists of goddesses, their areas of influence, and how they can assist you in your magick work. Now let's look at some of the aspects, powers, and attributes of the God.

Aspects of the God

Since the beginning of time, cultures around the world have honored a masculine force. The yang energy of the universe has been depicted in various guises and personalities, as individual deities with specific natures, characteristics, and responsibilities. The many faces of the God express qualities associated with the male archetype: strength, virility, daring, leadership skills, logic, protection, knowledge, and courage. The following list includes some of the god figures found in cultures around the world and the attributes connected with them.

GODS OF THE WORLD		
Name	**Culture**	**Attributes**
Adibuddha	Indian	ultimate male essence
Aengus	Irish	youth, love

GODS OF THE WORLD		
Name	**Culture**	**Attributes**
Apollo	Greek	beauty, poetry, music, healing
Bunjil	Australian	vital breath
Ea	Chaldean	magick, wisdom
Ganesh	Indian	strength, perseverance, overcoming obstacles
Green Man	Celtic	fertility, nature, abundance, sexuality
Horus	Egyptian	knowledge, eternal life, protection
Itzamna	Mayan	written communication
Lugh	Celtic	craftsmanship, healing, magick
Mars	Roman	aggression, war, vitality, courage
Mercury	Roman	intelligence, communication, trade, travel
Mithras	Persian	strength, virility, courage, wisdom
Odin	Scandinavian	knowledge, poetry, prophesy
Osiris	Egyptian	vegetation, civilization, learning
Pan	Greek	woodlands, nature, fertility
Shiva	Indian	destruction, transformation
Thoth	Egyptian	knowledge, science, the arts
Tyr	Teutonic	law, athletics
Vishnu	Indian	preservation, stability
Zeus	Greek	authority, justice, abundance, magnanimity

Archetypes transcend nationalities and religions, appearing in similar forms in many different cultures. For example, the Greek god Zeus corresponds to the Roman god Jupiter. You can see overlaps between the Egyptian god Thoth and the Greeks' Hermes. Mars and Mithras, both gods of war, were worshipped by soldiers in Rome and Persia, respectively.

Gaining the God's Assistance

On days when a witch wishes to identify with certain godlike qualities, she or he can ask for help from a deity who embodies those attributes. If you want to ace an exam, you can call on Mercury, Thoth, or Hermes to assist you. If you hope to overcome a formidable challenge or obstacle, ally yourself with the god Ganesh. Regardless of your goal or concern, you'll find a god who can provide the help you need.

In your grimoire, make a list of some gods with whom you feel a particular kinship. Also list some from whom you may seek assistance or think you might like to work with magickally. Then take time to learn all you can about them before you call on them for aid. Study the myths associated with them. Read about their powers and the areas in which they operate. If you are part of a coven or other group of magicians, discuss with them how they've worked with the Divine Masculine. The more you know about a particular god, the more effectively you can use his energy.

Note in your book of shadows which god(s) you called upon to assist your spellwork and why. Describe how you experienced his energy and how he made himself known to you. What transpired during the spell or ritual? What results came about?

Spell to Overcome an Obstacle

When a daunting challenge looms before you, call in some extra muscle to handle the task. Since ancient times, the people of India have drawn upon the strength of the elephant-headed god Ganesh to help them overcome seemingly insurmountable obstacles. You can too.

TOOLS AND INGREDIENTS

An image of an elephant or of Ganesh (for example, a magazine photo or small figurine)

An athame

1. Cast a circle around the area where you will do your spell.
2. Close your eyes and imagine you're in a dark, dense jungle. The vegetation is so thick you can see only a foot or two ahead of you. All sorts of dangers lurk unseen. Your situation seems impossible. You feel trapped and helpless.
3. Suddenly you hear the trumpeting call of an elephant—it's Ganesh coming to your rescue. He rushes toward you and lifts you with his trunk onto his back.
4. Explain to him the nature of your problem. Visualize yourself riding on Ganesh's shoulders as he marches into the jungle, trampling everything in his path.
5. With your athame begin slashing away at the vines and branches in your way (the dense vegetation symbolizes the obstacles facing you). Envision yourself hacking through the obstacles as space opens up before you. Feel Ganesh's strength, lifting you high above your problems.
6. Keep chopping away. You don't have to see all the way to the end, just tackle each obstacle as it presents itself.
7. When you feel ready, climb down from Ganesh's back and thank him for his assistance. You now realize you have the ability to handle whatever challenges arise.
8. Open the circle.

In your grimoire, describe how you felt performing this spell. Note your impressions, emotions, insights, visions, etc. Also write down how this spell and the deity's aid helped you overcome obstacle(s) in your life, and the results you experienced. You might want to paste the picture of Ganesh in your book or carry a small figurine in your pocket to remind you that you have a powerful ally on your side.

PETITIONING DEITIES

How can you get a god or goddess on your side? Many witches believe that divine assistance is always available to you and that the deities gladly offer their guidance, help, and energy to humans to use for positive purposes. Some view divine beings as higher aspects of human consciousness, which can be accessed and activated through magickal means.

If you want to connect with a particular entity, first ask that god or goddess to hear your request and come to your aid. One theory states that deities will not interfere with your own free will—you must ask them sincerely for help.

Honoring Deities

If you aren't accustomed to having a divine being as a partner in your spiritual pursuits, you may wonder how to go about petitioning your favorite god or goddess for assistance. Here are a few suggestions:

- Make an offering to the deity. Burning incense is a popular offering, although you may prefer a method that more specifically corresponds to the nature of the deity whose help you seek. Bacchus, for instance, is extremely fond of wine, so you could set a glass of good Cabernet on your altar and dedicate it to him.
- Place a picture or figurine of the chosen deity on your altar.
- Offer prayers, chants, poems, or songs to the deity.
- Light a candle in honor of the deity you wish to petition.
- Design and perform a ritual to the deity.
- Choose a gemstone for which the deity has an affinity, such as golden topaz for Amaterasu or moonstone for Diana, and place the gem on your altar.
- Plant herbs or flowers in honor of the god or goddess, or set a vase of flowers on your altar. Choose plants that correspond to the deity; asters, for example, are linked with the Greek goddess Astraea.

Which Deity Is the Right One?

Throughout history, people have linked gods and goddesses with certain qualities, skills, and powers, and their unique attributes can help you in your magickal work. If you're doing a spell for a particular purpose—and usually that's the case—your best bet is to request aid from a deity who has a special affinity with your objective.

- In love spells, seek aid from Venus, Aphrodite, Freya, or Aengus.
- For prosperity spells, call upon Lakshmi, Zeus, or the Green Man.
- Ask Brigid, Ceres, or Lugh for assistance with healing spells.

- If you seek protection, call on Artemis, Tara, or Horus.
- To gain wisdom or inspiration, ask Brigid, Cerridwen, Sophia, Mercury, Odin, or Thoth for help.
- Spells for courage or strength could benefit from the help of Mars, Sekhmet, or Ganesh.

Sometimes all you have to do to enlist a deity's aid is ask. However, you can show your sincerity by placing an image of the god or goddess on your altar, or in another place of honor. If the deity has a holiday associated with him/her, celebrate it. As suggested previously, you could also make an offering to a deity—incense, flowers, gemstones, etc.

Creating Altars to Deities

In addition to your primary altar, you may choose to create another altar and dedicate it to a favorite deity. This could be a more or less permanent altar, if your living circumstances permit, or a temporary one that you set up for a particular ritual and dismantle when you're finished.

- Place a statue, picture, or other image of the deity on the altar.
- If the deity you're petitioning presides over a certain sabbat or season of the year, put emblems of his or her special time on the altar.
- Drape the altar with a cloth in a color that reminds you of the deity: blue-green for water gods and goddesses, such as Neptune, Aphrodite, and Oshun; red, orange, or gold for fiery deities such as Apollo, Brigid, and Pele.
- If the deity has a connection with a certain direction, position the altar there. The archangel Michael, for instance, presides over the south, so an altar to him should occupy a south-facing spot.

You may want to include pictures of your favorite deities in your grimoire. Draw them yourself, or download them from the Internet. How about taking a photo of the altar you create to honor the deity and affixing it in your book of shadows? If you've composed a poem, song, or incantation to the deity, write that down too. What else did you do to petition a god or goddess? How did he or she respond?

The Charge of the Goddess

At some time, nearly every witch has likely experienced the desire to draw the energy of the Goddess or God into herself or himself. For the veteran priestess and priest, invoking the Goddess is often done as a part of ritual known as "drawing down the moon."

In this ritual, the priestess and priest work in tandem, with the priest invoking the great Goddess and the priestess receiving the energy of the Goddess into herself. The priestess then radiates this power outward through the circle. This sacred invocation is not exclusive to female/male working relationships. It is possible to attain divine consciousness on your own—communion with the deities is bestowed directly by the Goddess and not by any other person.

As we discussed in Chapter 1, the American-born folklorist Charles Godfrey Leland published accounts of interviews he said he'd conducted with an Italian strega (sorceress or witch) whose true identity remains unknown. Among the material Leland presented in his 1899 book *Aradia, Gospel of the Witches* was the earliest known version of the "Charge of the Goddess." The strega's particular tradition of Italian witchcraft focuses on the Roman goddess Diana, who gives birth to a daughter, Aradia.

This is perhaps an older tradition of Dianic witchcraft, which is now primarily associated with exclusively female covens. In the past, Dianic witchcraft was more closely connected with the worship of the moon goddess, personified by Diana and Aradia, than with a strictly feminine agenda. In this passage, Diana has instructed Aradia how to craft spells and ward off enemies, and now Aradia imparts her knowledge to others:

> *"When I shall have departed from this world,*
> *Whenever ye have need of anything,*
> *Once in the month, and when the moon is full,*
> *Ye shall assemble in some desert place,*
> *Or in a forest all together join*
> *To adore the potent spirit of your queen,*
> *My mother, great Diana. She who fain*
> *Would learn all sorcery yet has not won*
> *Its deepest secrets, then my mother will*
> *Teach her, in truth all things as yet unknown.*

And ye shall be free from all slavery,
And so shall ye be free in everything;
And as the sign that ye are truly free,
Ye shall be naked in your rites, both men
And women also: this shall last until
The last of your oppressors shall be dead;
And ye shall make the game of Benevento,
Extinguishing the lights, and after that
Shall hold your supper thus."

Following, Leland gave instructions for consecrating the meal, conjuring sacred cakes with wine, salt, and honey, and then forming them into crescent shapes before baking. Consider the age of this verse, and compare it to the more modern versions of the Charge of the Goddess found in other books—you'll see the evolution of the modern charge from its origins in the Aradia text. This evolution is an excellent example of how you can take wisdom that has been handed down over time and make it truly your own.

ANGELS

Virtually every faith speaks of angels in its legends, myths, and religious texts. According to most views, angels are considered cosmic messengers and spiritual guardians. They protect and guide human beings. They also serve as celestial helpers who carry requests between earth and the divine realm—the word "angel" derives from the Greek *angelos*, meaning messenger.

Guardian Angels

Spiritual and magickal traditions present many different conceptions of angels. In general, angels are considered the "good guys" in the universe. The simplest and most common image is that of the guardian angel, a personal celestial guide who may or may not have been human at one time. Your angel hears your prayers, watches over you, and helps you handle challenges in your life.

The Qu'ran tells us, "For every soul, there is a guardian watching it." Both the Old and New Testaments of the Bible regularly mention guardian angels. In the gospel of Matthew, for instance, St. Jerome explains, "Each one has from his birth an angel commissioned to guard it." The Talmud speaks of guardian angels being assigned both to individuals and to nations.

> *"Angels are anthropomorphic winged forms personifying divine will. Possibly evolved from Semitic and Egyptian winged deities, they appear in a number of religions as intermediaries between material and spiritual planes."*
>
> —JACK TRESIDDER, *THE COMPLETE DICTIONARY OF SYMBOLS*

Because guardian angels are believed to be the first-step intermediaries between humans and the divine realm, you can call upon your angel(s) whenever you need assistance, and feel confident that you'll receive guidance. Here are some ways your guardian angel(s) can help you in your magick work:

- In protection spells, ask your guardian angel(s) to keep you safe and sound in the face of challenges.
- If you're doing a travel spell, invite your angelic guide to accompany you on your journey.
- Want to send a message to the higher realms? Write your request on a slip of paper, and then burn it in your cauldron; as the smoke rises to the heavens it carries your request with it.

Angelic Hierarchies

Another theory proposes the existence of an angelic hierarchy, composed of many types of angels with varying roles and powers. The mystic Dionysius the Areopagite devised a three-tiered system for categorizing the heavenly entities. According to his system, each level contains three groups of angelic beings, each with their own powers and responsibilities.

- In the uppermost tier, the highest order known as seraphim wear red and cluster around the throne of God where they aid creation.
- Beneath them the cherubim, garbed in gold and blue, worship God and keep the Akashic records.
- Thrones, dressed in judges' robes, confer divine justice on those under them.

Below these three rarified orders, we find three more groups of angelic beings at the second level:

- Divine managers known as dominions wear crowns; they direct the other angels and govern the elements.
- Under them, virtues carrying white lilies or red roses work miracles throughout the cosmos.
- The powers, at the bottom of the second tier, fight evil in the universe.

Beings on the lowest tier maintain connections between the spirit world and the manifest one, and convey God's will to earth.

- Princes guide the nations and territories of the material world.
- Archangels aid the forces of nature and oversee the angels.
- At the bottom of the system, just above the level of human beings, angels protect people and convey messages to us from the higher levels.

This system says humans can only communicate with the entities on the lower two levels: angels and archangels. In earlier chapters, we've talked about calling upon the archangels Michael, Raphael, Gabriel, and Uriel through ritual. Guardian angels, it appears, are always with us, willing to lend a helping hand when we need it.

If you choose to work with angels and/or archangels, your encounters can be, well, heavenly! Describe your experiences in your grimoire. How did you contact and interact with the deities? Which deities appeared to you? Did you sense their immediate presence? What did you see, hear, feel, smell, intuit? How did their assistance enhance your magick work, your spiritual growth, and/or other areas of your life?

ELEMENTALS

Many beings that ordinarily remain unseen live side by side with us in the physical world. Folklore and faery tales frequently refer to these entities. Seafaring legends, for instance, often mention mermaids, and leprechauns appear with regularity in Irish lore. Most people discount these creatures as pure fantasy, but witches recognize them as elementals.

Sometimes called nature spirits, these nonphysical beings could be considered ambassadors for the four elements—fire, earth, water, and air—hence their name. Each resides within its element and possesses unique qualities characteristic of the element from which it harkens. If you befriend them, elementals will serve as devoted helpers and eagerly assist you in performing magick spells. But be aware: elementals can be tricksters, so approach them with care.

Salamanders

These fire spirits are naturally drawn to people who exhibit courage, creativity, passion, and initiative. When you do spells that involve action, inspiration, or vitality, salamanders can serve as liaisons, marshaling the forces of the fire element to assist you. Need an infusion of inspiration to complete your novel or a boost of stamina to win an important athletic event? Call upon these lively beings for help.

Paracelsus, the sixteenth-century philosopher, physician, and occultist, described them as looking like balls of fire or flaming tongues flashing across the landscape. Sometimes salamanders are depicted as lizard-like in shape. The ancients said salamanders hailed from the southern regions and brought nature's heat, without which warm-blooded creatures could not exist.

Gnomes

Gnomes are earth spirits. Sometimes called trolls, elves, dwarfs, or leprechauns, these practical, no-nonsense creatures may appear a bit gruff. However, they possess a wonderful appreciation for material things and can be valuable aides when you're doing prosperity spells. They have power over the plant and mineral kingdoms, so when you do magick with botanicals or gemstones, you're also working with the gnomes.

Legends say gnomes reside in caves or underground, where they guard hidden treasure. The ancient Greeks believed earth spirits known as hamadryads lived in trees, and if the tree was cut down the spirit died too. We find many varying depictions of gnomes in folklore, though often they're described as resembling small, sturdy humans, sometimes with coarse hair or fur—rather like Snow White's dwarfs—who come from the northern regions.

Undines (or Ondines)

Mermaids are the most famous of these water spirits. These beautiful but sometimes capricious beings are drawn to emotional situations and relate best to sensitive, intuitive, and artistic people. Invite these elementals to assist you when you're doing love spells.

Usually considered female, undines live in oceans, rivers, lakes, waterfalls, marshes, even fountains. Legends refer to them by many names, including naiads, water sprites, sea maidens, and selkies. Sometimes they're depicted as diminutive blue-green creatures who live under lily pads; other myths describe them as looking like incredibly lovely women with long hair and fishtails or scales, perhaps riding on the backs of dolphins. Undines care for the waterways of the world and all the marine life therein. (See my book *Mermaids: The Myths, Legends, & Lore* for information about undines throughout history.)

Sylphs

These air spirits gravitate to intelligent, literary, and analytical people. Their specialty is communication—call on them when you need help with negotiating contracts, handling legal issues, or managing other concerns that involve communication. Sylphs can also assist you in test-taking, public speaking, or writing.

As you might suspect, sylphs reside in the air. Legends depict them as delicate flying creatures who flit rapidly from place to place, riding the winds of the world. The tiny winged beings usually referred to as faeries are most likely sylphs. Some reports describe them as shimmering lights, rather like fireflies.

Thank Your Elemental Helpers

Make sure to treat elementals with consideration and respect—if they don't like you, they might play tricks on you. Always remember to thank the elementals that assist you in your spellworking and offer them small gifts to show your appreciation.

- Salamanders like candles and incense. Burn these to honor your fiery helpers.
- Gnomes adore jewelry and crystals. Bury a token in the ground as a way of saying "Thanks."
- Undines are fond of perfume. Pour a few drops of essential oil in a stream, lake, or other body of water.
- Sylphs enjoy flowers. Place fresh blossoms on your altar or lay them in a sacred spot outdoors as an offering.

Salamander Courage Spell

When you encounter setbacks, disappointments, or frustrating circumstances, ask the fire elementals to bolster your vitality, confidence, and resolve. Perform this spell on Tuesday or when the sun and/or moon is in Aries, Leo, or Sagittarius.

TOOLS AND INGREDIENTS
9 small red votive candles
Matches or a lighter
A magick wand

1. Arrange the candles in a circle around you, in a place where you can safely leave them to burn down completely.
2. Beginning in the east, light the candles one at a time as you move in a clockwise direction to cast the circle.
3. When all the candles are burning, stand in the center of the circle and face south.
4. Call out to the salamanders and tell them you have lit these 9 candles in their honor. Explain your situation and request their assistance, by chanting the following incantation aloud:

"Beings of fire
Shining so bright
Fuel my desire
Increase my might.
Help me be strong
All the day long
So in each deed
I'll surely succeed."

5. You may notice faint flickerings of light (other than the candles) in the room or sense the energy around you quickening. Perhaps you'll feel an excitement in the air. It might even seem a bit warmer. That means the salamanders are present and willing to work with you.

6. Take up your magick wand and point it toward the south. Your movements should be strong and purposeful, not wimpy. Envision yourself drawing powerful energy in though the tip of your wand. You might even see the wand glow or feel it tingle.

7. Now turn the wand and aim it at yourself. Sense the energy you've attracted from the south—the region where the salamanders reside—flowing from the wand into your body. Feel yourself growing more powerful, more confident, more alive.

8. Continue using your wand to pull energy and courage from the south in this manner for as long as you like. Remain in the center of the circle until all the candles have burned down completely.

9. Thank the salamanders for their assistance and open the circle, feeling renewed with vitality and confidence.

Elemental Exercises

To increase your awareness and ability to work with the elements, practice these exercises:

- Light a candle and focus your attention on the flame. See if you can make the flame move or flicker more brightly (without blowing or otherwise physically affecting it).

- Hold a crystal in your hand and close your eyes. Try to feel the crystal vibrating, pulsing, or otherwise resonating with energy.
- Sit beside a body of water. Cast your gaze slightly above the surface of the water and allow your focus to soften. Can you see energy swirling just above the water?
- Stand in a private spot outdoors, with your arms stretched out at your sides. Slowly bring your arms together and cross them in front of you, then open them again. Do this three times to raise the wind.

If you choose to work with spiritual beings, record your experiences in your grimoire. Who did you call to and why? What did you see, sense, hear, feel, smell, intuit? What impact did the entities have on your magick? What powers did they impart to you? Will you work with them in the future, and how?

Chapter 20

LOOKING TOWARD THE FUTURE

Once you've embarked on a magickal path, you will probably continue following it for the rest of your life. As is often said, magick isn't something you do, it's something you are. Having peeled away the veil of secrecy and glimpsed the mysteries within, you'll never see things as you did before. Now that you've become familiar with the hidden dimensions of the natural world, embraced the mystical forces that underpin our universe, and felt the power of the Goddess's touch, you can never go back to ordinary thinking.

No matter how long you study and practice the art of the Craft, you'll never know it all. You could be at it your entire adult life and still barely scratch the surface. It's like any other subject: The deeper you dig, the more you discover. Around each corner lies something new and awe-inspiring! Your grimoire is the place to describe your mystical discoveries, your experiences in the magickal realm, and anything else that you feel plays a part in your spiritual journey.

WORKING WITH OTHER WITCHES

If you've been a solitary witch until now, perhaps you're wondering what it might be like to work with other people who share your views. Maybe you've considered studying with a teacher who can help you advance more quickly and steer you away from some pitfalls along the way. Perhaps you know someone else who is following the Wiccan Way and you think the two of you could combine your talents to mutual advantage. Or you might want to join a coven, a group of like-minded folks with whom you can celebrate the sabbats and engage in magick and ritual practices.

It's nice to have "kinfolk" with whom you can share ideas and information. Also, you can learn from other people and they can learn from you, thereby expanding everyone's knowledge. In a world that still doesn't completely accept witches and magick, you may long for a community where you can feel safe, accepted, and valued. If you decide you want to share your magickal path with other people, do your homework in order to find the right folks for you to befriend. Each witch and each coven is unique, and it's important that your energies, beliefs, goals, etc. are compatible.

Some covens hold open circles and allow people outside their immediate membership to participate in some events or gatherings—for example, esbat rituals. That could be a good way to start exploring your options. Check out online resources, such as The Witches' Voice at *www.witchvox.com* to learn about possibilities in your area. My book *The Modern Guide to Witchcraft* offers more information about finding and joining a coven or other group of magick workers.

If you do start practicing with other people, you'll undoubtedly make many discoveries—about the Craft and about yourself. Doors will open into areas where you haven't ventured before. Record your findings in your grimoire. What did you experience when working magick with other people? How did you sense their energies and yours intermingling? Was the interaction uplifting, invigorating, peaceful, edgy, uncomfortable? Did a ritual or spell seem to have more power when you performed it with others? Note any impressions, insights, emotions, visions, sensations, etc. that seem relevant.

If you continue working with the same people over a period, you'll probably want to keep a running account of how you evolve as a group. Describe ways in which you support and enhance one another's workings, how you grow as a result of the group's input, challenges that arise within the group and how you solve them, and so on. In keeping with the tradition of secrecy, you may wish to mention other people by their Craft names, initials only, or pseudonyms to protect their identities should your grimoire fall into the hands of someone you don't want to know your business.

SHARING SPELLS AND SECRETS

As mentioned earlier, witches have often copied material from their teachers' grimoires. A High Priestess or Priest might make available some portions of her or his book to a chosen few within a small circle, as Gerald Gardner did in his Bricket Wood coven. In this way, ancient spells and incantations have been passed down through the centuries into the present day. This practice allows us to preserve witchcraft's rich heritage and observe its evolution over time. Everyone's experiences contribute to the development of the whole. Each witch is a torchbearer whose flame, when joined with others', lights up the world.

You may decide you want to let a magickal partner and/or the other members of your circle read what you write in your grimoire. Likewise, others in your group may give you permission to study their books. If you cast spells together, it can be useful to discuss what you did and what transpired. What went right and what went wrong? How might you do things differently in the future?

Depending on your personal perspective and preferences, you may choose to share your knowledge on a larger scale, as I do by writing books. A quick online search will reveal an amazing amount of information about all aspects of witchcraft, spellcasting, magick, the witchy life, and the occult in general. Maybe you'd like to contribute to an existing blog or even start one of your own. Now that Wicca and Neopaganism are becoming more accepted in many societies, lots of witches feel a desire to spread the word. Perhaps you will too.

Whether you decide to keep the contents of your grimoire private or share your experiences with other people is entirely up to you. So is the choice whether to hand down your knowledge to those who come after you or to have your confidences destroyed when you pass into the Summerland. If it is your wish, no one but you need know the secrets you keep in your book of shadows.

MORE THAN A BOOK

By now you've come to look upon your grimoire as more than just another tool. Few equally powerful methods of attaining self-awareness can be used so easily every day. This repository of your most private thoughts, spells, chants, musings, and meditations probably seems more like a friend than a book.

As you continue to learn, grow, and change, so will what you write in your grimoire. Looking back over earlier entries will reveal the arc of your journey and inspire you to keep going. Keeping your book of shadows will remind you of who you are during challenges and times of doubt. You also honor the precious moments in life by recording them. And, you preserve treasured memories for years to come.

Be passionate about yourself, even as you change, even in the face of the unknown. By writing your story, you may also become an inspiration for others. May your book of shadows deepen your knowledge of yourself, your aspirations, your dreams, and your loves. May it enrich your connection with the Goddess. May it comfort you in times of darkness and bring you joy in times of light. May it keep your secrets as would a trusted friend, protect the stories of your lifetime, and hold your personal mythology securely. Merry meet, and merry part, and merry meet again. Blessed be.

INDEX

ABOUT THE AUTHOR

Skye Alexander is the award-winning author of more than thirty fiction and nonfiction books, including *The Modern Guide to Witchcraft*, *The Modern Witchcraft Spell Book*, *The Everything® Wicca & Witchcraft Book*, *The Everything® Spells & Charms Book*, *Naughty Spells/Nice Spells*, *Good Spells for Bad Days*, and *The Everything® Tarot Book*. Her stories have been published in anthologies internationally, and her work has been translated into more than a dozen languages. The Discovery Channel featured her in the TV special *Secret Stonehenge* doing a ritual at Stonehenge. She divides her time between Texas and Massachusetts. Visit her at *www.skyealexander.com*.